TROUBLED FAMILIES
A TREATMENT PROGRAM

Matthew J. Fleischman, Arthur M. Horne,
and Judy L. Arthur

with chapter on School Intervention by
Frances C. Steinzeig

RESEARCH PRESS COMPANY

2612 North Mattis Avenue
Champaign, Illinois 61821

Copies of this book may be ordered from the publisher at the address given on the
title page.

ISBN 0-87822-271-5

Cover design by Jack Davis

Composition by Publication Services

Library of Congress Catalog Card Number 82-62573

We dedicate this book to our families.

MJF: Diane and Ross
AMH: Gayle, Sharon, Kevin, and Chuck
JLA: Dennis, Mom, Dad, Joyce, Becky, and Curt

Contents

Preface

The Johnson family came for counseling on the advice of their family pediatrician. Their daughter, Lori, had been labeled hyperactive. Her behavior was disrupting the family and causing considerable tension between the parents. The father assumed the mother was to "straighten Lori out," while the mother, exhausted at the end of the day, expected the father to take over as disciplinarian. In review, none of the family problems was major, just many minor antagonisms, aggravated by the parents' inability to deal with Lori effectively. Both parents wanted the situation to change.

The Watson family was referred by the school. Jeffrey was in constant trouble in the classroom and on the playground, and the school authorities had insisted something be done. Mrs. Watson was a single parent working in an office. She denied having serious problems with Jeffrey but did state that often he simply ignored her when she asked him to do something. With two other children and the demands of a job and a home, she had little enthusiasm for correcting Jeffrey. She knew he had stolen some items from local stores but didn't know what to do about the thefts.

The Anderson family was referred by the Welfare Office. There was suspected child abuse in this case, and the Welfare Office had counseled the Andersons to seek therapy rather than enter the court system. The parents were unemployed, though the father had been seeking work. The parents did not admit to child abuse but did say that they didn't know how to make the children mind them. They recognized they shouldn't hit their children but lacked any alternative methods of discipline.

The problems exhibited by these children and parents are typical of many families who seek or are referred for treatment. In fact, more than half of the referrals to child guidance clinics are for problems like defiance, fighting, lack of cooperation, and lying (Beck & Jones, 1973; Patterson, 1964; Roach, Gursslin, & Hunt, 1958; Rogers, Lilienfeld, & Pasamanick, 1954; Woody, 1969), behaviors we expect should be under parental control. In fact, for families who have been seen by counselors in family service agencies, and who have children in the home, Beck and Jones reported that 90% of their problems were child related. Yet before we jump to the conclusion that more and more adults are failing in their roles as parents, it is important to recognize that many social changes currently affect family life.

The extended family, in which parenting skills could be passed from generation to generation and the burdens of child rearing could be shared, has given way to the nuclear, and often isolated, household. The number of children living in single-parent households has increased 60% since 1960 (Sawhill, Peabody, Jones, & Caldwell, 1975), while the number of divorced women heading households nearly tripled in the same period (Schorr & Moen, 1979).

The number of women entering the job market has steadily increased until, at present, working mothers are in the majority. As a result, the roles and functions of family members are changing, but there are few guidelines or directions for managing these changes; as a result, families experience confusion and, at times, considerable disharmony as they try to adjust to their new lifestyle. In addition to the changing work roles of women, family workers are traveling longer distances to their employment, not only from suburb to city but in some cases from city to city, creating bedroom communities in which family members spend little time together.

The growth of electronic entertainment has shifted leisure time from more social to individual pursuits. Many young children now spend four to five hours per day watching television (Liebert, Sprafkin, & Davidson, 1982; White House Conference on Families, 1980).

Sex roles in society are changing. In previous decades a woman's role was primarily housewife and mother, while today many women are also pursuing careers outside of the home. In turn, many men are taking greater responsibility for child care. These role shifts, along with the availability of birth control and abortion, have influenced couples' decisions regarding the number and spacing of their children.

For many, these and other changes in societal and family structure have had little or no adverse effect on the quality of their family life. For others, however, these factors have increased family stress and left many adults unprepared to fulfill their roles as parents.

In addition, many families continue to be burdened by pressures that have always made child rearing more difficult: poverty, illness, emotional problems, physical handicaps, poor housing, unsafe communities, and the like. Yet despite these stresses and regardless of the types of problems that prompt families to seek help, it is our firm belief that parents can be helped to guide and nurture their children and bring the children's troubling behavior under control.

The program described in this book works to achieve this goal. It is based on well-established psychological principles of how behavior is learned and how it can be changed. Rather than attributing problems to individual or familial psychopathology, it emphasizes teaching the family to view problems in terms of behaviors to be encouraged or discouraged. Parents are then taught specific procedures for shaping behavior in more desirable directions. More than most forms of therapy, this program is directive and instructional and follows a step-by-step sequence for building skills and transferring responsibility for change and maintenance of change from the therapist to the family.

During the past two decades, this program has undergone extensive study in research laboratories, clinics, mental health centers, and protective services agencies. As a result of this research, the program has been modified to make it (a) more comprehensive and thus, hopefully, more effective; (b) usable by a wide range of service providers; and (c) easier for clients to understand and implement. Even though refinements continue to be made, we believe that this is an opportune time to publish this work. There has been a sharp reduction in the availability of various social services in the 1980s. The services left are expected to meet high standards of effectiveness and accountability. This program meets these needs because it:

- is aimed at a sizable population: children with behavior problems and their families;
- is time-limited;
- emphasizes home-based rather than institutional treatment;
- can be conducted in groups;
- can be used in a variety of social service and psychological settings;
- is goal oriented and easily evaluated;
- can be implemented by B.A.- and M.A.-level professionals.

The last point is particularly important. While the program can be employed by more advanced professionals, our primary intention in writing this book was to create a manual that could be used by mental health and social service workers who comprise the "line staff" of most community mental health centers, child guidance clinics, protective services agencies, juvenile departments, and school counseling services. Consequently, we have sought to make this work concrete and practical while at the same time avoiding a "cookbook" approach that is so specific it lacks the flexibility necessary for effective treatment.

The book is organized as follows. Chapter One gives a general overview of the treatment program, discusses how to adapt the program to the particular needs of each family, describes how to determine if this program is suitable for clients, and reviews settings and therapist and agency considerations. Chapter Two provides a historical perspective of the program's development and reviews the social learning and cognitive bases of the program. In Chapter Three, we describe the clinical skills you will need when presenting this program to clients. The treatment program is then discussed in Chapters Four through Eleven. We have also provided four ancillary chapters: working on school problems; conducting the program with groups of parents; adapting the basic intervention for the treatment of special clinical populations (e.g., stealing, hyperactivity); and, finally, techniques and strategies for working with difficult clients.

The authors wish to acknowledge the invaluable contributions of many others that have made this work possible. Gerald Patterson and John Reid laid the foundation upon which we built much of this program. Their contribution to the development of social-learning-based approaches to children and families is immense and deserves recognition. Robert Conger, past director of the Oregon Social Learning Center's clinical facility, also deserves special recognition, since he coauthored the original clinical manual from which this work, in part, descends. In addition, the staffs of the Oregon Social Learning Center and Family Research Associates must also be credited for their work on numerous drafts of the early treatment manuals. Ultimately, however, this work is a product of the authors. We alone assume responsibility for the changes we have made in the basic treatment model. While we gladly share credit for the book's basic strengths, we alone accept criticism for its weaknesses.

Besides those who have contributed to the development of this work, we also wish to thank all those who applied this program and were generous in their feedback. These include the staffs of the Helena, Montana, Family Teaching Center; the Jackson, Clackamas, and Lane County branches of the Oregon Children's Services Division; the Carl V. Morrison Center of Portland, Oregon; the Westend Creche of Toronto, Canada; and Eleanor McCabe and other doctoral students of the Department of Counseling Psychology at Indiana State University.

Lorna Limberg and Mary Lou Cooley deserve special mention for helping us through multiple revisions of the manuscript.

Chapter One

THE TREATMENT PROGRAM

In this chapter we describe the basic treatment program, beginning with an overview and a brief description of each of the treatment phases and sessions. Between-session assignments and the need for a flexible treatment plan are also covered. Next, we review the selection criteria for deciding who is appropriate for this form of treatment. We end with a discussion of the settings and users for whom this program is applicable.

OVERVIEW

Treatment is comprised of four phases, most of which contain several distinct sessions. Figure 1 presents a graphic overview of those phases and sessions, and what is accomplished at each point in therapy.

Pretreatment Phase

Initial interview (Session 1). The main objective of the first session is to prepare the family for treatment. This includes gathering necessary information about the presenting problem and other factors that will have a bearing on family participation, and presenting the program to the family so they understand what the treatment entails and what the likely outcomes will be. These pretreatment tasks are described in detail in Chapter Four. Two other objectives of this session are to develop a good working relationship with the family based on a sense of trust in your ability to help, and to strengthen the family's commitment to participate in and carry through with the program.

Intervention Phase

Setting up for success (Session 2). In working with families who have behavior problem children, it has been our experience that several issues must be discussed before parents can set about changing their child's behavior. One is the goals of the treatment program. You and your clients must reach a clear agreement on this issue before beginning. With many families, this may simply involve pinpointing or specifying appropriate behaviors to be increased and inappropriate behaviors to be reduced. In other families, there is considerable

Figure 1. Treatment Overview.

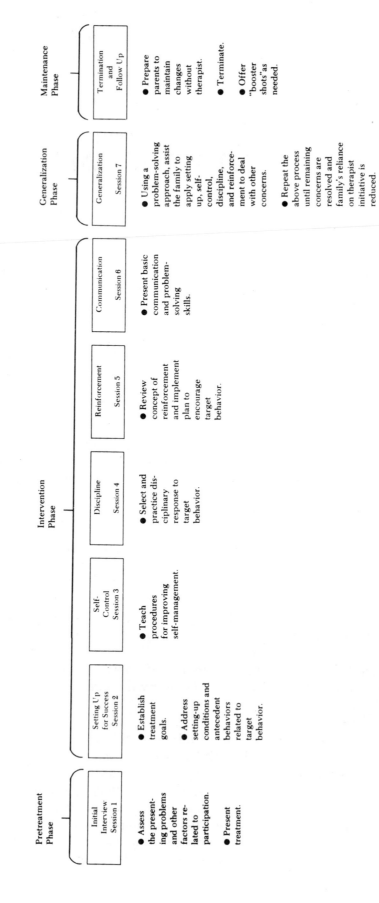

confusion or disagreement on what are appropriate expectations for the child. In these cases, the first step can involve education, guidance, and negotiation in order to achieve agreement concerning what is reasonable.

The other issue that must be considered is the process of "setting up for success." Social learning theory has long recognized the effect of the physical and social environment on a subject's behavior. For example, parents often complain that their child doesn't mind. Yet, when giving commands, these parents often fail to get the child's attention, are vague or unclear in what they want done, or sound hostile and demanding. Helping parents improve their commands is likely to have an immediate positive effect on the child's response. Other examples of setting up would be for the family to develop a daily household routine, arrange for the parents to have time away from their children, and organize the child's room so it is easier for the child to keep clean. Directions for conducting the second session are given in Chapter Five.

Self-control (Session 3). Having worked on setting up, the next step is to prepare the parents to cope with the stress of confronting their youngster's behavior. Parents who get enraged, depressed, or guilt ridden are less able to implement appropriate child-management programs. Thus, before helping parents gain more control of their children, we show them how to get better control of themselves. The program accomplishes this by teaching parents to be aware of their internal dialogue and then to modify that dialogue so it promotes greater calmness and self-confidence. In addition, we teach a simple relaxation procedure to reduce physical stress. Details of the session are presented in Chapter Six.

Discipline (Session 4). The third step in developing a plan for changing behavior is to identify how the parents have responded to past episodes of the child's misbehavior, and then to consider alternative ways of responding. Because different forms of misbehavior call for different forms of discipline, we offer six procedures from which to choose: withholding attention, Grandma's Law, natural consequences, time-out, taking away privileges, and assigning additional chores. In Chapter Seven, we review the various forms of discipline and describe how to prepare the parents to implement these procedures at home.

Reinforcement (Session 5). While being able to enforce limits is critical, parents also need to be more positive in general and to encourage specific prosocial behaviors in particular. Therefore, the fourth step covers the use of reinforcement. As part of introducing the family to reinforcement, we first explain what we mean by the term and, just as importantly, how parents and children can be shaped inadvertently to reinforce one another's undesirable behavior. Next, we teach the use of specific reinforcement procedures such as praise, affection, point systems, and an allowance to encourage certain desirable behaviors. Chapter Eight outlines how to present reinforcement concepts and how to teach families to implement a program of planned reinforcement.

Communication (Session 6). The final step in the intervention phase is to work on improving basic communication skills. Good family communication helps keep the channels open and prevents minor problems from becoming major ones. Perhaps even more important from the standpoint of this program is that good communication skills are essential if the family is to sit down and discuss how to resolve further problems. Thus, we introduce the family to concepts of verbal and nonverbal communication and to several dos and don'ts necessary for good communication skills. This material is covered in Chapter Nine.

Generalization Phase

By the end of the intervention phase, families will have been taught the essential concepts and skills for changing behavior and resolving conflicts. They should also be noting significant improvement with the problem they targeted for initial attention. However, most families still need assistance if they are to apply those skills to other concerns and eventually be able to carry on without further guidance from the therapist. Thus, the next phase is aimed at helping parents generalize what they have learned. Essentially, they are shown how the concepts and skills taught during the intervention phase can be applied to their remaining concerns. This is also the phase when the program can be extended to deal with the problems of siblings and/or troubles occurring at school or outside the home.

The length of this phase will vary depending on the parents' ability to assimilate the key concepts and procedures, the number and complexity of presenting problems, and the progress parents show in being able to generalize without extensive guidance. The format for these sessions is described in Chapter Ten. In practice, this format is repeated as often as necessary until all of the major presenting concerns have been addressed. Chapter Twelve explains how to extend the program to school problems, while Chapter Fourteen discusses how to intervene on such problems as stealing, setting fires, and lying.

Maintenance Phase

As the family's main problems show marked improvement and as the parents appear able to function with less direction, you should move towards termination. However, before doing so, it is important to make sure that the family can indeed maintain changes without regularly scheduled contact. To increase the likelihood of maintenance, you can assign the family specific tasks to complete and provide follow-up in person and over the phone, schedule "booster sessions" for continued support and training in problem solving, and build in natural support systems (family, neighborhood, peer groups).

It is important to realize that much of the activity directed toward maintenance occurs *after* formal termination. In our experience, depending on the population, up to half of the clients seen will need some limited posttermination counseling, usually in the form of what has been termed "booster shots." These booster shots typically involve a few telephone conversations or one or two face-to-face meetings where recent problems are reviewed and the family is helped to use their newly learned concepts and procedures in present situations. Chapter Eleven reviews general guidelines and specific procedures for both pretermination and follow-up contacts to strengthen maintenance.

BETWEEN-SESSION ASSIGNMENTS

Aside from the in-session meetings, an integral component of treatment is giving the parents, and often the child, daily assignments to perform. You can monitor these assignments through regular telephone calls and occasional visits to the home. Their purpose is to insure that in-session instructions are implemented in the home situation. For example, when parents are taught disciplinary procedures, they are asked to monitor and record their use of the correctional strategies during their interaction with the child. The assignments and the attendant record keeping also serve to provide you with ongoing reports of how well the parents are doing and whether the intervention is having the intended effect. An analogy we often use is that working with the program is like learning to fly an airplane. When the parents collect various types of information and share it with you, they are, in effect, reading data off various dials in the cockpit and enabling you to suggest appropriate corrections. Like the treatment sessions, the frequency of your calls will taper off as the parents become more proficient and begin to have the desired effects on the presenting concerns. Specific directions for designing and monitoring homework assignments are provided at the end of each chapter.

TREATMENT: STANDARDIZATION VERSUS FLEXIBILITY

We have described a logical order of presenting the treatment, but it is important to keep in mind the need for flexibility when putting this program into action. One advantage of a highly structured treatment model is that practitioners who are inexperienced with this model can follow our recommendations regarding an effective arrangement of the various program components.

However, avoid blindly adhering to what is described in the various clinical chapters. Rather, when designing a specific program be guided by the needs and limitations of your clients. For example, where parent-child conflicts, as opposed to antisocial behavior, are most pressing, communication skills might be taught immediately after the initial meeting. Or a child may be so unmanageable that the parents need immediate tools to get some control over the child's behavior if the family is to remain in treatment. In this case, it might be appropriate to move from targeting the initial goals directly to discipline, later returning to the sessions on setting up, parental self-control, reinforcement, and communication.

Another reason for program flexibility is that not all parents will have major problems in each skill area, nor will they need equally intensive direction with each component of the program. Some parents may have the most difficulty maintaining control of themselves, others are ineffective disciplinarians, and still others need to learn better communication skills. More often they have weaknesses in several areas. Thus, in designing the treatment plan for each family, you should attempt to place the greatest emphasis on those areas that need the most attention. You might spend two sessions on one procedure, monitor certain homework assignments more closely, or provide frequent home visits following sessions where the parents seem to have had more difficulty implementing a new technique. In general, however, we suggest that none of the program components be entirely omitted.

SELECTION CRITERIA

In most mental health or social service systems, a referral process is developed to facilitate client identification and selection. We have established a few basic criteria to help the staff evaluate the appropriateness of a referral. These criteria are as follows:

1. *The child is between the ages of 2 and early adolescence (13 or 14).* The current intervention program was designed and evaluated for this population. While this is a fairly broad age range, these children still depend heavily on their parents' support and, despite increasing peer influence as they grow older, are still under considerable parental control (or potential control as the case may be).

2. *The primary complaint is aggressive behavior, conduct problems, and/or parent-child conflicts.* The treatment program is geared toward the child who demonstrates *high rates* of aversive behavior in the home, community, or school setting. Usually, the parents are the primary "complainers," although teachers, counselors, caseworkers, or mental health clinicians may be equally distressed and concerned.

Following are characteristics or behaviors for which children are often referred.

Physical: hitting, kicking, tripping, shoving, throwing objects, and vandalizing or stealing property

Verbal: sarcasm, criticism, "putdowns," whining, complaining, yelling, defiance, interrupting, disrupting, noncompliance

Emotional: lack of affection, inappropriate or manipulative use of affection

Attitudinal: negative, defeatist

Obviously all children at one time or another engage in some of these behaviors; the essential point is the *frequency* with which they do so. Basically, the aggressive child exhibits deviant behavior far more often than does the nonreferred child.

These children can also be viewed according to the way different professions label them. Some examples are:

Professional field	Label generally used
Medical	Hyperactive, hyperkinetic
Legal-correctional	Out-of-control, child in need of supervision, incorrigible
Psychiatric	Conduct disorder, attention deficit disorder, oppositional disorder
Social Work	Social deviant, antisocial, child abuse (see Chapter Fifteen)
Education	Discipline/management problem, behavior problem, emotionally handicapped

3. *The program is not being used as the sole form of treatment for a psychotic, autistic, or severely retarded child.* The program could be adapted for use as a parent-education component of a more comprehensive psycho-educational treatment plan. If the program is used in this way, you should be prepared to place greater emphasis on how parents can teach new skills and behaviors to their children. This is only briefly covered within the "Setting Up for Success" session.

4. *The program is not being used as a form of crisis intervention.* Because the program is a sequential, skill-building method of resolving problems, it is not appropriate for a family on the verge of breaking up or if the child is an immediate danger to himself or herself or to others. However, once the crisis has been stabilized or resolved, this program could be used to help prevent the same problem from recurring.

5. *The family meets other criteria.* There are other considerations that weigh on whether a family is appropriate for this program. These include the parents' motivation to participate and apply what they learn, the degree of marital conflict, and the stresses and problems the family is encountering. In general, these considerations can be evaluated only during the initial meeting. They should not be considered reasons for exclusion until they have been discussed and the family has had an opportunity to learn about the program and decide whether it might serve their needs. Chapter Four reviews these issues further.

APPLICABLE SETTINGS AND USERS

The family therapy approach described in this book can be used by a variety of professionals and paraprofessionals working in a broad range of private and community agencies. The model is time-limited, structured, and, when presented in a clinically skillful manner, highly effective. Thus, it is particularly attractive to agency personnel who have heavy caseloads yet are under pressure to provide effective services. Since the model lends itself to being used in group treatment, agency workers can serve an increased number of families in fewer professional hours. Chapter Thirteen discusses the use of this program with groups. In addition to serving as a remedial program, the model can also be applied in a preventive context. It is well suited for parents whose children are not in trouble, but who wish to improve their parenting skills.

In the remaining sections, we will look at many of the diverse settings in which this model can be used, as well as some issues regarding agency philosophies and policies that have a strong bearing on how successfully this approach can be applied. Next, we briefly describe those persons we believe should be able to conduct this program successfully. Finally, we offer suggestions concerning how to use this program to maximize your learning and your clients' success.

Settings

The diversity of settings in which this model is applicable demonstrates the model's flexibility and its appropriate use with a variety of populations. The examples we describe are not exhaustive but provide a good mix of various settings.

Mental health centers. These centers will find the model useful with parents who need help to deal with a child who has been engaging in disruptive or delinquent behavior. Mental health workers will discover that the program can also help remedy the marital strife that child-management problems often cause. The model gives parents tools to communicate with each other and to solve problems together. This is an important consideration for mental health agencies faced with high recidivism rates. Finally, the model is instructional yet flexible enough to be helpful to many groups (single parents, adoptive parents, stepparents, extended family) and is suitable for both individual and group treatment.

The social learning model is especially well suited to the current commitment among mental health centers to provide preventive outreach services. The psycho-educational nature of this program not only makes it appropriate for those who wish to increase their parenting skills, but also for all groups of adults who work with children, such as day-care providers, recreational workers, and the like.

Children's protective services. These agencies become involved with children and their families when family relationships are so distressed that the children are considered to be in some danger. Parents who neglect their children or abuse them physically or emotionally frequently do so because they have no alternative behaviors available to them, not because they wish to harm their children. Also, as Patterson (1976) points out, children are both the architects and the victims of their relationship problems within the family. Many children who are physically abused by their parents also exhibit high rates of aggressive and socially inappropriate behavior. Thus, the social learning model proposes that negative relationships between children and other family members can result in the victimization of children in the home. This treatment program teaches parents alternative ways of responding to their children, which in turn results in a reduced level of inappropriate behavior by the children. The program is also beneficial to protective services workers because client cooperation and progress can be regularly monitored and evaluated. This is an essential ingredient of family treatment when the safety and well-being of the children is a primary concern.

Finally, many children must be removed from their homes either temporarily or permanently. Foster parents can benefit from this program when working with temporarily placed children. Adoptive parents can benefit from learning the techniques described in this program for long-term adult-child interactions.

Schools. School personnel are in a unique position because, of all the agencies in a community, only the school has access to all families at some time. This means that the parenting skills available in the social learning approach potentially can be offered to all parents. The educational nature of the program makes it suitable for use by school counselors and school social workers in parenting groups. In addition, many of the skills in the model can be used to improve teachers' classroom-management procedures.

Juvenile centers. Juvenile centers typically get involved with children in trouble at a later point than do the other agencies mentioned. For workers in these centers, the social learning approach can be applied in two ways.

First, these workers can be taught the basic principles and procedures of the treatment approach. For adults functioning in a surrogate parent role, the program can be applied, with the necessary alternatives, within the juvenile detention center. According to social learning theory, if the juvenile's original social environment remains unchanged, the social reinforcers that maintained the problem behaviors will still be present, and the same behaviors are likely to be repeated. Thus, the parents of the child in trouble should participate in a social learning training program at the same time the child is in the juvenile center. When the child is released, the parents can begin using the social learning techniques at home, and the family can continue to participate in an ongoing program. The agency worker, having been in contact with the child during detention, can serve as a liaison between the family and the juvenile center and will be in a position to insure the development of a coordinated treatment program.

A second way this program can be used by juvenile departments is to offer individual or group treatment to families whose children's behavior is deemed "incorrigible" or "out of parental control" but is not yet serious enough to warrant placing the children in detention.

The pastoral ministry. The local church is often the first resource from which parents seek assistance when their children exhibit behavior problems. Since the role of teacher is a familiar one for ministers, the psycho-educational nature of this program is well suited to this group. As with all psychological treatment, the opportunity for early intervention improves the chance of a successful outcome. Clergy could also offer training in parenting skills to groups of new and older parents. Not only would the usual advantages of group counseling be present, but the possibilities of social reinforcement from the church community are considerable.

Medical settings. Medical professionals can utilize this program in two ways. First, family practice physicians and pediatricians can involve psychologists and counselors directly and indirectly in treatment programs. For example, a "hyperactive" child may be seen first by a physician; if the physician fails to determine a physical basis for the uncontrollable behavior, the family can be referred to a psychologist or other mental health practitioner.

Second, social services departments in hospitals can employ this program as a community service comparable to the traditionally offered prenatal classes, which are educational and preventive in nature. The social learning approach could be adapted for use with both new parents and those who already have children. Making the principles of social learning available to parents at the outset of their parenting experience would provide them with skills for the important job of child rearing, a job for which most parents have had little or no training.

Practitioners in private practice. Private practitioners can use this program in individual family therapy. They, like the mental health workers, are likely to become involved with a family as a result of a child's being labeled out of control, deviant, delinquent, or some similar term. The reciprocal nature of the behavior between parents and children will soon become apparent in therapy. As social learning theory posits, *changes* of behavior in any one individual in the family will influence—and change—the behaviors of other family members. In addition to employing this program in a remedial context, private practitioners can make the psycho-educational teaching of parenting skills available as a preventive program to interested parents in both individual and group settings.

Agency Considerations

Included in the next chapter is a review of some of our efforts to disseminate this program. Our experience in those endeavors has taught us that the actual setting in which this program is installed is less important than the organization's commitment to making the program work. By commitment we mean the following:

1. The agency needs to recognize that the implementation of a new treatment model requires time before therapists become proficient in its use. Thus, the agency should allow sufficient time for trainees to study the material and should recognize that in the beginning the

trainees will work with only a few families. It is unrealistic to expect that staff can shift from one approach to another or learn a new treatment model without experiencing a temporary drop in productivity.

2. Because of the treatment model's systematic organization, therapists should be allowed to function in a similarly organized manner. Thus, therapists will need adequate time to plan and carry out scheduled sessions, make between-session phone calls, and often conduct posttreatment follow-up contacts. Agencies structured to deal primarily in crisis services may not be able to accommodate the program. In crisis-oriented agencies like child protective services facilities, use of this model is best attempted in a separate unit within the agency.

3. Adequate supervision must be arranged. Ideally, this is provided by an experienced therapist in a supervisory position. If that is not possible, a peer supervision model can still be used, assuming that time is scheduled to meet weekly, review progress, and discuss difficult cases. In our experience, this option works best if an agency supervisor participates in those meetings and is given responsibility for the overall functioning of the treatment team within the larger agency. The supervisor must participate in the training or self-instruction in the program and have an opportunity to develop personal skills within the program. Even if the supervisor sees only one or two families, or limits any clinical work to acting as an occasional cotherapist, it is quite possible to fulfill the responsibilities of both clinical and administrative supervisor to the team.

4. Sufficient supplies need to be available for the staff. There should be funds and machinery on hand to provide enough copies of handouts and monitoring sheets.

User Considerations

When you consider using the program, you must weigh the demands of this type of treatment and the level of skills it requires. We have found that specific educational training or advanced degrees are less important in carrying out the program than the level of clinical skills you possess. The basic counseling tools of active listening and clear communication are used throughout the treatment and should be adequately developed before you begin working with a family.

An understanding of cognitive and behavioral theory is necessary if you are to help family members make progress in this treatment program. Behavioral theory provides an understanding of reinforcement and punishment and the manner in which they shape behavior. It also gives you a rationale for contingency contracting, schedules of maintenance, modeling and rehearsing, and the extinguishing of behavior. Cognitive theory enables you to understand how beliefs about events affect the way people behave, including the A-B-C model of activating events, beliefs, and emotions. Both these theoretical positions are integrated into social learning theory. The ability to understand and employ these approaches is essential when working with the program; thus, we encourage you to become familiar with the references related to the subject, including work by Ellis (Ellis & Abrahms, 1978), Bandura (1977), Patterson (Patterson, Reid, Jones, & Conger, 1975), Meichenbaum (1977), and Mahoney (1974).

For the instructional sessions of the treatment, you should be able to model behavior in accordance with social learning theory, to use roleplays, to give clear and precise performance feedback, and to recognize and reinforce transfer of training to real life. Thus, although this is a clearly delineated, structured program, you should have a sound theoretical understanding of the approach and some basic listening and communication skills before instituting this form of treatment with a family.

If you elect to use the program, you must anticipate working directly with family members for a minimum of 1 hour each week for up to 3 to 4 months. Also, you should be available for telephone contacts between sessions and be committed to periodic follow-up contacts once the instructional sessions are completed. If you cannot devote this much time to the program, you probably will not find it suitable for your use.

In addition to time spent with clients, you should also allot time to prepare for sessions and to staff cases with other social learning therapists. The latter requires that you be able to discuss your case problems with co-workers in a way that encourages them to help you problem solve. In turn, you should support other co-workers who are using this approach and be prepared to offer constructive feedback and suggestions when necessary.

We recommend that in considering the use of this program, you assess its appropriateness in terms of the client population you serve, the level of agency support you can expect, and your own time commitments and skill level.

We have found that when line staff are given basic training and some in-house supervision, they can implement this program effectively. Like any new approach, a social learning program takes time and practice to master. To risk learning and using something new requires support from other key staff members. In the main, those who had that support did well. Those who did not, or who were expected to learn the program in addition to all their other responsibilities, had much more trouble.

The best way to learn this program is to read the entire book, paying particular attention to Chapters Two (background) and Three (clinical skills). When you are ready for your first client, carefully reread Chapter Four (the initial interview). Before conducting the interview, write any additional points, questions, rationales, or explanations you may need on a copy of the agenda form provided at the end of each clinical chapter (Chapters Four through Ten). The form serves as an outline for each session, listing the topics you need to cover, the skills you would like to teach, and any additional information you may want to include. While you may not be able to cover all the items listed, an agenda can help you keep on track during the session. Reread each chapter and clarify your agenda before each new session.

Chapter Two

DEVELOPMENT OF THE SOCIAL LEARNING FAMILY THERAPY PROGRAM

Social learning is a term applied to the process of people teaching people how to relate interpersonally. This learning process takes place within a social environment through observing, reacting to, and interacting with other people; in short, it is an education in human relations. People do not develop in isolation; rather, they are born into some social system, be it a traditional family or some other system of significant others. Virtually no one is exempt from this learning experience. Within such a social matrix children learn ways of behaving—termed behavior patterns—by receiving support for some actions and punishment for others.

The result of this selective social reinforcement is the gradual development of the behavior a person characteristically exhibits. A corollary can also be stated: without the opportunity of learning to perform in a particular manner, the individual will not develop specific social living skills. A social learning family treatment attempts to provide an environment in which effective learning can occur, alternatives for family interaction can be expanded, and new options can be presented. As a result, families are given the opportunity to develop new skills for dealing with the problems of living in close human relationships. This learning occurs in a systematic teaching-modeling program that emphasizes learning procedures derived from psychology and related behavioral sciences (Bandura, 1969, 1977; Ollendick & Cerny, 1981; Patterson, 1975).

Social learning theory began with the clinical application of principles derived from behaviorally oriented learning theories. Since its beginnings, social learning theory has expanded to include elements from experimental, cognitive, and social psychology. Behavior therapy in general, and social learning in particular, was originally a way of modifying discrete behavioral problems using techniques derived from learning theory. Through its evolution as a treatment discipline, behavior therapy has developed into a more general set of principles applicable to a wide variety of human problems. In its broadest sense, then, social learning therapy is not simply a series of techniques for treating families but is a systematic method of assessing family interactions, developing intervention strategies, and evaluating change.

HISTORICAL DEVELOPMENT

Social learning has been a major theory within psychology for several decades; its application to child and family concerns, however, is fairly recent, developing primarily since the 1950s and 1960s. In part, this increased interest in family applications resulted from studies demonstrating that a social learning approach could be effective with a variety of populations, including families, in diverse settings (Bandura, 1969). Also, during the 1950s, it became apparent that aiding families with child rearing and family relationship concerns within the community context was important: nearly two-thirds of all referrals by teachers and parents for mental health services were for children identified as out of control or unmanageable within the school and home (Roach, Gursslin, & Hunt, 1958). The need for more effective ways of dealing with family relationship problems was made more evident by several studies. Bahm, Chandler, and Eisenberg (1961) found that only a small fraction of the children referred for services actually received an offer of treatment. Levitt (1971) also reported that those who were accepted for treatment usually were given individual, traditional therapy which provided little or no help for socially aggressive children. Treatment of individual children by traditional methods did little to effect lasting change in their inappropriate behaviors either at home or in school (Meltzoff & Kornreich, 1970; Teuber & Powers, 1953). Further, if children were not treated, their conduct problems tended not to change (Morris, Escoll, & Wexler, 1956; Robins, 1966; Zax, Cowen, Rappaport, Beach, & Laird, 1968).

During the 1960s a number of behavioral treatment systems were developed in the area of marriage and family counseling. They shared a common grounding in social exchange theory, particularly the work of Thibaut and Kelley (1959), and were very similar in approach. In fact, they freely borrowed and adopted techniques from one another.

Since 1965, families with child management and family relationship problems have been studied by psychologists interested in developing methods to bring about effective change for the families. The predominant group for this work has been the Oregon Social Learning Center under the direction of Gerald Patterson and John Reid. The project initially pursued a series of studies examining a single family at a time in order to develop treatment methods based upon social learning principles, including training parents and others in the child's environment to act as agents of change. Early treatments included the use of "buzzer boxes" and M & M's candy but quickly moved toward employing basic point systems, modeling, time-out, and contingent attention (Patterson & Brodsky, 1966; Patterson, Jones, Whittier, & Wright, 1965; Patterson, McNeal, Hawkins, & Phelps, 1967). In the course of the project's development, research shifted from the psychology lab to the home and school in order to investigate and intervene in more naturalistic settings. Particularly important were efforts to develop and validate an observation system for recording the rate of naturally occurring positive and aversive behaviors (Reid, 1978).

In 1974, Patterson reported on the first large-scale application of this model to aggressive children. The subjects were 27 boys, ages 5 to 12, and their families. Results showed that approximately two-thirds of the treated boys evidenced at least a 30% reduction in their aggressive behavior as measured by home observation. In addition, parents' daily reports showed a 50% reduction in the occurrence of symptoms of primary concern to them. One year of follow-up data revealed that the improvements on both measures persisted. Interestingly enough, siblings' behavior also improved whether or not the therapists extended treatment directly to them. This fact seems to substantiate the notion that parents generalize the skills they learn and use them with other members of the family (Arnold, Levine, & Patterson, 1975).

While the main study was being conducted, several other studies were run to control for possible sources of bias. To determine whether improvements were due to spontaneous change rather than the treatment itself, six families were assigned to a waiting list while another six received treatment. Only the six who were treated improved (Wiltz & Patterson, 1974). To test whether families may have been responding more to the opportunity to meet with a therapist and share their concerns rather than to the specific content of the program, 12 additional families were randomly assigned to a realistic placebo therapy or to the actual program. While both sets of parents rated treatment positively, only the children in the social-learning-treated group had lower rates of observed aversive behavior at termination (Walter & Gilmore, 1973).

Besides the work on home problems that every child received, classroom intervention was required for 14 of the children. There, youngsters were given a daily work card on which teachers recorded points earned for appropriate behaviors. It was found that, with practice, teachers needed only a few minutes each day to carry out treatment effectively. In some families, where learning deficits were extensive, parents were taught to work as remedial teachers for their children (Patterson, Reid, Jones, & Conger, 1975).

In reviewing the work conducted through the mid-1970s, Patterson et al. concluded that treatment appeared to have the following effects:

1. Significant changes in the problem child's behavior were evident, which persisted during follow-up.

2. A modest reduction in coercive behaviors occurred for all family members, especially for siblings.

3. Parents' perceptions of their problem children became more positive.

4. Parental consequences for coercive behavior became less positive.

5. The punishment or negative consequences used by parents became more effective for controlling children's behavior.

6. Fathers tended to assume a more important role in controlling the children's coercive responses.

7. The majority of posttreatment ratings by the mothers indicated that the family was "happier," and all of them rated their children as being "improved."

The next step in the development and testing of the treatment program was to undertake a series of replication studies. The first of these was conducted in the same facility as the original study, but with a new set of therapists operating in an administratively and clinically distinct unit called the Family Center. There, using the same measures of outcome, home observations and parent reports, nearly identical results were obtained (Fleischman, 1981).

Later, the program was implemented in a new community-based facility in Helena, Montana. This venture was designed as a collaborative effort between the state of Montana and the Oregon Social Learning Center to create a model family treatment facility. There, at the Helena Family Teaching Center, over 50 families were treated and assessed with the same observation and parent report measures; again, the results were highly comparable (Fleischman & Szykula, 1981). Figures 2 and 3 summarize the results of these three studies. At the same time it is important to note that in Montana, despite many favorable circumstances that existed when establishing the Helena Family Teaching Center (legislative support, initially adequate funding, ability of Oregon staff to select Family Teaching Center therapists), implementation of the program and survival of the facility required extensive efforts aimed at developing community support, attracting referrals, and maintaining the clinical integrity of the program (Szykula, Fleischman, & Shilton, 1982).

Community and organizational factors that affect therapists' performance, and thus a program's effectiveness, were also noted in a recent replication and evaluation study. This study involved three mental health/child protective services facilities in Oregon. There, despite a 2-week in-service training period plus regular follow-up visits, trainees still had considerable difficulty implementing the program. Part of their problem seemed to be a need for more practice and supervision. However, the basic trouble seemed to stem from the difficulty of trying to learn a new treatment model while at the same time handling all the other demands of their jobs. Evaluation of actual audio tapes of treatment sessions revealed both quantitative and qualitative deficits in the therapists' performance compared to that of therapists working in the Oregon Social Learning Center's own in-house clinic. Also, treatment in the three new sites was considerably briefer; overall, therapists in these facilities held fewer sessions with clients during the generalization phase of treatment.

The net result was that while these therapists achieved initial improvements for their clients comparable to those achieved by research project therapists, they failed to extend those improvements past the 6th week of treatment. In fact, according to observation data, there was an actual deterioration from that point on: the net reduction in rates of observed aversive behavior from baseline to follow-up was

Figure 2. Naturalistic Observations of Total Aversive Behavior.

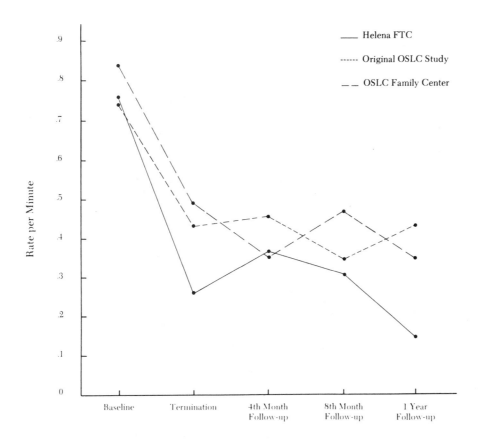

Figure 3. Number of Negative Symptoms Reported by Parents During Previous Day.

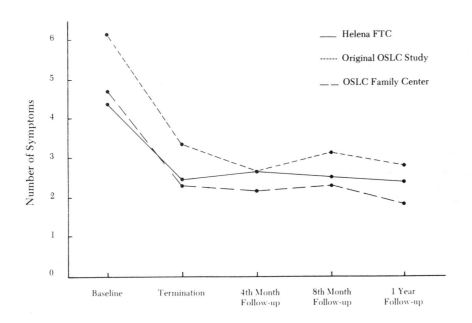

only 9% versus a 48% overall reduction for cases treated by the research project's own staff. Interestingly, despite the discrepancies in performance and outcome between research project and field site therapists on nearly every measure except observations (i.e., on parent-reported problem behavior, parent-reported positive behavior, mothers' ratings of treatment, proportion of families seeking additional help during follow-up, use of medication during follow-up, occurrence and severity of delinquent-type behaviors), the social learning treatment subjects showed greater improvement than the comparison sample of agency clients who received whatever other therapy or services were offered (Fleischman, 1982). Observation data collected after 6 weeks showed the social-learning-treated cases to have a larger reduction (44% versus 27%) in observed aversive behavior. However, after the 6-week period, the social-learning-treated cases began to exhibit more aversive behavior while the contrast-treated cases continued to improve; as a result the two groups showed little difference at termination. During follow-up, both groups deteriorated to the point that, by the end of follow-up, neither one showed much improvement from baseline.

These results demonstrated to us the need for continued refinement in the treatment program itself and the manner in which it is implemented. Several of these changes will be noted in this text, including greater emphasis on clinical skills, the generalization phase of the program, and working with difficult populations. Also, our efforts to disseminate the program have made us more aware that agency considerations such as administrative support for program change and sufficient time for staff to prepare for and learn the new program have considerable impact on how well therapists implement the program (Fleischman, 1982).

Indications that these efforts are in the right direction came from two recent efforts to disseminate this program, one in Oregon and the other in Montana. In the first, families with children between the ages of 3 and 12 who were considered at risk for protective placement out of the home were treated by a team of caseworkers using this program. These caseworkers were carefully trained and, most importantly, received ongoing supervision from an agency supervisor also trained in the model. The results were very promising. After the program's introduction, there was an 85% reduction in out-of-home placements for the target population. When the program was abruptly terminated 9 months later due to state-mandated layoffs of social service personnel, out-of-home placements rebounded to their previous level. Finally, while the great majority of the families were initially seen for child abuse, none were reported or investigated for further abuse during both treatment or 1-year follow-up, and none of the children were placed out of their homes.

The second study also involved protective services workers and families seen as a result of child abuse. Here a random assignment to social learning and control conditions was used. In addition, clients were first identified as more or less impaired on the basis of the number of prior episodes of abuse, extent of difficulty with housing or transportation, and whether the parent-child difficulty was seen as the central problem or only one of many. More and less difficult clients were balanced equally in the two treatments and the results were analyzed separately. Results showed that the social learning treatment had significantly fewer out-of-home placements with the group of abusive families seen as less impaired. For the most severely disrupted families, the two treatments were about equivalent (Szykula & Fleischman, 1983).

Together, these studies suggest that, while not a panacea, this program is effective in treating many children and families whose behavior is a serious concern to others and themselves. Further, the program can be implemented in real-world settings such as public social service agencies and conducted by their regular staff. There is room for further research and refinement; but in light of concerns going back over 20 years to develop more effective means for working with aggressive children and their families, it is clear that considerable progress has been made.

BASIC TENETS OF SOCIAL LEARNING THEORY

Almost all family therapy begins with a concern about one family member who is identified by either the family or some significant community agent as disruptive or disturbed. In the 1950s, the development of a systems perspective led to a greater recognition that an individual's behavior cannot be considered apart from the behavior of others in the family system. According to this view, the problem behavior of the individual is neither illogical nor crazy; rather, it is seen as a pattern of learned responses to the contingencies of that system. Furthermore, while the behavior of others within that system contributes to the individual's deviancy, the behavior of the individual contributes to and helps maintain the behaviors of others toward that person.

Maximizing Rewards/Minimizing Costs

This model, one that views an individual's behavior as a function of continuous, reciprocal influences rather than the surface manifestation of an underlying personality conflict, is very similar to a systems theory model. What differentiates social learning theory from systems theory models is the emphasis on how people learn to behave and how those behaviors, whether considered appropriate or inappropriate, are maintained.

A core concept of social learning theory is that individuals strive to maximize rewards while minimizing costs. Social relations are seen as satisfactory when a given relationship provides a high ratio of rewards to costs. Patterson (Patterson & Hops, 1972) further refined this notion of exchange with the concepts of reciprocity and coercion. Reciprocity refers to a pattern of social interaction in which two people maintain or control a relationship through frequent use of mutual positive reinforcement. Coercion, on the other hand, refers to an interaction in which each person uses aversive reactions to control the behavior of the other person.

Development of Behavior Patterns

While reciprocity and coercion describe styles of interaction, they do not explain how such patterns become stabilized. To understand this, we need to review some basic mechanisms through which learning occurs and how these contribute to the development of essentially positive or aversive behavior patterns.

Observation and modeling. Children learn new behaviors by observing others and modeling those whom they admire. Parents, siblings, peers, and the media are all potent influences for learning both prosocial and negative behaviors. Professionals working with children are particularly concerned about the amount of aggressive and violent models young children are exposed to on television and within families where physical conflict is frequent.

Positive reinforcement. Observing a behavior will have only a limited effect on how often it will be performed. For the behavior to be reproduced frequently, it must be reinforced. Positive reinforcement occurs when a particular consequence following a behavior increases the frequency of the behavior. For example, a young child who tries to dress himself and is reinforced by being praised by his mother will probably attempt to dress himself again. While positive reinforcement can be a very powerful tool for shaping behavior, its strength is greatest when the reinforcer is one the individual will work hard for and is given immediately after the behavior occurs. When first shaping a behavior, it is important to use reinforcers the individual desires and to reinforce nearly every occurrence of the behavior. Later, when the behavior is well established, only periodic reinforcement is necessary to maintain its frequency.

Extinction. Behaviors that are never reinforced will eventually stop occurring, that is, be extinguished. The child who gets good grades but receives no recognition for them will probably stop working as hard to get them. Because many well-established behaviors are maintained by very infrequent reinforcement, it may take a considerable time before extinction will occur. For this reason it is often advisable, when trying to eliminate an undesirable behavior through extinction, to also positively reinforce a competing desirable one.

Negative reinforcement. Negative reinforcement, often confused with punishment, is actually another form of reinforcement in that it strengthens or increases a behavior. We say we are negatively reinforced when something we do turns off something that is causing us pain. For example, in many cars, buckling the seat belt turns off an annoying buzzer; as a result, buckling up is negatively reinforced. Negative reinforcement can unwittingly lead to a cycle of unwanted interaction. For example, a parent may learn that the surest way to quiet a persistent child is to give in to the child's demands. While the parent may not be aware of it, the child is negatively reinforcing the parent for giving in by temporarily halting the whining and pleading after getting what he wants. However, by giving in, the parent is also positively reinforcing the child for persisting in the face of an initial refusal. This will result in an increase in the chance that the child will pursue demands even more persistently in the future.

Punishment. Punishment occurs when a behavior is followed by a loss of rewards or an increase in pain. Compared to extinction, it is usually faster and can be used in situations where it is not possible to withhold all of the naturally occurring reinforcers or wait for extinction to occur. However, punishment can have several unintended consequences. It can cause the person who is about to be punished to try to avoid the punishment, either by keeping the behavior secret or by staying away from the person doing the punishment. And it can lead to counter-punishment, which can rapidly escalate a situation. When this happens, the two parties strive to change each other's behavior by increasing the amount and intensity of their punishment. Such patterns are often at the heart of parent-child conflict (Patterson, 1976) and marital distress (Jacobson & Margolin, 1979). Furthermore, research on family inter-actions reveals that the family member who delivers the highest rate of aversives also receives the highest rate in return (Reid, 1967). As Lederer and Jackson (1968) aptly stated: "Nastiness begets nastiness."

Cognitive Approaches

Thus far, the discussion has emphasized how reinforcement and punishment play a role in shaping behavior. In the last dozen years or so, there has been a growing emphasis within social learning theory on the importance of thoughts, feelings, and other more complex cognitive events in controlling human behavior (Bandura, 1969). As a result, there has been a resurgence of interest on the development of clinical procedures for modifying the cognitive along with the behavioral components of problems. Mahoney and Arnkoff (1978) have classified cognitively oriented approaches as following one of three directions: cognitive restructuring, coping skills training, and problem solving.

Cognitive restructuring. The basic premise of cognitive restructuring is that maladaptive thoughts lead to maladaptive feelings, which in turn result in maladaptive behaviors. Both Ellis (1962) and Beck (1972) have identified series of irrational beliefs or distorted thinking. For example, you may believe that everyone you know must approve of and love you, or you may see a single negative event as part of a continual pattern of defeat or attack. Intervention usually involves educating the individual to take a more rational, analytic approach to events and to monitor and modify "inner-" or "self-talk." By doing so, subjects often find they can make dramatic improvements in their emotional states and interpersonal effectiveness. While originally used with adults, recent efforts with children have also been impressive

(Herman, Passmore, & Horne, 1982; Kirby, 1981; Kirby, Glynn, & Manos, 1980; Kirby & Horne, 1982; Meichenbaum, 1974, 1977).

Coping skills training. This is an extension of cognitive restructuring; once individuals have identified thought processes that lead to inappropriate feelings and behaviors, they can be taught skills to help them adapt to a variety of stressful situations. Coping skills include relaxation training, meditation, self-distraction, and performance rehearsal. Frequently, these techniques are taught by first having subjects evoke the stressful event in their imagination and then apply the coping strategy to reduce their stress. When this can be done successfully, the subject is helped to use the same strategy in the natural environment.

Problem solving. The impetus for a reemphasis on problem solving arose from D'Zurilla and Goldfried's (1971) observation that:

> Much of what we view clinically as "abnormal behavior" or "emotional disturbance" may be viewed as ineffective behavior and its consequences, in which the individual is unable to resolve certain situational problems in his life. (p. 107)

Spivack, Shure, and their colleagues, for example, have found that problem children could be differentiated from their normal peers by their lack of problem-solving skills. In addition, the researchers found that teaching problem children these skills led to positive changes in their behavior (Platt, Scura, & Hannon, 1973; Platt & Spivack, 1972a, 1972b, 1974; Shure & Spivack, 1972; Shure, Spivack, & Jaeger, 1971; Siegel & Spivack, 1976; Spivack, Platt, & Shure, 1976; Spivack & Shure, 1974). Blechman and her associates (Blechman, 1974; Blechman, Olson, Schornagel, Halsdorf, & Turner, 1976) have had good results teaching families to play board games that lead participants through the steps of problem solving and contracting.

Clearly, the use of cognitive restructuring, coping skills training, and problem solving is compatible with other elements of a social learning treatment. Moreover, they are highly complementary. Changing a child's behavior requires that parents alter their current responses to the child and create a social environment that is mutually reinforcing. At the same time, such a broadened approach recognizes that parent-child and parent-parent interactions are stressful at times and that helping individuals to cope with those stresses will have positive benefits for all. Finally, social learning theory argues that ultimately the family must enhance its skills at problem solving if long-term change is to be achieved.

Chapter Three

CLINICAL SKILLS

This chapter will familiarize you with therapist behaviors that we believe foster cooperation and facilitate change in clients. By developing and practicing these clinical skills, your success with this program will be enhanced. The rationale for emphasizing clinical skills is that the effectiveness of this program ultimately depends upon the family implementing the techniques they learn. While at first it may seem illogical that families seeking help would resist implementing treatment techniques, clients' hopelessness, fear, pride, or anger can act as barriers to change.

The notion of clinical skills is not new; it has been a mainstay of research, and clinical and counseling psychology, for years. Truax and Mitchell (1971) and Lambert, DeJulio, and Stein (1978) investigated what they referred to as interpersonal skills; Rogers (1942, 1957), Goodman (1972), and Dooley (1975) have looked at interpersonal traits. Lavelle (1977) studied therapist behavioral styles; and Alexander, Barton, Schiavo, and Parsons (1976) have researched therapist characteristics. Our interest in this area was sparked by findings that even among practitioners adhering to the program's content there was considerable variation in their ability to help clients. While we do not discount the effect of client variables, it appeared evident that certain therapists got better results despite client difficulties. To investigate these findings, we listened to over a hundred tapes of effective and ineffective social learning therapists (as determined by client outcome data). Using Flanagan's critical incident technique whereby actual work samples are studied for instances of desirable behaviors (Flanagan, 1954), we identified over 30 therapist behaviors that seemed to differentiate the two groups. Although these skills were identified in a post hoc fashion, we later found that many were in concordance with therapist variables identified in the clinical literature.

We grouped these behaviors into seven skill areas:

1. Building relationships
2. Gathering information
3. Maintaining structure

4. Teaching new skills
5. Insuring implementation of skills
6. Promoting independence and generalization
7. Handling resistance

In the remainder of this chapter we will discuss these categories, define the various clinical skills in each, and show how these skills can be used effectively with clients.

Unlike some clinicians, we do not believe that all skilled therapists are born with a set of characteristics or traits that makes them effective clinicians. While individuals have different competencies, new skills can be learned. However, we don't claim that performing the behaviors described in this chapter will automatically make a person "clinically skilled." Many variables affect the quality and clinical impact of these behaviors, including the timing of statements or gestures; the context in which they are performed; the types of problems being dealt with; and client variables such as temperament, personality, age, and sex. We do believe that with study, experience, persistence, and, most importantly, performance feedback (through colleagues, audio/video tapes, supervisors, and clients), you will be able to master the majority of the clinical skills discussed in this chapter.

BUILDING RELATIONSHIPS

In this program, as in other styles of family therapy, a good working relationship with clients is essential. Without it, clients are likely to withhold pertinent information, cancel sessions, resist implementing techniques taught during sessions, and/or drop out of treatment. The following activities help build positive relationships.

Communicate Empathy

Feeling understood is an essential ingredient in a trusting relationship. If you demonstrate your awareness of the clients' verbally and nonverbally expressed feelings, concerns, and views of the world, they will feel you understand them. This can be done by reflecting your interpretation of clients' thoughts and emotions. Here are some examples of reflective responses that communicate empathy. See if you can detect the feeling or thought being reflected to the client.

CL: I don't know how much longer I can take this!

TH: You're feeling really frustrated.

CL: You should have seen her!

TH: You must get embarrassed when she throws those tantrums at the store.

TH: (Observing client's expression) You look a bit skeptical. Are you worried that nothing will get Jeff to change?

CL: That house is a zoo!

TH: I'll bet sometimes you don't even want to go home after work, because you're afraid everyone's going to be fighting.

CL: He went to time-out without a fuss, and then came out and played nicely the rest of the day!

TH: I like your excitement. You sound very optimistic about time-out.

CL: I'm just exhausted.

TH: I know it's twice as difficult to deal with these problems now that Bill's gone. It's not easy being a single parent.

You needn't worry if your initial reflection is inaccurate. Families generally appreciate your attempts to understand them and usually will restate their sentiment: "No, that's not quite right. What I felt then was more like giving up!"

Empathic understanding need not be long winded. Examples include:

CL: I was so frustrated I just wanted to go to my room and cry.

TH: I can imagine.

CL: We had a great weekend camping.

TH: Sounds like fun.

CL: And then he went to bed without a fuss!

TH: Like icing on the cake, huh?

Empathy can also be communicated nonverbally. Haase and Tepper (1972) found that proximity, frequent eye contact, and leaning forward, in combination with being verbally empathic, produced the highest empathy ratings. Interestingly, therapists who did not maintain eye contact were scored very low, regardless of the level of their verbal empathy. D'Augelli (1974) also found low but significant correlations between frequency of nodding one's head and empathy ratings on the Truax and Carkhuff scales (1967).

Provide Reassurance and Normalize Problems

Many clients enter treatment with feelings of hopelessness, guilt, anger, or fear. Mothers and fathers may feel that they are bad or incompetent. Some parents will have labeled their child in deviant or otherwise unhelpful ways (a brat, a bully, "full of the devil," "a loser"), while others will have serious misconceptions of what is age-appropriate behavior. Assuring the family that the child's behavior and the parents' reactions to that behavior are normal helps parents see themselves and their child in a more positive light. Following are examples of providing reassurance and treating family problems as normal.

CL: When I tell him to do something, he acts like he doesn't even hear me.

TH: I know just what you're talking about. In fact, the most common concern of parents I work with is that their children won't "mind."

CL: She's such a pest. She won't leave me alone for a minute!

TH: The fact that most 3-year-olds have an attention span of only 2 to 5 minutes can be hard to deal with.

CL: I've tried yelling and spanking, but nothing I do seems to work.

TH: With the exception of watching how our parents raised us, most people don't have any training on how to be a parent. It's no wonder that sometimes we're not sure what to do.

When attempting to reassure your clients, be careful not to belittle their problems. Statements such as "Oh, most kids John's age talk back" or "That's really nothing to worry about" are likely to make parents feel that they are overreacting or cannot deal with their problems as well as other parents can, or that you do not understand the extent of their problems. Better ways to convey the same message would be:

TH: Even though most kids John's age do that, he does seem to be doing a bit more than his share.

or

TH: Although most adolescents sass back at times, it's sure hard for parents to know what to do.

Both of these examples acknowledge the parent's concern while stating that the child's problem is not unusual for a boy his age.

Use Self-disclosure

Family members are likely to feel more comfortable working with you if you are willing to disclose some personal qualities while maintaining a professional demeanor. One way this is done is by sharing feelings, thoughts, or problems you have had that were similar to those of your client. Examples include:

CL: It was so hard for me to stick to my word.

TH: I know how you feel. Sometimes I find it hard not to give in once I've withdrawn a privilege from my own kids. I really have to watch myself when that happens.

CL: I don't know if this day-care idea will work.

TH: When my daughter was Jill's age, I really worried she'd throw a fit when I left. And of course she did, but she quickly grew to like it.

Self-disclosure can also involve a brief mention of events that occur in your day-to-day life.

TH: That's neat that you're planning to take a weekend off. My wife and I went to the coast last weekend and really enjoyed ourselves.

CL: The week just went so well.

TH: When you told me on the phone how well Tina's behaving, it made my day. I feel really good about the progress you've made.

It is important, however, that the therapist and client roles not be confused. Your attention in the session should always be focused on your clients. Disclosures regarding problems should be brief and stated only when they relate directly to the client's situation, refer to past rather than current issues, and, when possible, allude to a positive outcome.

Define Everyone as a Victim

Family conflict usually involves deeply hurt feelings and frequent efforts to lay blame and assign fault. Thus, it is important to avoid the appearance of being for or against any particular person or faction within the family. This is best done by focusing on how each person is, in fact, a "victim" of the problem. Encourage individuals to describe how the problem affects them emotionally (do they become angry, sad, guilty?) and behaviorally (what unpleasant or undesirable behaviors occur as a result of the problem?). You need to be careful that when responding empathically to their statements you do not appear to be siding with the expressed point of view. Rather let the individuals know that you heard and understood how they feel without necessarily implying agreement. Examples include:

CL: He won't ever help me with the kids while I cook dinner.

TH: So when he comes home from working at the mill, he's tired and needs some time to relax, but that makes it difficult for you to get dinner on the table.

CL: We went shopping and then ran some errands for a couple of hours. She was so bad, getting into things and whining.

TH: It sounds like she was pretty bored and tired.

CL: He'll do anything to get me mad. If I tell him he's lost a privilege, he'll throw a tantrum just to get even.

TH: It sounds like he's testing you to find out if you really mean what you say and if you're going to carry through with the punishment.

Emphasize Positive Motivation

It's a sound working premise that clients are doing the best they can given the personal, social, and environmental conditions they are experiencing. Going beyond this, your relationship with each member of the family will be further enhanced if you actively work to ascribe positive and benevolent motivations and connotations to behavior and intentions that others view negatively. We have found that this is not always an easy task. To prepare yourself, we suggest that prior to each session you review what each person does that others dislike and identify a more positive interpretation. If you cannot do this, you will be unable to provide a convincing alternative to the old way of viewing the situation.

The following examples show how behaviors and intentions can be relabeled for the client.

CL: Unless my son turns around, he is heading for serious trouble. No one likes a kid with a big mouth.

TH: I'll agree with you that it is important for youngsters to show respect for their parents and for other adults. But I can also see that Jack's behavior suggests he has the self-confidence to stand up for himself and be a leader. What we need to do is to help him learn when to assert himself and how to do it most effectively.

CL: His dad just has no patience with him.

TH: Sometimes we get angriest with the people that we love the most. We have such high hopes for them and are consequently the most frustrated when things don't turn out the way we want them to.

Establish Positive Expectations for Change

Clients are often apprehensive or skeptical about treatment. Your goals should be to create an atmosphere that encourages the family to make changes, and to help them establish positive expectations regarding treatment outcome. This process is facilitated by expressing confidence in the program itself, in your personal ability to help the family, and in your belief that they will do well. In addition, their confidence will increase if you consistently reinforce their efforts and point to their successes.

You can encourage your clients with supportive statements such as the following:

CL: I don't know if you can help us. It just seems hopeless.

TH: We've worked with a number of families who are having problems similar to yours and had considerable success.

TH: You did a great job explaining time-out to him last week. I'm sure you'll do just as well when you explain the allowance system.

TH: After learning this program, you'll have the skills to deal with most problems that come up in the future.

CL: I think this will work.

TH: I like your positive attitude. It's going to be helpful in accomplishing your goals.

TH: I can assure you that what I'm going to teach you will make a big difference. Within a few weeks she'll learn to stay by your side when you take her to the store.

Match Your Communication Style to the Family

Matching your communication style to that of your clients will help insure that they understand what you say and, just as importantly, that they feel comfortable working with you. This includes gearing your vocabulary to their educational level and pacing your speech to theirs.

In addition, when instructing you should attempt to use examples personalized to the family's particular situation ("When John goes in his room and slams the door" rather than "When children get upset"). This technique helps clients relate to and understand new concepts, and conveys to them that you understand their concerns.

Following are two sample explanations that have been geared to the educational levels of the clients and personalized to address their specific concerns. *Example 1:* An explanation to a mother with a ninth-grade education who has been told by authorities that she must seek treatment in order to keep her 10-year-old son at home.

TH: What we will do is teach you ways to deal with problems, like getting Mark to go to school or help you more around the apartment. How does that sound to you?

MOTHER: OK.

TH: Good. I think you'll find that once you've learned how to help Mark stay out of trouble, the child welfare folks will close your case.

MOTHER: I don't know. I sure hope so.

TH: So do I. I'll bet right now you're feeling like that won't ever happen, that there will always be someone from an agency telling you what to do.

Example 2: An explanation regarding the benefits of treatment given to a set of professional parents seeking help with their child's temper tantrums.

TH: The focus of the program will be on teaching the two of you effective ways to intervene when Sara throws temper tantrums and destroys her toys. Since all 4-year-olds have tantrums occasionally, we probably won't eliminate them altogether. However, we will be able to bring them to an acceptable level. How does that sound to you?

MOTHER: I'm willing to try anything at this point. Sometimes I think Sara's behavior would be better if I quit my job.

TH: No doubt her behavior adds to your pressures, particularly when you're both working full time. You're probably worrying a lot about her behavior problems at the day-care center, which makes it difficult to concentrate on your work.

Use Humor

Using humor, and seeing the lighter side of events, can help clients relax and view their problems as less hopeless. It can also reduce anger or defensiveness. Care must be taken, however, not to make fun of the client's problems or feelings. Examples of how humor can be used include:

FATHER: And so Jesse and this other kid were about to get into it, so this other kid ran home and locked the screen door. Then he started calling Jesse names through the screen. Well, Jesse turned on the water hose and sprayed the kid. Naturally, he got the inside of the house, too.

TH: (Laughing) As you say this it sounds like something out of a Little Rascals film.

MOTHER: Sometimes I just don't know whether to cry or what.

TH: I recommend laughing.

GATHERING INFORMATION

Although many clients experience similar child-management problems such as noncompliance, temper tantrums, or lying, the way these problems are manifested will vary from family to family. For example, in one home a child's tantrums may result in both parents giving in to their child's demands, while in another it might bring on severe physical punishment from one parent, followed by soothing from the other. Such differences will require tailoring interventions to meet the particular needs of each family. To accomplish this you must have accurate information about the family's problems, relationships, and affective experiences. The following section describes several clinical skills that, when combined with the relationship-building skills discussed earlier, will enable you to gather important information while making your clients feel understood, accepted, and supported.

Use Open-ended Questions

An open-ended question is one that cannot be answered with a yes or no. Open-ended questions request information in a way that is specific enough for clients to understand what's being asked and general enough for them to answer as they wish. Open-ended questions tend to draw information out of the client, whereas questions that can be answered with yes or no often slow down or stop the dialogue and shift the burden of initiating conversation back to you. Examples of open-ended questions are:

"Tell me about your use of time-out last week" versus "Did you use time-out last week?"

"What happens when you tell him it's bedtime?" rather than "Did he throw a fit when you told him to go to bed?"

"How do you usually feel in those circumstances?" versus "Were you angry when that happened?"

Paraphrase and Summarize

To paraphrase means to repeat back to the speaker what you heard. To summarize is to reiterate the topics, decisions, or agreements previously made. Paraphrasing and summarizing can help clarify potential misunderstandings, get things moving following a pause or interruption in the dialogue, and show your clients that you are listening. Paraphrasing would sound like the following:

TH: (In response to client's extensive description of a recent experience in a store) So when he throws a fit in the store he screams, hits you, throws himself on the floor, and sometimes knocks things off the shelves.

CL: I decided she could start living by the family rules just like everyone else, so I put my foot down.

TH: So you decided to punish Allison for disobeying rules?

CL: The baby was crying, Joey was getting into my sewing box, and I was supposed to be getting dinner so my husband could get to his meeting by 7:00.

TH: So everybody needed your attention at once?

The following statements are good examples of summarizing:

TH: Let's see, we've covered where time-out will be, what he will be sent to time-out for, and how to send him. Let's talk now about how long each time-out should be.

TH: So, John, you'll be tracking Sue's behavior on Friday and Saturday for an hour, and Joan, you'll be tracking Monday,

Tuesday, Wednesday, and Thursday. And you both get Sunday off!

Open-ended questions, paraphrasing, and summarizing are general clinical skills used to gather information. The following three skills will help you gain specific kinds of information, regardless of whether you are conducting an initial interview, developing an intervention, or reviewing the family's progress.

Gather Information about What People Do

Whether you are just beginning the process of gathering information about their problems or reviewing last week's assignment, you must find out exactly what people do in problem situations. This is not always as easy as it sounds. Often people will describe their problems in terms of someone else's character traits ("He's defiant, lazy, rebellious"). Other times, their descriptions are simply too vague to give you an adequate picture of what is really happening ("She never listens," "She's just like her older sister"). Thus, you must be prepared to pursue the matter, asking people to be more and more specific about what they mean. The following example suggests how this might be done:

CL: He's so stubborn. Sometimes I think he does things just to upset me.

TH: What does Mark *do* when he's being stubborn?

CL: Well, when I tell him to do something he'll either ignore me or just come right out and refuse!

Often clients can give a more specific description of a problem or situation if they are asked to recall a recent occurrence of the problem. For example:

TH: I'm still a bit confused about how Michael defies you. Maybe it would help if you would give me a recent example of when he did this.

CL: OK. Just last night I told him to go to bed, but instead he decided to play his little game.

TH: So, last night when he played this game, a defiance game, what did he do?

CL: Well, he ran out of his room and hid under my bed.

TH: Good, now I'm beginning to get the picture. By defiance, what he's doing is not minding. In this case he didn't mind by running and hiding. Can you think of any other instances when he defied you?

With children in particular, it helps if you have them act out what typically happens. Other family members can be asked to take part in this roleplay. Once they have roleplayed, the entire family can critique the scene to insure its accuracy. In addition to being an excellent source of information for you, roleplays are often seen as fun by the family.

Gather Information about Cognitive/Emotional Reactions

Besides learning exactly what people do in specific situations, you also need to find out what each family member thinks and feels during those events. Some clients will have an easy time relating how they feel ("I get angry"). Others will be more aware of what they think ("I shouldn't have to put up with that foul language"). In either case, having such information will help you understand their view of the situation, including whether their reactions are based on objective reality or unwarranted assumptions. Later, you can incorporate this information in presenting the self-control methods described in Chapter Six. More immediately, reflecting back your understanding of their cognitive and emotional reactions gives clients the sense that you understand them. In the following example, notice how the therapist investigates both the client's thoughts and feelings while collecting information.

TH: Describe for me what the problem is at night with Dale.

CL: He screams for another glass of water and a kiss at least 10 times per night.

TH: What things are going through your head the first time he does this?

CL: "Please, not tonight" or "Here we go again."

TH: What about the seventh or eighth time?

CL: I get upset.

TH: What are you saying to yourself?

CL: Sometimes I think, "He's gonna get busted if he keeps this up."

TH: So you get angry? What about other times?

CL: The other night I just started crying and saying to myself, "I'll never have a peaceful night again" and "I can't take this anymore."

TH: At those times you start feeling hopeless.

Gather Information about Sequences and Patterns

Behaviors do not happen in isolation. They occur in response to some signal, event, or other behavior which, in turn, elicits further responses that set in motion a pattern or sequence of behavior. A typical sequence might be (a) mom asks son to pick up his toys, (b) boy refuses, (c) mom threatens, (d) son cries while simultaneously starting to work, (e) mom consoles son, (f) son distracts mom from insisting the chore be completed. When certain sequences appear to repeat themselves as discernable patterns, they are worth investigating. Questions that reveal such information include:

"How does the problem usually begin?"

"What usually happens next? What do you do then?"

"How do others get involved?"

"How do things generally end?"

Again, information about such behavior needs to be quite specific (i.e., what exactly do people *do*). Having the family roleplay or describe these sequences helps clarify patterns they may not have noticed previously. This information will help you discover the interpersonal payoffs each person receives for behaving in ways that maintain the problem. It also points out where in their interactions people need to change their own behavior if they want to change that of another.

MAINTAINING STRUCTURE

Compared to other styles of family therapy, this program is both more directive and more instructional. Thus, unless you maintain control of the pace and direction of treatment, you will have difficulty covering the material during the allotted time. We have identified several clinical skills that will enable you to keep your sessions on task and facilitate the participation of all family members.

Share the Agenda

Each clinical chapter of the book is accompanied by an agenda that summarizes the tasks for the session. While clients are not usually given a copy of this form, it is important to let them know what you would like to accomplish during that day's session. Sharing the agenda also allows them to ask questions about topics that will be discussed or to add items they would like covered. Sharing an agenda with a client during the initial meeting might go as follows:

> TH: What I'd like to do today is find out what problems you are having with your son, Shawn. I'll be asking you to be very specific about what he does and also what things you've tried in the past to correct the problem. Then I'll spend a few minutes explaining this program. By the end of the hour, we'll be able to decide if this program can help you with the problems you've described, and you can decide if this is the type of treatment you're interested in. How does this sound to you?

Agendas can be flexible; you may cover topics in a different order than originally planned, or you may find that you cannot cover the entire agenda during the session. However, do not hesitate to refer back to the agenda if the conversation seems to bog down or the family starts to get off the subject. For example:

> TH: I'm really anxious to teach you what to do when Josh does mind you, so perhaps we should move on.

TH: Great. I think you've agreed on how to use time-out with Susan. Now I'd like to talk about your assignment for the next week.

On occasion you will also need to postpone or abandon your agenda. This will be due to one of three things:

1. At the start of the session you discover that the clients did not understand how to carry out a key aspect of the program that was taught at a previous session. In this case you will need to reinstruct them before proceeding.

2. The clients clearly do not understand or are in direct disagreement with what you are presenting. In such cases it is counterproductive to move on. The clients' concerns should be addressed and resolved before continuing with your agenda. Further discussion on dealing with comprehension problems and resistance are found later in this chapter.

3. On occasion, crisis situations will arise that interfere with the clients' ability to absorb and implement new material. However, take care before abandoning your agenda because of a client crisis. If you fall into the trap of consistently putting out "brush fires," you will not have time to teach the family ways of preventing future crises.

Deal with One Issue or Task at a Time

Jumping from topic to topic without coming to any conclusions or agreement can be confusing for client and therapist alike. If you find this situation happening, take a moment to state clearly the topic at hand, then stay with it until it has been covered. Confusion may also arise when clients jump ahead or ask questions that are linked only tangentially to the subject you are discussing. Acknowledge their concern, but don't allow yourself to become sidetracked. In the following example, notice how the therapist tactfully steers the conversation back to the main point.

CL: What if I'm not home one evening to review his performance?

TH: Good point. That's something we should talk about. But first I want to make sure we finish the list of privileges Jerry can earn if he does his homework each day.

Break Complex Problems into Manageable Units

Clients usually enter treatment with a host of complex problems. Breaking these down and exploring each part separately helps clients see things in more manageable terms. In addition, it helps you gather the specific information necessary to determine an appropriate intervention. The following example illustrates how a therapist focuses on one of many complex problems mentioned by a client.

CL: He's just been so upset since his dad left. He does everything he can to make me feel guilty. He blames it all on me. Besides that, he's ruining all of his friendships, and he's just destroying himself.

TH: It sounds like Mark is having a lot of problems right now. Let's talk for a few minutes about the things he's doing that lead you to feel guilty.

This same strategy can be used when developing the intervention. If you break the intervention down into logical steps and determine solutions to each step before proceeding, your clients will have a better understanding of what they are to do. It is also more likely that you will have developed a sound intervention. Here is an example of breaking down several steps of an intervention:

TH: You have several decisions to make regarding the use of an allowance system: how much Linda can earn, what she must do in order to earn it, and how often you will be paying her the allowance she's earned. Let's start by deciding how much money you would be willing to pay her, say each week, for doing assigned chores.

End Sidetracking

While it is expected that clients will wander off the topic occasionally, frequent sidetracking interferes with accomplishing the treatment goals. We have several suggestions about bringing clients back on task.

1. Summarize what the person has just said and follow your summarization with a transitional statement that returns you to the topic at hand: "So you'll be having lots of company next month. Learning to use time-out with John now should make that go easier for you."

2. Apologize for interrupting and refer back to the agenda: "Sorry for interrupting, but I just looked at my watch. We've got 20 minutes left, and we have three more things to cover today."

3. Empathize with the client, relating the task at hand to a specific concern: "I can tell that his acting out is very upsetting to you. The techniques I'm teaching you today will help reduce this problem and help you feel better."

4. Refrain from making verbal and nonverbal gestures that inadvertently reinforce the person's sidetracking: head nods, comments such as "Uh-huh" or "Really?"

Give Everyone a Chance to Participate

Part of structuring is to get everyone to participate. Unless they do, you won't know how they feel about some issue or whether they understand what you are asking of them. In the following examples, the therapist uses direct questions to call on quieter family members without putting them on the spot.

TH: Sometimes fathers have a different perspective. Tom, as Julie's father, how do you feel about the situation?

TH: Anne, we haven't heard your position on this topic. Do you have any thoughts you'd like to share?

TH: Hank, you haven't said anything. I'm wondering if your perception of this is the same as Ruth's?

In contrast, you may be faced with family members who dominate the conversation or try to talk for others. In these cases, you will need to alter the balance in the discussion without angering or humiliating the speaker. Using a pleasant tone of voice, let the speaker know you understand the stated view or concern, and then firmly redirect the conversation. Avoid direct confrontations such as "I was asking Terri" or "Terri can speak for herself." Examples include:

TH: (To husband) Larry, what do you do when Molly refuses to do what you ask?

WIFE: It all depends on what mood he's in. Sometimes...

TH: Excuse me, Margaret, I know that as an observer you know a lot about how Larry and Molly interact with each other. But for right now I'd also like to hear how Larry sees the situation. Larry, what do you do when Molly disobeys you?

TH: (To wife) So what are your thoughts, Sally?

HUSBAND: Mike can be tough to deal with.

TH: I understand your feelings Jerry, but Sally may have a different perspective. Let's see how she views this situation. Sally, what are your thoughts?

TEACHING NEW SKILLS

The focus of this program is to teach the family new ways of interacting. Thus, more than other family therapy programs, this one calls on your skill as an instructor. To be an effective teacher you must make learning new skills interesting and relevant to your clients, clearly communicate concepts and instructions, and insure that your clients understand the information. We believe that the instructional skills discussed next will enable you to teach your clients more effectively.

Describe Skills in Specific, Nontechnical Language

Strive for brevity, simplicity, and clarity. You should use common, understandable language, and steer clear of jargon. Finally, illustrate points by using client-relevant examples, such as:

TH: When Clare gets home, you should say "Clare, you weren't home from school on time so you will have to clean the bathroom."

TH: You said Jason loves it when you praise his schoolwork, so your approval is very reinforcing to him.

Provide Rationales

To spark the interest of clients, tell them why concepts and tasks are important and how they relate to the clients' situation. The following explanation shows how this can be done.

TH: The discipline method I'm about to describe to you is called "time-out." It has several advantages over most other forms of punishment. First, it is nonphysical. You said in our first meeting that spanking Shawn doesn't get him to mind you and that you feel guilty after using physical punishment. Once you start using time-out, you'll find you won't need to spank him anymore. Second, time-out can be used for even minor misbehaviors; therefore, you can correct Shawn before he gets really out of control. That should keep you from getting so upset with him that you get one of those headaches you told me about.

Model the Skill

Demonstrating the skill helps the family understand what you are talking about. You can model by taking the role of one of the family members and acting out examples of specific statements or actions. In some circumstances it is useful to model both appropriate and inappropriate behaviors so that your clients can observe the difference, as in the following examples:

TH: First I'm going to do it the wrong way. See if you can notice what's wrong. "If you don't shape up you're not going outside to play!" Now here's a better way of saying it: "When you've cleaned your room you may go outside to play."

TH: Compare "My God, you actually cleaned your room!" to "Your room really looks nice."

In addition to modeling newly taught skills throughout the sessions, you should try as much as possible to demonstrate appropriate communication skills, empathic understanding, and positive relabeling.

Check for Comprehension

New topics should not be addressed until clients have demonstrated their comprehension of previous topics. You can check for comprehension through questioning and rehearsing. Avoid questions that require a yes or no answer; clients may say they understand when in fact they don't for fear of appearing ignorant. Open-ended questions encourage the client to give more elaborate answers, enabling you to pinpoint any areas of confusion. For example:

"What things will Martha be sent to time-out for?"

"What are some things that would be reinforcing to her?"

"What will you do if you find yourself getting tense?"

A second method of determining your clients' level of comprehension is to have them rehearse how they will implement procedures and use social learning concepts at home. While roleplaying is one of the most useful instructional techniques, many clients report feeling self-conscious, nervous, or silly when asked to practice skills in sessions. To alleviate some of this tension, we have several suggestions.

- Don't make a big production out of roleplaying. Clients are more likely to cooperate, particularly during their first visits, if the term "roleplay" is avoided. Rather, ask such questions as "What would you say if Jeremy were teasing his sister?...Is that how you would say it?...No?...How would you say it?" or "What would you do if Alice got right up to your face, like this, and said 'I hate you'?" By keeping the situations spontaneous, you will find that clients often slip into roleplaying naturally.

- Make rehearsing fun. By exaggerating the roles you play and making it funny, clients warm up faster.

- Once your clients have demonstrated a behavior that they will exhibit at home, reinforce their efforts: "You were so convincing, for a second I forgot we were in my office." Provide positive feedback about their performance: "That was great, Joan. You sounded firm yet you remained very calm."

- If clients express discomfort over rehearsing, reassure them that their feelings are quite natural and that it will get easier for them to roleplay.

Couple Negative Feedback with Positive Statements

After rehearsing and when reviewing their prior week's performance, you may need to give clients corrective feedback that could be construed as criticism. To minimize defensiveness, embarrassment, or anger, you should accompany the correction with reinforcement, empathy, reassurance, or a statement of confidence. When sensitive issues are sandwiched between positive statements, clients are more apt to hear the feedback and react to it in a calm and rational manner. For example:

TH: You've really learned to give clear and polite, but firm, commands, George. I think the area we need to work on more is reinforcing the children when they do obey you. I know you said that sometimes you feel silly, but I'm convinced we can figure out some ways you can reinforce them that you'll feel good about doing.

A second way to provide constructive feedback without upsetting clients is to begin by ascribing benevolent motivations to their behavior. Relabeling their actions reduces the likelihood that clients will feel criticized or blamed, and it allows them to save face in front of other family members. For example:

TH: (To mother) It sounds to me as if you were trying to communicate to Melissa that you really care about what happens to her. But to Melissa it seemed as though you were just lecturing.

INSURING IMPLEMENTATION OF SKILLS

As a skilled social learning therapist, you will not only teach and have your clients practice new skills during sessions, but you will also take steps to help them generalize these skills to their interactions at home. Even clients who understand topics covered in the sessions can have difficulty implementing new procedures outside the therapeutic setting. There are several reasons for this fact. First, many people find it difficult to focus on behavior change when they are also confronted with a host of problems unrelated to parent-child conflicts, such as unemployment, poor transportation, or medical problems. Second, some enthusiastic clients will set up programs that they cannot carry out realistically; for example, a parent who works two jobs agrees to observe her child's behavior for 3 hours each day. Third, some clients may understand what to do but lack the motivation to change. And finally, some clients will achieve a conceptual understanding of the concepts they have been taught but be unable to apply them to their own problems. The following four clinical skills will help you prepare the family to use the social learning and cognitive techniques at home.

Personalize In-session Rehearsals

Generalizing newly learned skills to home situations is more likely if in-session rehearsals match home conditions as closely as possible. Thus, rehearsals should be based on problems actually experienced by clients, should incorporate the emotional and cognitive aspects of the situation, and should include forces external to the family that influence their behavior. The following example illustrates how this can be done:

TH: What I'd like the two of you to do is imagine an evening when you both get home from work feeling rushed; John, you're expected to go to a union meeting that night, and Donna, you're upset because your boss made you work late. OK?

CL: OK.

TH: Now suppose Terry isn't home when the two of you get there, and he's left no note saying where he's gone. Donna, you're worried that something might have happened to him. John, you're getting angry because dinner is being delayed, and you're going to be late for the meeting.

JOHN: A *very* similar situation happened just a couple of weeks ago.

DONNA: That's right.

TH: (Acknowledges parents by nodding head and continues) After 45 minutes, Terry walks in. John and Donna, can you tell me how you could use the self-control techniques in this situation?

Preproblem Solve Potential Difficulties

Once you have taught the family new techniques and they have determined specifically how they will implement them at home— where time-out will be, who will track behaviors—explore any potential problems they will encounter. While the difficulties discussed will vary among families, common deterrents include:

- Carrying out interventions and maintaining self-control in the face of additional pressures such as financial problems, visitors, or medical problems.
- Scheduling days so that daily tracking and/or performance reviews can be done.
- Handling unanticipated obstacles, as when the boss wants you to work on a night that you promised to take the children to the movies.

The best way to discover likely problems is to have the family members describe exactly how they will carry out their plans ("Tell me when you will review the monitoring sheet each day") and to ask questions regarding logistic and emotional deterrents ("When will you review the sheets if something disrupts your schedule and you can't do it at 7:30?" or "How will you handle the reviews if you've had a bad day and Joan didn't earn her reward?"). Clients who think about and solve difficulties in advance are better equipped to handle them when and if they occur in the home. In addition, this process usually points out to clients their unrealistic expectations and gives them a chance to readjust their program, increasing the possibilities of success.

Solicit and Anticipate Concerns

It is important that client concerns be raised and discussed. If clients harbor reservations about some step, they are less likely to implement that part of an intervention. You should invite clients to express their concerns by asking questions like "How do you see this working in your family?" "What problems do you foresee if you were to try this?" "How do you feel about that idea?" or "You look a bit skeptical. Why don't you tell me what your concerns are?"

If you suspect your clients have a concern or doubt, you needn't wait for them to raise the issue. Rather, bring it up yourself; assure them their concern is normal as you address the subject. For example:

TH: Parents often worry that their child won't think time-out is much of a punishment. But you know, what we've found is that children Joey's age really don't like being taken away from their parents' attention and all of the family activities... even for 5 minutes.

Predict Feelings and Behavior Changes

There is an advantage in being a bit of a Svengali and predicting both positive changes and temporary problems the family will experience because of the treatment. Predicting positive changes in behavior or feelings can make clients more sensitive about noticing improvements, and recognition of positive change is a primary motivation for clients to continue implementing the program. Examples of positive predictions include:

TH: In addition to using self-control techniques with your children, I think you'll notice yourself trying out these skills in other stressful situations.

TH: Parents usually tell me that within a week or so of using time-out their child goes in without a fuss. Some kids even time themselves out!

TH: When you begin using relaxation, you'll notice yourself being less tense by the end of the day.

Warning clients about temporary problems will keep them from getting caught off guard and will help them maintain better self-control and implement appropriate techniques more effectively. In some cases, warning clients of potential difficulties enables them to take steps to prevent or minimize them. While your predictions will vary depending upon the age of the child, the presenting problems, the punishment and reward techniques chosen, the family's routine, and the temperament of various family members, some common predictions include the following:

1. There is usually a temporary escalation in the child's misbehavior following implementation of consistent punishment.
2. Parents often feel anxious or awkward when first implementing techniques.
3. Parents may not want to give the child an earned reward because of some other misbehavior the child committed.
4. After things improve, there will be some backsliding.

Accurate predictions increase your credibility. Clients frequently make statements like "You were right about her trying to get out of going to time-out by saying she likes it" or "It's like you said, I actually look forward to his coming home each day."

PROMOTING INDEPENDENCE AND GENERALIZATION

While your initial goal is to help the family reduce their presenting problems, a second and equally important goal is to teach them skills for resolving future conflicts with little or no professional assistance.

Encourage Client Initiative

From the outset clients should be given a central role in setting goals, developing interventions, and initiating solutions. While the program's instructional format puts you in a teaching role regarding the presentation of concepts and techniques, you should encourage clients to interject their ideas about material covered and to decide how they will apply techniques to their situation. It is important that they do not see you as "the person with all the answers."

While some families will readily take the initiative, others are more hesitant to do so. One way to encourage input from clients is through the use of prompts and leading questions. These are statements and questions that help the client narrow down and assess options. For example, after explaining time-out, you could say:

TH: Where would you have time-out in your house?

In a situation where a client cannot think of any work chores for the child to do, you might say:

TH: Are there any things around the kitchen, garage, or yard that could use some attention?

When the parents are considering dessert as a reward for their child, you could prompt the parents to see whether they might feel guilty giving dessert to the rest of the family with no strings attached by asking:

TH: Is dessert something the rest of the family would get anyway?

For clients who have difficulty responding to prompts, you can encourage them to take more initiative by providing them with choices. For example:

TH: You could use either the bathroom or the laundry room for time-out. Which do you think would work out best for you?

By providing quality options, clients are assured of picking one that should succeed; at the same time they are getting practice evaluating for themselves what methods they will try.

Reinforce Client Initiative and Give Credit for Positive Changes

You should be alert for signs that your clients are generalizing skills they have learned to novel situations. At the same time, ascribe any changes in the targeted behavior to their efforts.

TH: John, Nancy told me you used time-out with Jill in the store with a lot of success. That's great. Why don't you tell me about it?

CL: You've really helped us out.

TH: Well, thank you. But you are the ones who've really made it work. You've taken away privileges if they weren't earned, and you've let Nick know when you appreciate what he has done.

Interpret Situations from a Social Learning Perspective

Use social learning interpretations to describe incidents in terms of modeling, reinforcement, and punishment. If clients are encouraged to analyze their own behavior accordingly, they will be better equipped to work out possible solutions to future problems. The first example shows a therapist making a social learning interpretation; the second example illustrates how clients can be prompted to think in terms of these principles.

TH: When you pick up Katie she stops whining and that's reinforcing to you. But without realizing it you're teaching her that all she has to do is whine and she'll get picked up.

TH: Joan, when David threw the tantrum in the store, and you took him to the car for time-out, what were you teaching him?

CL: That he can't get away with that in public any more than he can at home.

TH: How is that different from what you used to do in those situations?

CL: Well, I used to reinforce his tantrums by giving in and buying him candy.

TH: Right.

HANDLING RESISTANCE

Despite the best efforts of therapists using this program, client resistance often proves to be a treatment obstacle. Resistance can occur in a variety of ways including nonparticipation of family members, withholding of pertinent information, talking about the past rather than the present, placing blame on others for one's own problems, failure to complete assignments, session cancellations, and direct challenges and confrontations.

Determine Why Clients Resist

The implications of client resistance vary from one theoretical orientation to another. Social learning theory assumes that client ambivalence, skepticism, and caution are reasonable given the risk involved in making changes. After all, while one's lifestyle may be uncomfortable, it is still predictable. Change brings about unpredictable consequences which have the potential of being more painful than the status quo.

Resistance also can be an outgrowth of pride. For some people, seeking help is an admission that they cannot solve their own problems or that they are at fault in some way. When we recognize that family conflict often produces considerable anger and blame, it is easy to understand how people take the position that, if changes are to be made, others should take the first step.

Clients will also resist the program if they do not understand what treatment will entail and how it can benefit them, or if they have had a bad experience with previous counseling. Finally, some people do not voluntarily seek treatment, but are coerced into doing so by schools, courts, or welfare agencies. It would be surprising if people under these circumstances were not resistant.

Despite these situations, we believe that under the right conditions families will enter into and carry through with treatment. The therapist must assume the responsibility for creating conditions in which clients feel safe to disclose their problems and initiate change. Use of the relationship-building skills described earlier will help you do this.

Make Sure It Is Not a Comprehension Problem

Before discussing some specific ways to deal with client resistance, it is important to stress that you should not always attribute a client's nonperformance to a lack of motivation. Rather, nonperformance is often the result of a communication and comprehension problem; the clients may not adequately understand the techniques or what they are expected to do. Besides the points listed previously under "Teaching New Skills" and "Insuring Implementation of Skills," you are encouraged to make it easy for clients to admit their confusion or misunderstanding. This can be done by reassuring them ("We really covered a lot last week. Did you have any difficulty remembering parts of what we discussed?"), sharing the responsibility ("I may have explained it in a way that was confusing to you"), and asking open-ended questions to find out where the confusion arose ("Last week we set up a point system. Can you tell me what problems, if any, you had with that?"). Avoid questions that put clients "on the spot" and make them feel as though they're being tested ("Can you tell me what reinforcement is?" "What were you supposed to do at home last week?").

If a comprehension problem does exist, it is a good idea to go through a review before moving on to new material. During this review you may need to:

1. Use simpler language to explain concepts;
2. Slow down the pace of instruction;
3. Cover fewer points during the session;
4. Use more examples to illustrate points;
5. Incorporate more modeling and rehearsal;
6. Engage in more extensive preproblem solving before sending them home to use the techniques.

Contact the clients within 24 hours to check for problems. If they are still confused, be prepared to make a home visit.

The remainder of this section reviews several clinical skills for dealing with clients when they appear either unmotivated or actively resistant. We assume that if you spend considerable time developing a relationship with clients early in treatment, many resistance problems can be circumvented. We concur with Alexander et al. (1976) in that therapists must build a trusting relationship with clients before efforts to teach concrete skills will have a positive impact. Those authors contend that without such a relationship, clients tend to challenge or refute their therapist's suggestions, observations, and directions.

Discuss Client Concerns

If clients do not cooperate, it may be because they have a concern that they have not expressed or that you have failed to grasp. Whatever the case, it is best to ask them about the problem in a nondefensive, nonconfrontative manner. Remember that many people cannot immediately pinpoint what is bothering them. On the other hand, even if they know what the problem is, they may be reluctant to say so without considerable reassurance from you that it is all right to be open.

Once the concern is clarified, it needs to be addressed sincerely and honestly. For example:

TH: (On the phone) I wanted to give you a call and find out if the self-control method is working for you.

CL: Well...I didn't get a chance to begin yet.

TH: Hmm...Sue, I think I'm hearing some concern about using the self-control program. Can you tell me what you're thinking?

CL: I guess the problem is I just don't see how changing my "self-talk," as you call it, will really make a difference.

TH: You know, you might be right. It may not work for you at all, or maybe it will only have a limited effect. What I'd like to suggest is an experiment where you try it for just a few days to see what happens.

Relate Tasks to Client Goals

When clients do not see how a specific task relates to one of their goals, they are unlikely to cooperate for long. Thus, in working with resistant clients you need to keep making that connection clear. A client's goals refer to more than just a list of specific behavioral changes. For most clients, these goals also include feeling better about oneself and the rest of the family, and receiving greater support from others. In this regard, you will do well to emphasize some of the more nonspecific, "warm fuzzy" outcomes of treatment that clients can expect to gain ("When you use time-out consistently, he'll see that you mean what you say. It will be showing him you really do care about what he does" or "You're such an important person in her life, when she hears you say nice things about her it's bound to increase her self-confidence").

Relating goals to treatment tasks is more difficult if family members disagree about those goals. In the following example, the father wants his son to obey, while the mother is concerned about the father's often harsh reactions to the boy. Note how, in addition to addressing everyone's concerns, the therapist relabels behaviors to give the family more common ground for understanding.

TH: One of the ways we can set ourselves up for success when we ask children to do something is to try and follow certain basic rules about giving commands. The number one rule is "first get the child's attention" (looking at the mother). This way both of you can be sure that Greg really did hear what you've asked him to do, and (looking at the father) there is less chance that later he can pretend he didn't. In either case, both of you will find it easier to support each other knowing that Greg has been given a fair chance. Can both of you see why this rule is helpful not only to Greg but to the two of you?

Modify Tasks and Assignments

Families will resist tasks and assignments that they feel are too difficult or impractical. Therefore, both in planning new assignments and reassigning tasks that were not done, you should review with family members what obstacles they foresee and have them decide what they can realistically accomplish. Once the family states what they feel is reasonable, they are likely to be more committed to carrying it out.

In addition, tasks and assignments should take into account well-established family roles. If the husband is the acknowledged head of the house and the wife is the primary caretaker of the children, you might have her take responsibility for tracking the children's behavior. The husband, in turn, could be asked to look over the tracking forms each evening and be supportive of his wife's efforts.

Following this chapter is a list of the major clinical skill categories and the specific behaviors involved. We do not expect you to keep all of these skills in mind while concentrating on delivering the program. Rather, we suggest that you make an audio or video recording of your sessions with families. By reviewing these recordings, you can keep track of which skills you use and begin to recognize where your delivery might be improved. Novice users of the program often are pleasantly surprised to discover that even with their first clients they already exhibit many of these skills and that with practice their proficiency increases rapidly.

Building Relationships
   Communicate empathy
   Provide reassurance and normalize problems
   Use self-disclosure
   Define everyone as a victim
   Emphasize positive motivation
   Establish positive expectations for change
   Match your communication style to the family
   Use humor
Gathering Information
   Use open-ended questions
   Paraphrase and summarize
   Gather information about what people do
   Gather information about cognitive/emotional reactions
   Gather information about sequences and patterns
Maintaining Structure
   Share the agenda
   Deal with one issue or task at a time
   Break complex problems into manageable units
   End sidetracking
   Give everyone a chance to participate
Teaching New Skills
   Describe skills in specific, nontechnical language
   Provide rationales
   Model the skill
   Check for comprehension
   Couple negative feedback with positive statements
Insuring Implementation of Skills
   Personalize in-session rehearsals
   Preproblem solve potential difficulties
   Solicit and anticipate concerns
   Predict feelings and behavior changes
Promoting Independence and Generalization
   Encourage client initiative
   Reinforce client initiative and give credit for positive changes
   Interpret situations from a social learning perspective

Handling Resistance

    Determine why clients resist

    Make sure it is not a comprehension problem

    Discuss client concerns

    Relate tasks to client goals

    Modify tasks and assignments

Chapter Four

INITIAL MEETING
WITH THE FAMILY

In this session you will meet the family and prepare them to begin treatment. You have five major tasks to accomplish:

- Welcome the family and explain the session agenda.

- Investigate the presenting concerns.

- Inquire about any other factors that may affect the family's ability or willingness to participate.

- Describe the treatment program, including rationale, expected benefits, material covered, and effort required.

- Discuss concerns related to their participation.

Individuals seeking help typically are anxious about what will happen and skeptical that any program will really help. Accomplishing the listed tasks should address many of these concerns. In addition, always keep in mind that one of your primary objectives is to build a positive relationship with the family.

In general, the material in this chapter can be covered in 1 to 1½ hours. Some families, however, may require more time; thus, you should be prepared to complete the tasks in a second meeting. It is important not to rush through crucial sections, nor should you leave the family with the impression that they did not have enough time to give you necessary information, express their concerns, or learn about the program before making a commitment.

We recommend that if you are seeing the family alone (i.e., not in a group therapy format), and if the target child is 8 years old or older, you invite the child and older siblings to attend the first session. By having the child or children in this session you will get a first-hand impression of some of the family conflicts; more importantly, you will be able to involve the child or children in the change process. Children under 8 years are usually not verbal enough to participate and are unable to sit through an entire session. This is not, however, a hard-and-fast rule. You may choose to meet with the entire family during this session to decide whether the children, regardless of age, should be included in future sessions. If you decide not to include younger children in this first session, you should schedule one short meeting with them in order to get a first-hand impression of their behavior. Specific directions for observing or interviewing the children are provided at the end of this chapter.

Working with children in attendance is little different from working with parents alone. You will need to guard against letting parents ventilate an unending stream of complaints about the children in their presence. Similarly, you may need to make greater efforts to include the children in the conversation. Our experience has been that if you approach concerns from a nonblaming stance, review positive as well as negative behaviors, and accept everybody's positive desires for change—as well as their natural fears in this regard—then the children become helpful participants.

BEGINNING THE SESSION

Materials Needed

You should have the following listed materials ready for use when you begin the session. The Therapist Agenda is found at the end of the chapter. The intake form should be whatever form you (or your agency) use to summarize basic information about the family (names, address, ages, etc.); the release of information forms should be those forms that are needed to gain access to records held by schools, medical facilities, or other helping agencies.

- Therapist Agenda with notes
- Intake form
- Release of information forms

Welcome the Family and Explain the Agenda

When the family comes into the treatment room, introduce yourself and then spend a few minutes in social conversation, making an effort to speak to each person. The family members are more likely to be at ease and better able to accommodate themselves to your purpose if they know what to expect. Explain that today you want to accomplish several tasks:

1. To learn about some of the problems and concerns that brought them to see you and to discover the strengths that each person has and the strengths they share as a family.

2. To explain what the treatment is, what the benefits might be, and the effort it will require of them.

3. To decide together whether this program is appropriate for them or whether referral to a different resource might be better.

We usually find it helpful to stress that the purpose of this session is simply to find out about the family and that no decision or commitment to enter treatment is expected at this point.

If there are children present, you may want to take a few moments to present some ground rules. Those ground rules include:

1. Everybody gets a chance to speak.
2. When others are talking, listen quietly.

Children are usually very attentive at this point, so use this as an opportunity to praise how well they are doing. Then, every few minutes, if the children continue to be attentive and follow these rules, stop what you are doing and reinforce their behavior.

Should children become disruptive, give them one firm but pleasant warning that at any subsequent outburst, they will be asked to leave the room and you will continue without them. In 5 to 10 minutes, children can be readmitted; however, if they need to be sent out a second time they should remain out for the rest of the session.

Check for Concerns about Entering Treatment

Ask if the family has any concerns or questions. If the family was coerced into seeking treatment, acknowledge their probable wariness and emphasize that before starting both they and you must decide whether the program is appropriate. Raising the issue in this fashion should help allay any mistrust or resentment.

GATHERING INFORMATION

Review the Presenting Problem

You are now ready to inquire about the problem that led them to seek treatment. A good opening is: "Tell me about the problems that led you to decide to come in." Most parents quickly identify something their children are doing as the major concern. Occasionally, parents will describe the problem in terms of their inability to deal with their children. In either case, the discussion quickly focuses on problematic child behaviors.

Less frequently, parents will state that they were coerced into coming, either by an outside party or a spouse. In such cases, you will need to shift the discussion to the particular parent and child behaviors that prompted the demand that they seek treatment. Investigate the presenting problem along the following lines:

1. What are the specific problem behaviors and what are the settings in which they are most likely to occur?
2. What are the typical interactional sequences around the problem?

3. How does each family member respond cognitively and emotionally to the problem?
4. What would they like to see happen instead?
5. How have they tried to deal with the problem behavior or to encourage more appropriate behavior?

The following sections should help you gather more complete information in these five areas.

Problem behaviors and settings. Your objective is to get an exact picture of what the child does that is causing a problem. Useful questions include:

"Tell me exactly what he does."

"Describe a recent incident."

"How long has the problem been occurring?"

"When did it start or when did you first notice it?"

"How often does this occur on the average in an hour, day, week, or month?"

"Is it more likely to happen at certain times of the day?"

"Is it more likely to happen in a particular setting, such as while you and she are shopping or in public, while driving, or while visiting friends or relatives?"

In addition, you can ask the parents or child to demonstrate a typical incident.

Interactional sequences. Your objective at this point is to find out if the problem tends to occur in a typical, repetitive pattern and how the problem expands to include the entire family. Questions useful for investigating the first issue are:

"Describe a typical incident. What starts it off? What happens next? And then? And then? How does it typically end?"

Questions for the second issue include:

(To seemingly uninvolved family member) "Where are you when this takes place? How do you hear about it? What do you do?"

Cognitive and emotional responses. The next set of questions will help you determine what members of the family are thinking and feeling, both when they are actively involved in the conflict and later when they think back, reflect, or brood over the matter. An assumption of this program is that people's ability to respond effectively may be impaired because of what they tell themselves or feel about their problem. Of special concern are thoughts that generate extreme anger, depression, self-doubt, and anxiety. Useful questions in this regard are:

"When _____ did _____, how did you feel?"

If individuals have difficulty recalling their feelings, rephrase the question as follows:

"Think back to when _____ happened. Try to get a really good picture of that situation. Can you see it now? All right, what are you feeling?"

When a family member begins to share a feeling, it is important for you to discover, identify, and link the associated thoughts with the feelings.

"When _____ did _____ and you were feeling _____, what were you thinking?"

As you begin to elicit these feelings and cognitions, it is important to convey a clear sense of empathy and to reassure the person that many people feel this way. Also, explain that one objective of this program is to help people feel better about themselves and each other as they learn to deal with their problems. You will need to emphasize at this point that perfect harmony will never occur. All families have some conflict, but the goal is to have the conflict become less frequent and more manageable.

Desired behaviors and prosocial opposites. These questions will encourage the family to think in terms of more desirable behaviors that may or may not be occurring and that could replace the problem behaviors. Examples include minding rather than defiance, waiting to be recognized rather than demanding attention, or asking for something in a neutral or positive tone rather than whining.

"What is it that _____ has done at times rather than _____ that you would like to see happen more often?"

Be wary of demands that the other person simply stop the problem behavior. For example, rather than select "not fighting" as the behavioral opposite of fighting, behaviors such as sharing toys, taking turns, and playing by oneself might be chosen. Because thinking in these terms is often difficult, you may have to prompt the family. You might have the parents recall an instance when their son or daughter behaved well, and then have them identify what exactly it was that he or she did that they appreciated. Incidentally, don't overlook asking the children to identify what they would consider more appropriate behavior for themselves. Finally, once the family has identified positive behaviors, get an estimate of the present frequency and the situations or settings in which they are most likely to occur.

Current ways of dealing with problems and encouraging appropriate behavior. Questions that should be asked include:

"What do you do when your son or daughter does (the presenting problem)?"

"What effect does that have?"

"Is that the way you usually respond?"

"Besides trying to deal with the problem after it has occurred, have you ever tried to prevent or avoid the problem? How did that work?"

"How have you tried to encourage your son or daughter to (the prosocial behavior)? How has that worked?"

Investigate Other Behavior Problems

After discussing the problem that led them to seek help, repeat the same line of inquiry for other issues. This can include other problem behaviors of the targeted child, conflicts with the other children, and problems raised by the youngsters. If not specifically mentioned, inquire about troubles that might be occurring outside the home, including stealing, setting fires, wandering away from home, and problems in school. If school problems are mentioned, have the parents sign a release of information form for the school records.

Inquire about Developmental, Health, and Medical Concerns

Make a brief check on the youngster's development, including significant milestones (when the child first walked and talked, early school adjustment, significant illnesses, current health). If there are any outstanding signs or concerns, you may want to suggest that a physical examination or a comprehensive developmental screening be scheduled. Also, check whether the parents have discussed their problems with the child's physician and whether the child has been or is currently on any medication or a restricted diet for behavior problems or hyperactivity. If the youngster is on some form of medication, or if the child's physician is involved, obtain a release to consult with doctors.

Inquire about Past or Current Help

Ask the parents if they have previously sought help or are currently doing so for any of the problems mentioned. If they answer yes to any of these questions, find out the time, place, and name of the service provider, what was done, and any results. If they are currently receiving treatment, you will want to make sure that your program will not conflict with that service. Ask them to sign a release of information form and contact the necessary persons before offering your own services.

If the family has participated in a series of treatments that have not helped, you will need to take special note of why they felt it failed. Later, when you describe the program and the effort required, you should make sure that they are committed and that they will work to overcome any obstacles to their full participation.

Check for Parental Conflict

If the child is present, you should excuse the child while you pursue this issue and the next two topics related to parental agreement and support. If the prior discussion has not uncovered any major conflicts between the parents about child management, it is appropriate to raise the issue at this point to get specific information about the nature of any conflict, areas of disagreement, and so on. At the same time, reassure them that their conflicts are normal and shared by many parents. A possible lead-in sentence is:

"Often when parents are having some problems with the children, they develop different opinions about how to deal with the issue."

If differences surface, acknowledge that some conflict is to be expected. After all, parents frequently see the children under different circumstances; some children play one parent off against the other; and, most importantly, parents bring different expectations about child rearing to their marriage. Convey these notions to the family, checking for their agreement, or at least openness, to what you are saying. Incidentally, if you are seeing only one parent in a two-parent family, be careful not to side with the parent who is present. The person may go home and announce that the therapist agrees the spouse is the cause of the problem.

Once you have opened the discussion regarding parental disagreement, extend your questioning to the general state of the marital relationship itself. If the parents are having marital difficulties, ask if they are considering marital counseling or separation and whether they believe they can make a mutual commitment to work on the child's problems at this time. If they feel they can, you should continue with this program. If they are doubtful, you will need to talk with them about the possibility of seeking marital counseling, from yourself or from someone else. It is important to recognize that while some of the children's problems may arise from serious parental conflict, often the marital conflict may result from the parents' inability to handle their children, which may generate anger, guilt, and depression in the parents. Acquiring the skills to resolve one set of problems can lay the foundation for resolving others.

Inquire about Parental Sources of Support

There is growing evidence that parents who are isolated or lack basic social support from adults risk having more problems with their children. Indeed, Wahler (1980) has noted a direct relationship between day-to-day fluctuations in children's behavior problems and the frequency and quality of contacts the parent has with others outside the home. Wahler and Moore (1975) also noted that parents who were socially isolated at the beginning of treatment, and who did not break out of that isolation during treatment, had great difficulty maintaining treatment-based improvements.

As you can see, it is important to inquire about the frequency of, and personal satisfaction derived from, adult contacts parents have outside the household. These can include relations with close relatives and neighbors, participation in church or social organizations, and work- or school-related contacts. If the parents report that they have few, if any, regular contacts with other adults, you will need to address this issue during treatment. You might help parents locate ongoing support groups, child care, educational or employment opportunities, and the like. We also recommend group-based treatment for isolated single parents (see Chapter Fifteen).

Inquire about Other Problems Confronting the Family

Unless it has already come up in the conversation, it is a good idea to find out if the family is experiencing other problems or stresses. These can include depression or other emotional problems of the parents, financial worries, alcoholism, possible relocation, or serious illness. Also, check whether the parents themselves have been or are currently in therapy for any other problems. The purpose of such questions is to determine whether parents can realistically commit themselves to working on the children's behavior.

Yet the fact that the parents are facing other difficulties does not mean you should automatically defer treatment. As long as the parents feel that other concerns will not interfere with their performance, you should proceed. However, you also might want to assist them in finding other needed services, and, on occasion, help them decide which concerns should be handled first and which can be dealt with while they participate in this program.

PRESENTING THE PROGRAM

The next major task is to present the treatment program. While to some extent you may need to sell the family members on participating, your main goal should be to make them intelligent and committed consumers.

In describing the program, we suggest that you organize your presentation into four steps. Those steps are:

1. Point out the strengths and positive qualities you see in each individual and in the family as a whole.

2. Assure them that it is normal to have problems, and link that fact to the need for new skills and behaviors.

3. Describe the treatment, giving details of what it involves, how it relates to the problems noted, and how each individual will benefit from participating.

4. Discuss any concerns you or the family may have regarding their participation.

Describe Family Strengths and Positive Qualities

To put the treatment on a positive note, identify and stress the strong qualities of each individual and the family as a whole. Share your optimism that their problems can be solved and that essentially you see them as good, well-intentioned people. Qualities worth emphasizing are concern, caring commitment, and their ability to carry on under truly difficult conditions. Coping ability is a particularly important quality to convey to families who appear overwhelmed by a myriad of stresses.

Where there is considerable anger and hostility, use the relabeling skills described in Chapter Three. A highly critical parent can be described as "very concerned about the children's welfare." A parent who is remote or very quiet can be identified as one "who is unsure how to share feelings." Hostility or defiance might be relabeled as "testing limits," while adolescent rebellion might be more appropriately defined as "the difficulties of moving from childhood to adulthood." New labels are not always automatically accepted by the family. However, relabeling can open the door to change.

Normalize Problems and Link to the Need for New Skills

With parents of younger children, an effective tactic is to discuss how parents are never formally trained to be parents. Point out that there has been a tremendous change in our society between the way the parents were raised and the world in which their children are growing up. Similarly, parents often receive conflicting advice, and they bring different expectations to the task of child rearing. When faced with these difficulties, it's hard for anyone to know what to do.

With parents of older children, greater emphasis can be given to the developmental process and how each new phase requires that parents adapt to changes in their children. In addition, children are constantly adapting themselves to a larger social environment. For families who have a handicapped child or who have undergone divorce or remarriage, such events can be interpreted as creating even greater challenges.

Describe Treatment

You do not have to give a step-by-step description of the program. But it is essential when explaining treatment to personalize it to the family's particular concerns and needs. Points you may wish to cover include:

1. The program will focus on dealing with problems clients have already described.
2. It will start by taking a look at some things that might make the situation better.

3. You will review ways of becoming less upset when these problems occur in order to deal more effectively with the situation.

4. You will review various procedures for handling the problems and agree on what to do when the problem reoccurs.

5. You will talk about how to encourage their youngster(s) to behave even better.

6. The family will practice how to communicate and solve problems so that in the future they can solve problems on their own.

The final part of describing the treatment is to discuss the effort and time required. Typically, we describe treatment as requiring 3 to 4 months with weekly meetings at the beginning and less frequent contact as treatment progresses. Contact is gradually reduced to insure that the family can maintain the improvements. In addition to these sessions, the family will have weekly assignments, which can include keeping records of the targeted behaviors, implementing the procedures learned in the sessions, and evaluating how well these procedures work.

Discuss Practical and Therapeutic Concerns

Ask the family if they have any questions about the program or concerns regarding their participation. If they seem confused or express reservations, you will need to pursue the matter. Assuming that you are able to satisfy their concerns, it is also important that you present any questions you may have regarding their participation. There are two general concerns you might need to address: practical matters and attitudes toward change.

Practical matters include whether they can attend sessions regularly, set aside time during the week to practice skills and carry out assignments, work together, and turn their attention to the child-management problems in the face of other pressing concerns. You will also need to find out whether the child might be an immediate danger to himself or herself or to others.

The second concern deals with a more subtle issue. While most family members harbor anger, frustration, or despair when entering treatment, individuals who maintain these attitudes are poor candidates for the program. Thus, you should be alert for clients who firmly believe that everyone else is to blame for their problems, who see no need for change in themselves, who believe their situation cannot improve, or who feel that this program is identical to one they have already tried and discarded. If you encounter families who take these positions, it is best not to argue but rather to discuss the fact that neither you nor they can change everyone else. However, since the situation is not good at home, it may be worth their time and effort to attempt to improve matters. The program may be similar to others they have tried but there are differences, such as the setting, the therapist, the age of their children, and perhaps the seriousness of the problem. Finally, mention that their situation reflects an old saying: "If you don't change the direction you're headed, you're likely to get there." Ask them if they like where the family currently is heading. If not, they can work with the program to change that direction. If these points don't persuade the family to participate, it may be best to let the natural consequences take place.

Successful participation in treatment does not require that clients believe the program will work or that it will be easy. Rather, clients need only commit themselves to attend the sessions, carry out the assignments, and withhold final judgment until they have had a reasonable period of treatment. While there is no fixed script for addressing these concerns, the following order of discussion is one we have found effective.

First, briefly state your concerns about the family's participation in the program, citing your reasons. At the same time, assure them that their attitudes or beliefs are normal and avoid labeling any person negatively.

Second, have clients respond to your concerns; listen as empathically as possible. If part of the problem is a misunderstanding about what the treatment will involve or attempt to achieve, address that issue. For example, a client who has had a previous failure in getting help may need to be told how this program differs.

Third, if the clients' responses reveal a fixed attitude or belief, or if they are unwilling to see things differently, suggest that they view the program in terms of a choice. The choice is to enter treatment, attend the sessions, carry out the assignments, and judge for themselves if the benefits are worth the effort. If the clients decide the benefits are not worth it, they can go back to the old way of doing things. When making this suggestion, recognize that clients must choose to change their behavior and that the ultimate responsibility for change lies with them.

If at the end of this discussion the clients still refuse to consider changing their current attitude, it is probably best not to proceed at this time. However, you might suggest that the clients think things over and consider the choice offered by the program. If they are unwilling to do even that, you should conclude the session, either offering to help find another referral source or leaving the door open for them to return.

CLOSING

Schedule the Next Session

If you have worked with the entire family in this session, and they have agreed to participate, schedule the next session. Because momentum is important, we suggest that you plan to meet as soon as possible. If you saw only the parents and have not previously met the children, you should see them next. Directions for conducting the session with the children are provided at the end of this chapter.

Close on a positive and friendly note.

OBSERVING AND INTERVIEWING CHILDREN AND PARENTS

Given the instructional orientation of the treatment, we do not usually involve children under 8 years of age in the regularly scheduled meetings. Nonetheless, there are advantages to observing the child in the parents' presence before you begin the formal intervention. While structured and unstructured observation using a formal system for coding the child's and parents' behavior are standard features of most laboratory-based behavioral treatment programs (Forehand & McMahon, 1981; Reid, 1978), in clinical practice they are less commonly used. It requires considerable effort to learn the code, collect sufficient data to establish reliability, and analyze and interpret the results. Consequently, we suggest a less formal observation procedure that we have found useful in several ways. First, the procedure gives you a first-hand picture of parent-child interactions and some idea of the child's specific problems and strengths. Second, it assures parents that while they, rather than their child, will be seeing the therapist, you have not overlooked meeting the child. Third, it allows you to see if the child exhibits any bizarre behaviors, thoughts, or mannerisms or appears unduly anxious or fearful. Should you note anything unusual in this regard, seek additional consultation before proceeding with the program.

With very young children (5 years old and younger), we suggest you observe the child under three conditions: (a) playing with the parents, (b) playing independently, and (c) responding to a series of simple parental commands. With older children, we suggest a brief interview centering on what changes they would like to see in their family and what they might like from their parents in terms of reinforcers. The latter can include both social reinforcers and special activities the children would enjoy. Specific directions for observing or interviewing the children are provided on pages 63, 64 and 65.

After your observation or interview you should give the parents a brief report on what you noted. It is important to accentuate the positive. Problems should be dealt with as something to be expected in light of the presenting problem and as affirmation of the family's decision to seek assistance. Schedule the next session for as soon as possible and close the session.

DIRECTIONS FOR OBSERVATION OF PARENT-CHILD INTERACTIONS WITH CHILDREN 5 AND YOUNGER

Task 1—Parent-Child Play

Directions: Ask the parents to play with their children, using a variety of age-appropriate toys provided by you or brought by the parents. We do not recommend that commercial games be used, as they tend to restrict interactions. Instructions to the parents:

1. Allow the children to guide the direction of the play. Participate but do not structure the activity.

2. Follow what the children do, attending enthusiastically. Refrain from giving commands unless necessary to prevent the play from becoming destructive. Do not use the time for any formal teaching.

3. Maintain the play for 10 minutes.

Note the following:

Were the children able to enter into the play with the parents?

Were the children able to continue playing without being distracted or constantly moving from object to object?

If more than one child was involved, were they cooperative or competitive?

Was the play reasonably peaceful or excessively active or violent? If excessively active, could the parents assert control?

Were the parents able to follow the directions to participate without structuring the play?

How well did the parents attend and express enthusiasm and warmth to their children?

Task 2—Independent Play

Directions: Ask the parents to tell their children to play by themselves without disturbing you or the parents. Provide the parents with something to read or a form to complete so that they are not involved with the children. Allow 10 minutes for this activity.

Note the following:

How well were the children able to entertain themselves for the entire period?

How well did the parents ignore the children or redirect them to continue their playing if necessary?

Task 3—Response to Parental Commands

Directions: If there are toys to be picked up, ask the parents to have the children put them away. Other possible commands are to have the children rearrange chairs, draw a picture, or put on their coats.

Note the following:

How many commands were given?

How many times did the children comply (within 10 seconds)?

What percentage of the time were the children compliant?

Were the commands clear?

Were the parents firm but positive in giving commands?

Did the parents allow enough time for compliance?

Did the parents follow through by repeating the request once if necessary?

If the children continued to disobey, what did the parents do?

DIRECTIONS FOR INTERVIEW WITH CHILDREN 6 AND OLDER

Introduce yourself to the children and chat briefly about things appropriate to the children's level of interest. As the children relax, explain that you want to ask some questions. These should be covered in a conversational manner, in a style that builds rapport. The questions, with space for your comments, are:

1. In the children's opinion, why are the parents seeking help? _____
_____
_____
_____

2. What problems do the children see or have at home and school? _____
_____
_____
_____

3. What would the children like to change about themselves and about the way the family gets along? If the children are vague, mention some of the problem areas noted by the parents and ask how the children would like to see those things change. _____
_____
_____
_____

4. How would the children like their parents to act differently towards them (more hugs and kisses, more approval and recognition)? Are there any special activities that the children would like to do more often, either individually or as a family? _____
_____
_____
_____

5. Any other observations or comments regarding the children relevant to treatment. _____
_____
_____
_____

THERAPIST AGENDA: INITIAL INTERVIEW

Agenda	*Notes*

Beginning the Session

Welcome the family and explain the agenda:

Learn about their concerns and discover their strengths

Explain treatment

Decide whether the program is appropriate

Check for concerns about entering treatment

Gathering Information

Review the presenting problem:

What are the presenting problem behaviors, and in what settings do they usually occur?

What are the interactional sequences?

How does each family member respond cognitively and emotionally?

What would they like to see happen instead?

How have they tried to deal with the problem or encourage appropriate behavior?

Investigate other behavior problems (Need release of information from school?)

Inquire about developmental, health, and medical concerns (Need release of information from physician?)

Inquire about past or current help (Need release of information from other service providers?)

Check for marital problems or parental conflict over child management

Inquire about parental sources of support

Inquire about other problems confronting the family

Presenting the Program

Describe family strengths and positive qualities

Normalize problems and link to the need for new skills

Describe treatment:

Give general description of program that is personalized to their concerns

Explain the time and effort required

Discuss practical and therapeutic concerns

Closing

Plan to observe the children and schedule the next session

Express confidence in the client

Chapter Five

SETTING UP FOR SUCCESS

This chapter describes the first intervention session. With this step, you will begin the process of teaching basic child-management skills. There are five major tasks you need to accomplish:

- Complete the Goal Setting Form. This form will list three to five areas of concern and the behaviors the family would like to see changed.

- Select or target one of the identified behaviors as the initial focus of change.

- Introduce the concept of "setting up for success" and apply it to the target behavior.

- Prepare the family to begin tracking the target behavior and their effort at setting up for success.

- If the child is not present, prepare the parents to explain to the child that they will be tracking the child's targeted behavior.

As with the intake session, children may be involved at this time if they are mature enough to pay attention to the tasks and to listen without becoming disruptive. In fact, the children's presence may actually encourage cooperation among family members and help clarify treatment goals. Also, when children understand the process of "setting up for success," they may help generate ideas to facilitate change in the family's situation.

Before teaching the concept of "setting up for success," you will help the family decide exactly what the treatment goals will be, that is, what behaviors family members would like to see occur more often and what amount of change they would consider satisfactory. Clarifying treatment goals in terms of behavior serves several purposes. First, the established goals can be consulted periodically to assess treatment progress. Second, they provide a basis for evaluating treatment outcome. Third, redefining problems as discrete behaviors to be changed often makes overwhelming concerns seem more manageable. Fourth, goal setting begins to bring the family together to work on problems everyone has identified. Fifth, knowing in advance what behaviors the family wants to change or encourage will make the task of treatment more manageable for you.

Once the family has established some concrete treatment goals, your task will be to teach them to apply the concept of "setting up for success" to their first concern. "Setting up for success" means to change some of the conditions that contribute to or reinforce the problem behavior. Behavioral psychology has emphasized the role that such events and conditions play in controlling behavior, yet many behavioral and social learning programs stress only consequent events in behavior change. Setting up for success attempts to correct this weakness.

The procedure is important in another way. It appears that in families with few child-management problems parents frequently use what we call setting-up activities to deal with problems. They establish routines and plan activities in order to facilitate cooperation and prevent many parent-child conflicts. They express their expectations in a way to encourage compliance, and they recognize their children's limitations and are constantly teaching them new skills and behaviors. As the parents you see in therapy become more familiar with the idea of setting up, their parenting style should begin to resemble that of parents who have fewer problems.

The following section provides a description of the procedure known as setting up for success. You will learn a variety of approaches that can be used in this technique and ways of presenting these approaches to your clients.

Following this discussion, we present the activities for the session step by step, from establishing treatment goals, to introducing the basic concept, to practicing the technique with clients. The chapter closes with suggestions for a between-session review of your clients' efforts at setting up for success.

UNDERSTANDING SETTING UP FOR SUCCESS

As previously noted, setting up for success means altering the antecedent events and setting conditions that have an effect on the behaviors families would like to change. There is no single approach to setting up; it requires basic problem solving in several areas. The following sections illustrate these areas and give sample solutions.

Rearranging the Environment

We are all aware at some level of the effect our physical surroundings have on our behavior. By physical surroundings we mean the setting (house, room); objects in the setting (toys, books, furniture); and environmental factors (noise, lighting). Often, by changing certain aspects of the physical environment, we can increase the chance that a desirable behavior will occur. For example, you are more likely to bake a cake if you have all the ingredients at home than if you have to run out to the store for them. Altering the physical setting can also discourage undesirable behaviors. For instance, a toddler is less likely to break expensive items if they are placed out of reach. Other ways families can rearrange their environment to deal with certain problems include:

- Encouraging a youngster to do homework by creating a quiet, well-lighted place to work;
- Putting up hooks and hangers at the right height for a child to make it easier for the youngster to keep the room neat;
- Making sure the child has some toys that encourage quiet and/or cooperative play.

Developing Consistent Routines

Routines and schedules help children know what to expect and tend to reduce conflicts over such issues as getting off to school, homework, and chores. Once expectations exist regarding when certain activities should occur, parents often find they need to do less reminding and nagging. Routine schedules could include:

- Arranging a set nightly bedtime routine such as a bath by 8:00 p.m., then a story, and finally a drink of water before being put to bed;
- Scheduling a weekly family night where the entire family shares fun activities;
- Scheduling a 15-minute "quiet time" (i.e., a time when children are not to bother the parent) when a parent returns from work so he or she can shift gears before turning attention to family members.

Making Sure Commands Are Clear, Polite, and Understood

Parents who have trouble with compliance almost always benefit by learning to give better commands. The key steps in giving good commands are:

1. Get the child's attention by moving closer, calling the child's name, and waiting to be acknowledged.
2. Tell the child exactly what you want done and how you want it done.
3. Specify when you want it done.
4. Keep your tone of voice firm but polite.

Teaching New Skills

Often children fail to do something not because they won't but because they don't know how. In such cases, parents can approach the problem as an opportunity to teach skills. The steps in teaching desired behavior are as follows:

1. Identify the skill to be taught.
2. Break the skill down into a sequence of steps.
3. Have the parent demonstrate each step. If the task is complicated, only one or two steps should be demonstrated at a time.

4. Have the child practice the step.

5. Have the parents comment on the child's performance, remembering to reinforce effort and give corrections without being critical.

6. Continue to monitor until the child can perform the entire task alone.

Some skills parents might want to teach are doing household chores, greeting guests, answering the phone, responding to teasing, taking care of personal hygiene, and cooking.

Treating Each Other with More Care, Respect, and Love

An absence of positive interactions and an increase in negative, coercive interchanges make it difficult for family members to work together. Any plan that encourages family members to use more positive statements and fewer negative ones will help. The family may agree to refrain from saying certain critical remarks or decide to give each person at least one sincere compliment or statement of appreciation each day.

Strengthening Marital Ties

Childhood behavior problems wear on the marital relationship. While marital therapy is beyond the scope of this program, there are steps within the framework of setting up that can help. The key seems to be the parents' willingness to acknowledge that their relationship could be better. If they seem willing to work on this issue, there are two approaches you might consider.

The first is relatively simple. Ongoing parent-child conflicts tend to focus the parents' attention on the children. With nearly the entire day taken up by the children's problems, little time or effort is left to do things as a couple. To restore a more healthy balance, suggest that parents schedule time to be together without the children. They might make a weekly "date" to go out for dinner and a movie, visit friends, or prepare a candlelight dinner after the children go to bed.

The second approach is aimed at rapidly improving the parents' daily interaction through what Stuart (1980) refers to as a "caring days" system. "Caring days" can increase the number of times parents do little things for each other to show their care and concern. The only requirement for these "caring" behaviors is that they be (a) positive, (b) specific, (c) small, and (d) not the subject of recent conflict. To set up a "caring days" system, each of the parents is asked to identify 10 to 20 behaviors that he or she would like the spouse to do. These behaviors are listed on a sheet of paper and posted. Each day, the husband or wife marks down whether the partner performed any of the desired behaviors by recording the date after that behavior. By doing so, the parents not only obtain a record of each other's efforts, but become more observant of how the other tries to please. We have noticed that parents in conflict are often quite willing to please their partner if they know precisely what the partner wants and that their efforts will be recognized. Stuart (1980) gives the following examples of caring behavior that parents might list:

- Ask how I spent the day.
- Offer to get the cream or sugar for me.
- Listen to "mood music" when we set the clock radio to go to sleep.
- Hold my hand when we go for walks.

Improving Parental Coordination

It is important that parents work as a team. This means they need to communicate with each other, delegate responsibilities, and support each other's efforts. The following examples show them how this could be done:

- Two working parents divide up the evening child-management tasks. The parents agree that the father will supervise the children as they set the table and do the dishes, while the mother prepares dinner and gives the youngest child a bath.

- Two parents agree that the one who gives the child a command is responsible for enforcing it. The other parent, however, will not allow the youngster to come to him or her to get out of the task.

Encouraging Parental Growth and Well-being

Isolation from other adults, frequent stress, personal problems, and a lack of personal satisfaction with one's life make it hard to be an effective parent. While it is important to focus on parent-child concerns, it is also important to recognize the benefits of dealing with these other areas. Parents need to be encouraged to grow and to develop themselves. Once they realize the importance of satisfying their own needs, there are a number of ways they can enrich their lives. Examples include:

- A single mother joins a group for single parents at the local YMCA.
- A mother signs up for a class on assertiveness training for women at the local community college.
- The parents of a handicapped child join a support group composed of parents in a similar situation.
- A single father arranges for his mother to take the children one evening a week while he goes out with friends.

BEGINNING THE SESSION

Materials Needed

Gather the following listed materials to use in this session. The handouts, blank Goal Setting Form and Program Monitoring Form, and Therapist Agenda are provided at the end of the chapter. The sample Goal Setting Form appears as Figure 4 in this chapter.

- Therapist Agenda with notes

- Completed intake form
- Handout for Parents: How to Complete the Goal Setting Form
- Sample Goal Setting Forms
- Blank Goal Setting Form
- Handout for Parents: Setting Up for Success
- Blank Program Monitoring Form

Welcome the Family and Explain the Agenda

After greeting the family and conversing with them briefly, explain that today you will work together to develop a set of treatment goals. They will then learn a new concept—setting up for success.

COMPLETING THE GOAL SETTING FORM

Having gone over the session's agenda, the next step is to begin the goal setting process. Explain that setting goals helps you understand exactly what changes the family would like to see happen as a result of treatment. In addition, goal setting helps family members clarify for each other exactly which behaviors they feel are problems and which behaviors they would like to have occur more often.

Review the Handouts

Give the family copies of the goal setting handout and sample forms (Figure 4) to look over. Then, following the steps listed on "How to Complete the Goal Setting Form," walk the family through the process of identifying their major concerns, identifying prosocial behaviors they would rather have occur, and setting treatment goals. This entire task usually requires 20 to 30 minutes. The following suggestions should help you through this process.

Enter family concerns (Step 1). Ask the family to determine their major concerns. You should have a good idea what those concerns are from the information you gathered during the previous session. Besides making sure that their goals are described in behavioral terms, you should see to it that no individual is labeled negatively and that they all agree on the treatment goals. The first objective can be met by making sure concerns are stated in a positive or neutral manner, while at the same time not identifying any one individual as the problem. Thus "compliance" is preferable to "Sherry's disobedience."

In most cases there will be a general consensus regarding major child-management problems. On occasion, however, parents will disagree about what the problem is. If this happens, try to focus on general concerns that both parties can agree on. The following is an example of how this could be done:

TH: Josh, you seem concerned that Mark is watching too much TV on Saturdays instead of helping you out in the yard. Theresa, Mark's watching TV doesn't bother you, but it

Figure 4. Sample Goal Setting Forms.

Family _Johnsons_   Therapist _Brad Finley_   Date _10/2_

CONCERNS	Bedtime	Compliance	Chores	School attendance
DESIRED BEHAVIOR	Kisses mom goodnight and then stays in room alone with night light on.	Does what she's told to do without arguing. Completes the task. Begins to comply within 15-20 seconds.	Keeps bedroom picked up and bed made each day. Toys and hobbies are put away before dinner and again before bedtime.	Goes to every class except when excused for health reasons.
CURRENT LEVEL	Never	1-3 out of every 10 commands	2 days per week	Absent at least once per week
CHANGE EXPECTED	4-5 nights per week	6-8 out of 10 commands	5 days per week	Absent only once or twice per month
MORE THAN EXPECTED CHANGE	6 nights per week	9 out of 10 commands	6 days per week	Absent no more than once per semester

CONCERNS	Togetherness			
DESIRED BEHAVIOR	Whole family does pleasant activities (e.g., games, hikes, movies, dinner out) together that all members want to do.			
CURRENT LEVEL	Once a month			
CHANGE EXPECTED	Once every 2-3 weeks			
MORE THAN EXPECTED CHANGE	One or more times per week			

75

does upset you when he forgets to feed the dog or take out the garbage. It seems that you're both bothered by Mark's neglecting his chores. Is that right?

If one parent sees an issue as a problem and the other parent is not bothered by it, point out how, when one spouse is upset because of a problem, it often ends up affecting the other parent ("When Mark fights with the neighbor boy, Theresa gets so upset that she is on edge all night, which is upsetting to you"). Once this point is accepted, we suggest a compromise in which each partner identifies a particular concern, and both concerns are entered on the form.

In cases where the child objects to the parents' concern, you should acknowledge the child's point of view and attempt to explain how the youngster will benefit from working on the issue. For example:

> CHILD: Skipping school's no big deal.
>
> TH: I know that sometimes going to school is a drag for you. You also said you and your dad have gotten into some really heated arguments about your skipping classes. I think we can stop those fights if you're willing to work with your dad on this.

If the child continues to object, do not get into a debate. Rather, write down the parents' concern and continue to identify other family concerns.

Finally, when including the target child or siblings in treatment, we recommend that you include at least one of their concerns as well. By doing so, you will be communicating to all family members that treatment will help each of them obtain desired changes. In addition, by including the children's goals, you are more likely to gain their cooperation and increase their participation in future sessions.

Once the family has determined their major concerns (clients generally list three to five), have them write these issues on one or two blank Goal Setting Forms in the boxes labeled *Concerns*. At this point they should use words that are relevant to them, which may not necessarily be behavioral terms. For example, they may put down "pleasant evenings" instead of "getting child to bed by 8 p.m."

Specify desirable behavior (Step 2). Start with the first concern, and have the family describe the behavior they would like to target for change. The emphasis should be on behavior they want to encourage or increase rather than on behavior they would like to eliminate. The description should be clear and specific. If the family is having difficulty being specific, you may need to:

1. Ask some leading questions: "What exactly does Sherry do when you tell her it's bedtime?" and "What would you like her to do?"

2. Give examples: "Some parents want their children to go to bed without having to leave on a light or keep the door open, while others would be content if their child were willing to stay in the bedroom alone. What would you like Sherry to be able to do?"

3. Paraphrase, using behavioral terms: "So at her bedtime, you would rather that she just kiss you goodnight and allow you to leave the room?"

When parents differ on standards, we believe it's better to emphasize their common aims rather than to emphasize their differences. If one parent does not agree with a particular standard that the other parent wants to set, clarify the concern and work to negotiate a compromise. After you have worked out a complete definition, commend the parents for their ability to come to an agreement. Have them write the definition on the Goal Setting Form in the box labeled *Desired Behavior*.

Determine the frequency of the desired behavior (Step 3). Continue working on the first concern. If you did not find out in the initial interview how often the desired behavior occurs, ask the family to determine how frequently, on the average, the desirable behavior has occurred in the recent past, say, the last 2 months. To get an accurate rate, you may want to ask them to describe how often the behavior occurred during a specific time period ("How many times did Sarah do what you asked this morning?" or "Did Peter feed the dog yesterday? How about the day before that?"). The rate can be specified in a variety of ways, such as the number of times per day or week, or as a percentage (20% of the time or 2 out of every 10 opportunities). Once this is determined, have them write this rate in the box labeled *Current Level*.

Set realistic goals for change (Step 4). Next, ask the family to decide what they would consider a marked improvement. This prediction should be based on a reasonable expectation, taking into account how severe the problem is, how hard it has been to deal with in the past, and the family's determination to change the situation. Clients should be supported in establishing goals for meaningful change; at the same time they should not expect that problems will never occur. You can help circumvent calls for 100% change by prefacing this step with statements such as:

TH: I'd like you to think about what you would consider a big improvement, given that we'll work on this concern for 2 months. Keep in mind, though, we all have some bad days, so we can't expect total perfection.

Once your clients have decided on a reasonable level of change, enter it in the row marked *Change Expected*.

Select more than expected change (Step 5). Staying with the first concern, estimate the specific results that might be obtained if "more than expected change" were achieved. As stated before, we do not encourage clients to expect perfection, even at this level of goal attainment. For example, on Figure 4, the sample Goal Setting Form, the second concern on the form is labeled "Compliance." Note that at the level of *More Than Expected Change* the criterion was placed at "9 out of 10 commands" instead of "10 out of 10 commands." Once you have determined the appropriate criterion for this level, enter it in the box *More Than Expected Change* at the bottom of the page.

After finishing with the first concern, repeat Steps 2 through 5 with the remaining concerns.

IDENTIFYING THE INITIAL FOCUS OF TREATMENT

It's impractical to target several behaviors for change simultaneously, so you will need to have the family decide where they want to begin. There are some general suggestions you should follow when targeting concerns.

First, pick the concern that is causing the greatest anger and tension in the family. By reducing a major source of irritation, you will be setting up yourself and your clients for success. You will also enhance your credibility as someone who can help them solve their problems, increase their self-confidence, and strengthen their commitment to make positive changes.

Second, if several behaviors are of equal concern, pick the problem that occurs the most frequently. This will give your clients more opportunities to apply the skills they learn in this session. The more the family tries out these new skills, the more noticeable the changes will be.

Third, if possible, avoid starting with a behavior that occurs mainly outside the home such as vandalism or fighting at school. Not only are these behaviors harder to control, it is more difficult to see any day-to-day progress. Once the parents have learned and successfully applied the social learning techniques to other in-home behaviors, you can then target behavior problems that occur outside the home.

We have one final suggestion. The most common complaint of parents who have children ages 3 to 9 is either noncompliance or directly related behavior such as arguing, defiance, tantrums, dawdling, or doing tasks poorly. As a result, we strongly suggest that, if this behavior has been targeted by the family, they choose compliance as the first target concern. Resolving this issue can lower the family's level of conflict and stress dramatically. In addition, noncompliance, being a common problem, is something parents can readily learn to handle.

Once the family has selected their first problem concern, you are ready to teach them how to set up for success.

INTRODUCING SETTING UP FOR SUCCESS

Introduce the Concept

Explain that you would like to review with them a process called "setting up for success." Setting up for success means to take a preventive approach to problems. It is part of a treatment plan you will be developing with them that will also include how to deal with current misbehaviors and how to encourage more positive behavior.

Review the Handout

Give each person a copy of the "Setting Up for Success" handout and ask them to look it over briefly. When they are ready, give a one- or two-sentence explanation of each category followed immediately by hypothetical examples (examples for each category are provided earlier in this chapter in the section called "Understanding Setting Up for Success").

To see if your clients understand the concept, give examples of problem situations and ask them to describe how the setting contributes to the problem. Next, ask them to think of possible ways the situation can be set up for success. For example:

TH: Let's take the situation where a mother has problems with her 4-year-old son when taking him on long shopping trips in the afternoon. Can you tell me how she's not setting up for success?

CL: Well, kids don't have a long attention span, so the boy's probably bored. Besides, she definitely shouldn't take him out if he hasn't had his nap.

TH: That's right. Now suppose the mother had to get the shopping done; how could she have set up the situation for success:

CL: She could have taken several short trips instead of one long one, or taken toys along that the boy could play with.

You can use the following examples to review setting up.

- A child who regularly takes 3-hour naps in the afternoon won't go to bed without a fuss.

- Ten-year-old Johnny is left alone from 3:00 p.m. until 6:00 p.m. when his mother returns from work. A neighbor has accused Johnny of stealing something from her unlocked car.

- Sue's father drops her off at school 45 minutes early while on his way to work. About once a month Sue is reported truant.

- Bobby's mom gives him 75¢ every day to buy his school lunch. However, he doesn't appear to be eating lunch, because he comes home from school and proceeds to eat two sandwiches. This ruins his appetite for dinner.

Once parents have demonstrated that they understand the concept, ask them to describe instances in which they have previously set up situations for success. If they can't think of any, be prepared to offer examples of how you feel they have used the concept, either from what you have observed or inferred based on the information collected. You can also prompt them to recall ways they have used setting up in the past. For example:

> TH: Let me guess, when Jason was only a baby, you had to be careful that he didn't eat anything that would make him sick. Can you remember some of the things you did?

Brainstorm Ways to Set Up for Success

The next step is to apply the concept of setting up to the concern that the family has just selected. Explain that to do this they should look at each category listed on the handout and brainstorm ideas about how they might set up for success. They don't need to come up with suggestions for each category. *However, if compliance is the targeted concern, we strongly recommend that work on giving good commands be included.* As the family brainstorms, make sure everyone gets a chance to contribute and write down all ideas. If people are having trouble thinking of things to do, prompt them ("You mentioned that sometimes one of you will tell Marla to do something and the other one, not knowing that's the case, will tell her she doesn't have to. Can you think of a way to prevent that from happening so often?")

Discuss Ideas and Select the Most Practical

Discuss each of the setting-up ideas in turn, asking the family to consider each idea in terms of its advantages and disadvantages. Close the discussion by summarizing which ideas or combinations of ideas seem most reasonable to try. Have them record these on the "Setting Up for Success" handout.

INSURING IMPLEMENTATION

Review and/or Practice Selected Procedures

Carefully review each of the selected procedures to insure that the family members know exactly what is involved. While they cannot roleplay such things as rearranging the environment, developing a routine, or improving parental coordination of child-rearing responsibilities, they should be able to describe in detail what exactly will be done ("We will get a new toy box so the toys can be put away"), who will do it ("Mom will go out and buy it"), and when it will be done ("She'll buy one within the next 3 days"). If the parents are implementing the caring days technique, they should develop and exchange their lists of caring behaviors.

In cases where the selected setting-up procedures include giving good commands, complimenting each other, or teaching new skills, this review should also include some in-session rehearsal. During rehearsals you should:

1. Model how the behavior should be performed;
2. Have the parents roleplay the procedures;
3. Discuss their performance and reinforce their efforts;
4. Have them repeat the skill until their performance is satisfactory.

If the parents will be working on how they give commands, you should illustrate each of the key steps in giving good commands by first modeling an inappropriate way, followed by an appropriate way. Next, you should have the parents rehearse the appropriate method. The steps for giving good commands are:

1. Get the child's attention.
2. Say exactly what you want.
3. Say when you want it done.
4. Be polite but firm.

If children are present for this session, the parents should practice with them, while you observe and give feedback.

Problem Solve Potential Difficulties

Before turning to the assignment, ask the family what obstacles or problems they foresee in carrying out their setting-up procedures. Respond empathically to any problems they anticipate, then ask what they can do to avoid those problems or minimize their effect on following through with setting up.

GIVING THE ASSIGNMENT

Explain the Assignment

The parents' assignment for the upcoming week will be to track both their child's behavior and how well they implement the setting-up procedures discussed during the session. You will want to take a few minutes to explain the purpose of tracking. First, regular tracking will help them notice when the problem behavior does and does not occur. This is essential, since the effectiveness of the treatment program will depend on the parents' ability to identify negative and positive behaviors consistently and to provide consequences in the ways you will be teaching them. In addition, the parents' weekly tracking sheets will help you determine when progress is being made, when further instruction is necessary, and/or when it is appropriate to modify the current program to suit the family's needs.

Fill Out a Program Monitoring Form

On a blank Program Monitoring Form, starting with Space 1 and working down the form, enter the behaviors that the clients are

Figure 5. First Sample Program Monitoring Form.

Day or Date	3/4	3/5	3/6	3/7	3/8	3/9	3/10
1. *Complies* _____ _____	ℍℍ	ℍℍ II	ℍℍ ℍℍ	IIII	IIII	II	ℍℍ I
2. *Does not comply* _____ _____	ℍℍ III	ℍℍ I	ℍℍ	ℍℍ I	ℍℍ	ℍℍ II	IIII
3. *Get child's attention before giving command*	A	A	A	B	B	B	A
4. *Say exactly what I want done* _____	B	C	B	C	B	B	A
5. *Say when I want it done* _____	B	A	A	B	B	A	A
6. *Be firm but polite* _____ _____	A	B	B	D	C	D	B
7. _____ _____ _____							
8. _____ _____ _____							

Things to Remember

Complies means:
a) *starts task within 30 sec.*
b) *doesn't argue*
c) *finishes task*
Does not comply means:
a) *doesn't start task right away*
b) *argues, debates, whines*
c) *doesn't complete task*

grade A=did all but once or twice
grade B=did all but 3 or 4 times
grade C=did about 1/2 the time
grade D=less than 1/2 the time
grade F=didn't do at all

trying to increase and decrease, such as compliance and noncompliance. Often it is helpful to break down targeted behaviors into components. Doing chores could be broken into the various tasks, such as making the bed and taking out the garbage. You should enter one component per space. Finally, in the remaining spaces, list each of the setting-up ideas they decide to try, such as giving good commands or supporting each other's commands. (See Figures 5 and 6.)

Figure 6. Second Sample Program Monitoring Form.

Day or Date	2/1	2/2	2/3	2/4	2/5	2/6	2/7
1. *Makes bed in morning before school*	+	+	—	+			
2. *Sets table without being reminded*	+	—	—	+			
3. *Puts dirty clothes in hamper*	—	—	+	+			
4. *Get John up in morning by 7:00*	+	+	+	+			
5. *Make sure dinner is ready at 6:00 every night*	+	—	+	+			
6. *Take hamper out of my bathroom and put it in the kids' bathroom*	+						
7.							
8.							

Things to Remember

Bed: Sheet and covers must
be pulled up and smooth
Pillow should be under
covers.
Table: Must be completely
set by 5:45.

Explain How to Track

Point out that there are a number of ways to track, or monitor, what happens in the coming week. To record the target behavior and its negative opposite, counting with hatch marks is often easiest. Other ways include yes/no, stars, happy/frowning faces, or letter grades (A, B, C, D, F).

It is not necessary to use the same system for each item monitored. For example, the parents might choose to record their child's compliance and noncompliance behaviors with hatch marks, while grading themselves once a day on their ability to set up for success. It's important not to make the tracking system used too complicated. At the same time, it should be sufficiently detailed that parents can detect and record gradual behavior changes. If children are present for this session, be certain to involve them in the process of selecting a tracking system. They frequently enjoy the tracking process and like to choose the recording method to be used.

If compliance is the behavior being monitored, it is important to set some simple rules about what that involves. The following definition is the one we suggest. Review it with the family and summarize it in the *Things to Remember* section.

1. The child should start to obey within 30 seconds of when the command is given.

2. There should be no arguing, whining, or pouting.

3. It is OK for the child to ask the parent a question, about the command but the parent has the final say on how the child should comply.

4. If the child is to stop doing something, repeating it later that day is an automatic "not complying."

Finally, have the parents decide who will do the tracking and when it will be done. Child behaviors should be tracked as they occur. The parents' setting-up efforts should be monitored at least daily. Decisions about the when, where, how, and who of monitoring should be summarized in the space *Things to Remember* at the bottom of the Program Monitoring Form.

Practice Tracking

Once you have written down on the monitoring forms all the items to be tracked in the upcoming week, have your clients do some practice tracking. By doing so, you will be able to note and correct any comprehension problems that still exist. You can make up relevant examples and have the clients show you how they would mark their monitoring forms. Examples should cover instances of targeted behaviors and descriptions of setting up for success. In the following illustration, the parents will be tracking whether their child complies or does not comply with requests.

TH: I'm going to describe a situation, and I want you to write down how you would track that on your form, OK?

CL: OK.

TH: You say to your daughter, "Sarah, please put your toys away now. It's time for dinner." Sarah answers, "But can't I play for 5 minutes more? Besides, I don't want to eat dinner." You say, "No, I want the toys put away now." Sarah then puts all her toys away.

CL: Let's see. I would put a mark in the "comply" box.

TH: Perfect.

Give several examples until you are confident the clients understand exactly what they are to record as correct behavior and misbehavior, as well as how to track those behaviors on the monitoring form. Next, if the parents have decided to use letter grades to evaluate their own performance, give them several relevant examples of setting up for success and have them grade the quality according to the criteria they have previously determined. For example:

TH: Let's practice how you will be grading yourselves on setting up for success. Suppose that twice in one day you found yourself yelling at Sarah to do something. How would you grade yourself?

CL: Let's see. If, over the whole day, I get upset only twice when giving Sarah a command, I'm supposed to give myself a "B."

TH: Good.

CL: Yes, particularly since now I yell at her a lot more than that.

Give at least one example of each setting up for success item the parents have written on their monitoring form. The clients should be able to grade themselves realistically using the criteria they have established.

Problem Solve Potential Tracking Difficulties

Before sending the family home, it's helpful to talk about any potential problems that might interfere with their tracking. This is similar to the preproblem solving they did earlier for the setting-up task; now, however, the focus is on the tracking assignment. By considering potential problems and solutions before they go home, the family will be better prepared to cope with any difficulties and will not have the excuse that they didn't know what to do.

Prepare Parents to Explain Tracking

If the child is not participating in the sessions, the youngster should still be told by the parents that they are concerned about some of the problems in the home and will be working to improve matters, including, for now, tracking both the positive and negative behaviors in question. Because this discussion can be a touchy issue, you will need to spend a few minutes preparing the parents to make the explanation in a calm and objective manner. The child needs to see tracking as a technique that can help resolve or remedy family problems and not as simply a new form of punishment.

The parents should pick a neutral time to give the explanation, one in which the child is not misbehaving, upset, tired, or distracted. Parents should keep their explanations brief, matter-of-fact, and at the child's level of understanding. It should *not* turn into a nagging session or lecture. Many parents find it useful to have their monitoring form in front of them to use as a reference when they give the explanation.

We also recommend that you have them rehearse the explanation. If the child becomes argumentative, parents should be instructed not to try to justify their actions, argue, or plead with their child to listen. Rather, they should end the discussion and proceed with the tracking assignment. If their child later asks to discuss the matter, they should do so, but only if the child remains cooperative.

We also suggest that parents share their monitoring forms with their child at the end of the day. They should use this time to praise their youngster for appropriate behaviors performed and to give feedback in a matter-of-fact way about inappropriate behaviors. Again, this should not turn into a scolding session. As with the initial explanation, parents should only review the day's progress at a time when everything is calm and when there are no distractions. If you and/or the parents are not sure that the parents and child can sit down calmly to review the daily tracking, it may be best to recommend that the tracking form just be posted in a place where the child can see it, such as on the refrigerator or bulletin board.

CLOSING

Once you've discussed the family's concerns and have solved potential difficulties, they should be ready to go home and begin the program. It will be important that you call the family during the week to check on their progress, to find out whether they had any difficulty implementing the program, and to check for any emotional or practical concerns that may have surfaced.

Before sending the family home, set up times that you can talk individually to the parents on the phone. If appropriate, you may want to speak to the youngster as well. Explain that these calls should take 5 to 10 minutes. Write down the scheduled times on your calendar and ask the clients to write down the times on their monitoring form. Make sure that you have a copy of their assignment sheet so that you will be able to monitor their performance accurately when you talk to them on the phone.

If the family has no further concerns, close the session by expressing your confidence in their ability to carry out the program.

MAKING BETWEEN-SESSION CALLS

When you talk to parents over the phone, make sure you both have copies of the monitoring form. Together, review the following items:

1. The child's negative and positive behaviors the parents are monitoring. Neither they nor you should necessarily expect any

improvements at this point. Change should be expected by Session 3 or 4. In addition to getting the counts of those behaviors, ask them to describe one or two positive and negative incidents.

2. Their daily ratings of their setting-up efforts. Besides listing how they evaluated their own performance, have them describe what they did. Reinforce their efforts in this regard.

3. Whether they have any problems or concerns. If they do, address them as well as you can. If the problems are complicated, you might mention you will make a note of them and work on the concerns at the next session.

Finally, close with a statement of support.

HANDOUT FOR PARENTS
SETTING UP FOR SUCCESS

Before tackling a problem, it sometimes helps if we can step back and look at what may be contributing to the situation. We can then work on changing those things first. Here are some ideas you might want to consider.

1. *Rearrange the environment.* Are there items you could acquire or ways you could rearrange your home to make the desired behavior easier to do?

_____

_____

_____

2. *Develop consistent routines.* Children are more comfortable if they know what to expect. Take a look at the most common problems and see if a set routine might help resolve them. _____

_____

_____

3. *Make sure your commands are clear, polite, and understood.* The way we tell children to do something has a big impact on their compliance. Key things to do are: (1) get the child's attention; (2) say exactly what you want; (3) say when you want it; and (4) be polite but firm. _____

_____

_____

_____

4. *Teach new skills.* Sometimes children don't perform the way we'd like because they lack the skills, not the motivation. In what areas could your children use instruction? _____

_____

_____

_____

5. *Treat each other with care, respect, and love.* This may mean biting your tongue, or, conversely, mentioning behavior that may otherwise be taken for granted. _____

_____

_____

6. *Strengthen marital ties.* When your marriage is strong, it is easier to work together to solve child-management problems. What are some ways you could strengthen your relationship? _____

_____

_____

_____

7. *Improve parental coordination.* How can you share responsibilities and support each other's efforts? _____

_____

_____

_____

8. *Encourage parental growth and well-being.* We all need time for ourselves, away from our children. What are some personal interests you could pursue? _____

_____

_____

_____

_____

HANDOUT FOR PARENTS
HOW TO COMPLETE THE GOAL SETTING FORM

1. *Enter concerns.* Determine your major concerns and list them on a blank Goal Setting Form in the boxes across the top labeled *Concerns.* The concerns listed should include at least one or two items that the entire family has agreed on. You can also include some individual concerns of each family member.

2. *Specify exactly what behavior you would rather see occur.* Starting with your first concern, write the specific behavior(s) in the box labeled *Desired Behavior.* Each behavior should be written clearly and simply, so that anyone can read it and understand what behavior you would like to encourage.

3. *Estimate how often the desired behavior happens now.* Once you have decided, in general, how often the desired behavior happens (once a day, twice a week), write this figure in the box labeled *Current Level* under the first concern.

4. *Set realistic goals for change.* Decide what you would consider to be a marked improvement in the desired behavior at the end of several months of treatment. Be realistic, taking into consideration how severe your problem is now. Try not to expect perfection. Enter what you think is a reasonable level of change in the box labeled *Change Expected.*

5. *Select what would be more than expected change.* Estimate how often the desired behavior would occur if the level of improvement were much more than you expected. Enter this in the box on the bottom row labeled *More Than Expected Change.*

GOAL SETTING FORM

Family _____ Therapist _____ Date _____

CONCERNS				
DESIRED BEHAVIOR				
CURRENT LEVEL				
CHANGE EXPECTED				
MORE THAN EXPECTED CHANGE				

PROGRAM MONITORING FORM

Program _____ Dates _____ to _____

(beginning)   (end)

Day or Date

1. _____						
_____						
2. _____						
_____						
3. _____						
_____						
4. _____						
_____						
5. _____						
_____						
6. _____						
_____						
7. _____						
_____						
8. _____						
_____						

Things to Remember

_____   _____
_____   _____
_____   _____
_____   _____
_____   _____
_____   _____
_____   _____

THERAPIST AGENDA: SETTING UP FOR SUCCESS

Agenda   *Notes*

Beginning the Session

    Welcome the family and explain the agenda

Completing the Goal Setting Form

    Review the handouts:

        Enter family concerns

        Specify desirable behaviors

        Determine the current frequency of the desired behavior

        Set realistic goals for change

        Select more than expected change

Identifying the Initial Focus of Treatment

    Select the first concern to be addressed

    Pick the concern that:

        Is causing the greatest anger and tension

        Occurs the most frequently

        Occurs within the home

        With younger children, focus on compliance first, if it is one of their problems

Introducing Setting Up for Success

    Introduce the concept

    Review the handout:

        Brief explanation

        Examples of "right" way and "wrong" way

        Have family identify how they have used this concept

    Brainstorm ways to set up for success

    Discuss ideas and select the most practical

Insuring Implementation

    Review and/or practice selected procedures

    Problem solve potential difficulties

Giving the Assignment

Explain the assignment:

To track selected concerns and setting-up efforts

Rationale is to determine progress, identify need to modify program

Fill out a Program Monitoring Form

Explain how to track

Review definition of compliance (if compliance is the targeted problem)

Practice tracking

Problem solve potential tracking difficulties

Prepare parents to explain tracking to the child:

Discuss how and when to explain

Rehearse what the parents are to say

Review how to handle arguments

Plan on a daily review of the monitoring forms

Closing

Arrange for between-session phone calls

Express confidence in the clients

Chapter Six

SELF-CONTROL

The objective of this session is to teach parents how to modify their cognitive, physiological, and emotional responses to their child, with the expectation that in so doing they can remain calm and in control of themselves during periods of conflict. The major tasks to be accomplished during this session are:

- Review the prior week's assignment and family performance.
- Instruct the parents on the relationship among thoughts, emotions, and behaviors.
- Teach self-control methods, including (a) changing self-talk and (b) relaxation procedures.
- Prepare the parents to use these self-control procedures at home.
- Develop the assignment.

As in previous sessions, children mature enough to understand and listen to the activities being presented should be encouraged to attend this session, particularly for the units addressing problem-solving activities and relaxation training. In general, however, this session is a little more difficult for children to follow than the two preceding sessions.

As previously noted, one of the ways this program differs from other child and family intervention programs is its focus on personal self-control. You may, after reviewing this chapter, decide not to train families to use these techniques. However, in our experience there are good reasons for teaching the family calming techniques.

First, these methods help parents acquire the emotional composure needed to implement a behavior change program for their children and for children to develop an awareness of how they respond to conflict. Second, even parents who seem fairly composed have benefited from the time and attention devoted to their emotional well-being.

Finally, a frequent side benefit of teaching self-control is that the participants often are able to use these techniques in situations other than parent-child conflicts. In many cases, family members who have difficulty controlling emotional responses in the home may have similar difficulty outside. After progress has been made with the child-management concerns, you may want to help individuals who have self-control problems generalize their new skills to other areas.

Following is an overview of the specific self-control techniques to be used. You will learn when to use particular techniques and the procedures for presenting these techniques to the family.

After the self-control techniques are presented, the activities to be covered during a self-control session are described in detail. This is followed by a discussion of the between-session activities for you and for your clients.

UNDERSTANDING SELF-CONTROL TECHNIQUES

A variety of self-control techniques is available to therapists. They range from simple relaxation exercises to elaborate biofeedback methods. While the specific procedures described here have been used to help troubled families, they can also be generalized to situations outside immediate family concerns. The following material should be considered as an overview of a particular self-control process and of the steps necessary to teach families to use it rather than an in-depth explanation of cognitive theory, research, and practice.

Cognitive Techniques

The work of Albert Ellis (1962, 1969), Aaron Beck (1972), Maxie Maultsby (1975), and others has demonstrated that there is a relationship among what we *think* about a situation, how we *feel* about the situation, and how we *behave*. Essentially, they all suggest that our thoughts dictate emotions and behaviors. For instance, if we view an event or person in hostile terms, we are likely to express anger and aggression. Similarly, fearful thoughts often breed anxiety and withdrawal. On the other hand, thoughts that emphasize our ability to cope and remain composed engender good self-control and facilitate rational and effective responses. We can conceptualize this process in terms of an A, B, C, D sequence in which:

A   Something happens.

B   A person has thoughts about the situation, including beliefs, perceptions, and attitudes.

C   Based upon the evaluating thoughts, the person feels a particular way.

D   The person acts/behaves consistently with those feelings.

For example, a child may arrive home late from school and offer no explanation. This is Step A. The parents may begin to think of the child as disobedient, irresponsible, uncaring ("He's a selfish brat," "I hate that," "He's just trying to show who's boss"). This is Step B. As the parents think these thoughts, they will feel themselves becoming angry. This represents Step C. As a result, the parents are likely to deal with the child by yelling, spanking, or imposing harsh consequences they may later regret. They have arrived at Step D. Thus, as you work with parents on self-control issues, it's important to help them (a) become aware of how their thoughts and beliefs affect their behavior and (b) modify these thoughts to improve their self-control. There are several ways to accomplish the second objective.

The most direct method for modifying self-talk is to help parents recognize negative self-statements they currently generate (anger, depression, guilt). They can then replace those thoughts with other equally valid but less upsetting self-statements. For example, when a child comes home late, rather than tell oneself that this "proves he's irresponsible and unmanageable," the same incident can be interpreted as "he's just checking to see if I'll follow through with what I've said I would do." The parent handout "Sample Thought Menu" at the end of the chapter gives several additional examples of both negative and positive thoughts.

For parents who have difficulty substituting thoughts, you may want to use an alternative method. Teach them to ask themselves during moments of conflict whether what they are thinking and doing is *helping them reach their goal.* If they decide it is not, they are to consider what they might think and do that would help. In a sense, this procedure has the parents shift their self-talk from self-defeating thoughts to more goal-oriented problem solving. The model is similar to the steps of William Glasser's Reality Therapy (1965). Specifically, this technique involves having parents learn four basic questions which they ask and attempt to answer themselves:

1. What is my goal?
2. What am I doing now?
3. Is what I'm doing helping me to achieve my goal?
4. If it isn't, what do I need to do differently?

The parent handout "Problem Solving" gives an example of how these questions should be framed and answered.

In addition to the previously mentioned techniques, relabeling can also have a strong impact on everyone's self-statements. As described in Chapter Three, relabeling is a method of redefining negative situations and attributions as either positive or neutral. By using relabeling, you will be modeling more appropriate and positive ways for clients to view disruptive situations and behaviors. You may find, as we have, that family members who are at first reluctant to accept the reinterpretation of a behavior or event later spontaneously begin describing the situation from the new perspective.

Relaxation Procedures

Many family members find that in stressful situations they experience such physical tension (rapid heartbeat, headache, muscle tension) that they cannot maintain their self-control. Others report that they suffer from chronic anger, anxiety, or depression and are thus easily set off by the slightest event. For these parents, learning to relax can be essential in gaining greater self-control.

There are many relaxation procedures. The one we recommend initially combines controlled breathing while counting to oneself. The steps for completing this procedure are described in detail on the parent handout "How to Relax," provided at the end of this chapter. This method has several advantages. First, concentrating on counting clears the mind of extraneous and aggravating thoughts that may be distracting or upsetting the clients. Second, methodical breathing physically calms and relaxes them. Finally, it can be done without drawing attention to oneself and can be learned without extensive training (Maultsby, 1975).

BEGINNING THE SESSION

Materials Needed

The following listed materials should be on hand when you begin the session. The handouts, and Therapist Agenda are found at the end of the chapter. The blank Program Monitoring Form is at the end of Chapter Five.

- Therapist Agenda with notes
- Notes from the initial interview
- Copy of previous week's Program Monitoring Form
- Handout for Parents: Sample Thought Menu
- Handout for Parents: Problem Solving
- Handout for Parents: How to Relax
- Blank Program Monitoring Forms

REVIEWING PAST EFFORTS

The opening review is designed to set the stage for presenting the topic of self-control and the importance of becoming less emotionally upset by another's behavior. Because it is such an important subject, and a potentially sensitive one, a careful lead-in is crucial. We have outlined the opening part of the session to help you set the stage.

Review Efforts at Setting Up for Success

After welcoming the family and engaging in initial social talk, ask to see last week's Program Monitoring Form and review the family's attempts at setting up for success. Commend family members for their efforts, regardless of whether they reported positive changes.

If the parents did not attempt the setting-up assignment, or made only the most cursory efforts, it's important to determine if their poor performance is due to a motivation or comprehension problem. If they did not understand the assignment, you should reexplain the concept of setting up for success and reinstruct them regarding tracking behaviors. If they appear to have a motivation problem, probe to find out what their concern is. Once the concern has been addressed and the parents have resolved to continue, help them determine what they can do to carry out the initial assignment. Ultimately, you must decide whether it is best to spend the rest of this session reviewing last week's material, or whether you should proceed and expect the parents to do two sets of assignments in the coming week.

Review the Child's Behaviors

On the Program Monitoring Form, the parents should have tracked one problem behavior and its prosocial opposite. Review the data, asking the parents to describe some of the situations they recorded. Be sure to include situations in which the child behaved well; use these instances to suggest that the parents should be encouraged by such behaviors. Statements like the following help parents pay greater attention to and appreciate the positive behaviors of others.

> TH: So, on Monday Marianne went to bed when you told her to, without fussing and fighting. I'll bet you were happy about that.

If the parents do not list any instances of positive behaviors, elicit and list any examples that occurred but were not recorded.

Draw Out Emotional/Cognitive Responses

After reviewing the situations listed by the parents on the monitoring form, you will need to get a clear understanding of the feelings the parents experienced and the thoughts they had during each situation. Once you understand exactly what each person *did* in the situation, probe to find out first what the parents were *feeling* ("How did you feel when she broke the toy?" or "From your description, it sounds like you were pretty angry"). Some parents will report they felt very angry, while others will say they felt impatient, annoyed, frustrated, guilty, tired, or depressed. As they describe their emotions, reflect back what you hear to show you understand what they were feeling ("So, when Susan doesn't pick up her toys, you get irritated and resentful"). Check to make sure your reflections are accurate. If they are not, shift your statements until they correctly reflect both the content and the intensity of the parents' feelings. For example:

> CL: I couldn't believe Scott actually ripped up all of his books.
>
> TH: That's the kind of thing that would make a lot of parents furious. I'll bet you were pretty mad.
>
> CL: Well, I wasn't exactly mad…
>
> TH: How did that make you feel?
>
> CL: I just didn't know what to do.
>
> TH: So you were a bit overwhelmed.
>
> CL: Exactly.

If the child is present, identify the feelings he or she might have had when the parent became upset.

> TH: (To child) And I'll bet you were feeling pretty unhappy, too. Can you remember?
>
> CHILD: I remember mom looked real mad, and I felt terrible.
>
> TH: (To child) You felt terrible and wished you two could get along better.

Once the clients agree with your statements, expand your reflections to include thoughts that were likely to accompany the content and feelings reported.

> TH: And you start telling yourself, "What do I do now? I'm at the end of my rope. Nothing works."
>
> CL: (Nodding in agreement) Uh huh.

Link the Prior Discussion to Today's Agenda

As you talk about problem situations, let the parents know that you understand how upsetting their child's behavior can be. You can see how they might lose their tempers or repress their feelings. Point out that the child often responds in the same way. State that you also hear them saying that, just as they want the other person's behavior to improve, they also wish they were in better control of themselves during those times. Explain that today they are going to learn ways to remain calm under conditions that previously would have been very upsetting.

INTRODUCING THE CONCEPT OF SELF-CONTROL

Explain the Role Emotions Play

Explain that having feelings or emotions is good, and that one purpose of an emotion is to motivate us to take some action. Fear, for example, motivates us to leave a dangerous situation. It's healthy to have a normal fear of heights and of cars, as long as that fear does not become debilitating or overly restrictive. In families, the situation is much the same. Feeling annoyed or disappointed by something a child has done helps motivate parents to remedy the problem. However, when parents allow themselves to become so upset or overwhelmed that they overreact, the consequences can be unfortunate. Parents may say or do something they soon regret (strike the child, humiliate or say hateful things, impose punishments they cannot enforce). Often after they calm down they feel guilty about their actions and hesitate to deal with the youngster for fear of repeating the last episode. For the child, seeing a parent lose control is frightening and anxiety provoking. Also, the parents are modeling behavior for the child to imitate. The cycles of overreaction and avoidance mean that the parents cannot deal with the child in a way that will achieve lasting improvement in behavior. As a result, the best emotional state for dealing with conflict is the middle ground: not so overwhelmed that one is unable to respond nor so upset that one overreacts.

Explain How Thoughts Determine Emotions

Explain that one of the recent trends in psychology is the notion that the thoughts people have learned to think and tell themselves play a part in determining their emotional responses. For example, a mother observes her son dumping his books on the floor and tells herself, "That child is just so inconsiderate of my feelings—he really doesn't care at all about me." As a result of these thoughts, she is likely to feel either very angry or hurt and depressed. On the other hand, if she looks at that same episode and tells herself, "I'm going to have to help him learn to put his things away—we can't have a mess like that every evening," then most likely she is going to feel calm and determined to do something about the situation. You might find it useful to diagram the thought/emotion relationship on a blackboard or on a piece of paper, with the thoughts described on the left and an arrow leading to the right, pointing to different resulting emotions.

Thoughts	*Lead to*	*Emotions*
That child is inconsiderate and just doesn't care at all about me.	→	Anger, hurt, depression
I'm going to have to help him learn to put his things away.	→	Calm, determined
My mom's unfair. She never lets me do anything.	→	Anger, hurt
Mom's tired and really busy. It would help if I did the extra work.	→	Calm, helpful

Next, illustrate your explanation with several personalized examples.

TH: Similar thoughts and emotions happen to you, I'm sure. In fact, a few minutes ago you were telling me that when Joanie comes home late from school, you start thinking things like, "I know something must have happened to her. What's she getting into now?" You become worried and sometimes angry. Suppose in the same situation you told yourself, "This keeps going on and on; there's nothing I can do about it," how would you feel then?

CL: Depressed, hopeless?

TH: Right. I think we all might feel that way if we talked to ourselves like that.

Teach Procedures to Modify Self-talk

Earlier, in the "Understanding Self-control Techniques" section, we outlined two procedures for modifying self-talk. One was based on a sample thought menu and the other on following a sequence of problem-solving questions, originating with "What is my goal?" Use whichever of these procedures you feel would be more effective with your client or whichever you feel more comfortable in teaching. We believe both to be equally effective. The problem-solving approach might work best with clients who like to feel they are taking charge. For clients who are not yet oriented toward problem solving, the sample thought menu may be more effective.

Depending on the procedure to be used, give the parents a copy of the appropriate handout. Review it with them and discuss any questions they have about how to use the procedure. If they are employing the "Sample Thought Menu," they should fill in the space at the bottom of the page with the upsetting thoughts they have and calming thoughts that would be helpful in the situation. If they are using the "Problem Solving" handout, have them go through an imaginary internal dialogue around some situation, following the steps described on the handout. To help them with this, you might recall a situation during the previous week that upset them and triggered negative self-statements.

Explain the Physical Tension/Emotional Self-Control Connection

Explain that many people experience physical reactions to stress. Their muscles tighten, their heart rate increases, their breathing accelerates, their voice rises, or they may start to shake or break into a sweat. When these symptoms occur, they find it hard to maintain any semblance of self-control. Thus, restoring some calm to the body is a necessary first step before many individuals can achieve greater control over their self-statements. For these individuals, you will be introducing relaxation.

To find out whether the parents would benefit from relaxation training, ask them how they react physically during various conflict situations in the home. If they report any of the symptoms previously described, they should be provided with relaxation training.

Teach Relaxation Procedure

Give the family a copy of the handout "How to Relax." Read it over with them and take them through one practice episode. You will be giving verbal directions while they follow each step in the procedure. The entire practice rarely takes more than a few minutes. At the end of the procedure, ask them how it worked for them, review any problems they mention, and have them practice again. If your clients report severe physiological signs of stress such as migraine headaches, you may want to consider one of the more extensive relaxation procedures published in audio cassette form by either Research Press (Box 317720, Champaign, IL 61820) or BMA Audio Cassettes (200 Park Avenue South, New York, NY 10003).

INSURING IMPLEMENTATION

Rehearse Use of Self-control Procedures

Ask the parents to list several situations in the upcoming week in which their child is most likely to do the targeted misbehavior. Once they've identified several of these situations, lead them through a covert rehearsal of their self-control procedures. In a covert rehearsal, participants imagine themselves experiencing a situation and using all of the procedures that they have just learned. Usually their imagination will be guided by your presentation. Covert rehearsal is an excellent way to emphasize all the points previously covered and to make sure that parents are prepared to carry out the procedures. It also allows you to rehearse the cognitive aspects of an intervention as well as the behavioral responses. The following is an example of how a covert rehearsal might be conducted with the use of self-control procedures.

> TH: I'd like you to imagine a situation where you've told your son to pick up his toys. Let's imagine that you've told him three times, and he still hasn't done it. (Pause) You begin to think, "I'm sick and tired of always having to tell him what to do. How come I never get any cooperation from him?" At this point you start asking the four questions. "What is my objective? What am I trying to do? I'd like him to learn to pick up his toys, so is getting upset and angry going to help? No. What's the first thing I should do? Calm down, just relax. I'll do some of that breathing." And you breathe in and out slowly. (Speaking more and more slowly) Each time you breathe in, you count to 10. Then exhale... breathe in, counting to 10. There, now you're feeling much calmer. You walk to your son, and you say, "Andrew, I told you to pick up your toys. I want you to do it now." You think to yourself, "Hey, that worked. I was much calmer and much more in control of myself. It will take a while to teach him to pick up his toys, and we're still learning things to do, but this went well."

After leading the parents through covert rehearsal, if the child is present, repeat the process with the youngster using examples from the child's perspective. Then have the parents pick another problem situation that is likely to occur in the upcoming week and describe how they will use the techniques of self-talk and relaxation training.

Problem Solve Potential Difficulties

Ask the family what problems they foresee in carrying out the procedures they have just learned. Common situations you may need to discuss include using self-control procedures outside the home and deciding what to do when clients lose their tempers. Should the latter occur, reassure the family that there will be times when they will find it difficult to use the self-control techniques described; when this happens, they should not worry about it. Relapses and difficulties are to be expected. With practice, however, they will become more proficient.

GIVING THE ASSIGNMENT

Explain the Assignment

The assignment for the upcoming week is to apply the procedures covered in the session and to continue tracking the child's targeted behavior as before. However, if in the previous week the parents did not monitor their child as they agreed to do, you may need to renegotiate or simplify how they will track behavior in the upcoming week. The child's behavior they agree to monitor should be listed on the Program Monitoring Form.

The parents should also continue tracking their efforts to set up for success. We recommend that if during the previous week the parents were monitoring several different setting up for success behaviors ("Get my child's attention before issuing a command," "Say exactly what I want," "Be polite but firm"), they should condense those items into one category ("Give good commands" or "Set up for success"). This one item should also be entered on this week's Program Monitoring Form.

In addition to tracking their child's behavior and their continued efforts to set up for success, the family should monitor their self-talk. The manner and amount of tracking they choose to do will vary, but we recommend that they implement one of the following methods. They can evaluate the helpfulness of their self-statements by grading them using an A, B, C, D, F system or by rating each day's performance with a plus or minus sign. A second option is to record each time they find themselves using calming or upsetting thoughts. Finally, some people find it useful to record their calming and upsetting thoughts in a journal. If they choose the letter-grade or plus/minus sign method, they should enter *Self-Talk* on the Program Monitoring Form. If the second method is used, they should have two lines for *Calming Thoughts* and *Upsetting Thoughts* on the form. If the child is interested and able to track his or her own self-control, a space should also be provided on the form.

Those parents who will be using the relaxation technique should also track how many times each day they use it. Have them enter *Relaxation Technique* on their form. If they do not feel the need to use the technique on any given day, they should be instructed to put *NA* for *Not Applicable* in that day's box. Finally, instead of or in addition to having them use the methods already mentioned (or with clients who do not have the time or inclination to do more extensive tracking), you may ask them to rate, on a scale of 1 to 100, how upset they got with their child each day. (See Figures 7 and 8.)

Practice Filling Out the Monitoring Form

Once the parents have determined what methods they will use to track the child's and their own behavior, have them practice filling

Figure 7. Third Sample Program Monitoring Form.

Day or Date	3/11	3/12	3/13	3/14	3/15	3/16	3/17
1. *Complies*	✝✝✝ ✝✝✝	✝✝✝ I	✝✝✝ II	✝✝✝ II	IIII	✝✝✝ III	
2. *Does not comply*	IIII	II	II	IIII	✝✝✝ II	II	
3. *Good commands*	A	A	A	A	B	A	
4. *Calming thoughts*	A	B	B	C	C	A	
5. *Upsetting thoughts*	A	B	A	C	D	A	
6.							
7.							
8.							

Things to Remember

Complies means:

a) *starts task within 30 sec.*

b) *doesn't argue*

c) *finishes task*

Does not comply means:

a) *doesn't start task right away*

b) *argues, debates, whines*

c) *doesn't complete task*

out the monitoring form. Describe several example situations and have the parents mark on their form exactly how they would track them. In the following example, the parent practices tracking both his own and his child's behavior.

TH: Let's say that you want Joe to quit fighting with Molly, so you tell Joe, "You'd better shape up, fella." Joe continues to tease his sister and you feel yourself starting to clench your jaw. Then you say to yourself, "I'm getting tense. I need to

Figure 8. Fourth Sample Program Monitoring Form.

Day or Date	2/8	2/9	2/10	2/11	2/12		
1. *Makes bed before school*	+	+	—	+	+		
2. *Sets table without reminder*	—	+	—	+	+		
3. *Puts dirty clothes in hamper*	—	—	—	+	—		
4. *Setting up for success mom/dad*	A/A	A/B	C/C	A/A	B/A		
5. *John's self-talk*	A	B	C	A	B		
6. *Parents' self-talk mom/dad*	B/B	A/B	C/D	A/A	C/B		
7. *Mom's relaxation technique*	1	2	0	2	1		
8.							

Things to Remember

Bed: Sheet and covers pulled up and smooth
Table: Set by 5:45

relax, and then go in and stop their fighting." Tell me, how would you mark Joe's behavior?

CL: I'd mark down here (points to correct spot on the monitoring sheet) that he didn't mind me.

TH: Right. How would you rate your setting up for success, your self-talk, and your relaxation?

CL: Good. I did a good job. I'd say that's a plus for me.

TH: Right. You did well on self-control. Now let's talk about your process of setting up.

Practice until the clients demonstrate that they understand how to complete each component of the monitoring form.

Problem Solve Potential Tracking Difficulties

Spend a few moments discussing any problems they foresee in completing the Program Monitoring Forms every day. Let them tell you how they will resolve the matter and still provide enough data to measure how well the program is working.

CLOSING

Arranging at least one between-session phone contact is recommended. It should take place within 1 or 2 days, so that problems, if they arise, can be caught early. Schedule that contact and decide who will make the call. Enter the time on your calendar and ask the clients to write it on their monitoring sheet. Close the session with an expression of confidence in the clients.

MAKING BETWEEN-SESSION CALLS

When talking with the parents by phone, you should cover the following items:

1. Ask for the data on the negative targeted behavior and its prosocial opposite. Comment on any changes. If the child's behavior has not changed, reassure the parents by explaining that noticeable changes are not expected to happen until after the next session.

2. Inquire about the ratings they gave themselves for setting up for success. Ask for specific examples of what they did in this area. Reinforce their work.

3. Ask for the ratings, counts, or examples from their log concerning their use of the self-talk and relaxation procedures. Have the parents describe an incident where the child did the targeted misbehavior, then ask them the following questions:

"What was the situation when the targeted behavior occurred?"

"What did the child do?"

"How physically upset did you become?"

"Did you try to relax?"

"What were you thinking?"

"Were you able to use the calming self-talk?"

"How upset did you get?"

"What, if anything, would you do differently to stay calm in the future?"

4. If the child agreed to monitor self-talk, speak to him or her, raising questions similar to those listed in 3.

It is important that you express optimism and give the family practical suggestions for their problems and concerns where necessary.

HANDOUT FOR PARENTS
SAMPLE THOUGHT MENU

The two columns below provide examples of thoughts that can lead to a loss of self-control and alternative thoughts that can help people remain calm and in control.

Upsetting thoughts	*Calming thoughts*
"I can't stand it when he acts like that. It drives me crazy!"	"I don't like it when he acts like that, but I can handle it."
"This child is a monster. It's ridiculous what he gets away with."	"This is a child who's trying to get his own way. My job is to stay calm and help him learn better ways to ask for what he wants."
"What if he never changes?"	"He's learned to act this way. I just have to stay calm and help him learn better ways to behave."

Now think of times during the past week when your child performed the targeted misbehavior. Write down the upsetting thoughts you had in the column below titled *Upsetting thoughts*. Then list some alternative, calming thoughts that you could use instead in the column titled, *Calming thoughts*.

Upsetting thoughts   *Calming thoughts*

HANDOUT FOR PARENTS
PROBLEM SOLVING

Here are problem-solving steps to follow when you find yourself becoming upset; Use these steps each time a critical situation occurs.

Step One: What is my goal?

Step Two: What am I doing now?

Step Three: Is what I'm doing helping me to achieve my goal?

Step Four: If it isn't, what do I need to do differently?

Sample

A father trying to read the paper is interrupted by his child scuffling with the family dog. Irritated, the father then engages in the problem-solving process:

1. *What is my goal?* My goal is to have my children mind me and for us all to get along better.

2. *What am I doing now?* I'm getting mad that she's playing with the dog while I'm trying to read the paper.

3. *Is what I'm doing helping me to achieve my goal?* No, if I continue to get mad, we'll have an argument, I'll probably spank her, and then the whole family will be upset.

4. *What can I do differently?* First, I'll relax myself a little. Then I'll go in and clearly state that I want her to take the dog outside to roughhouse. Then I'll relax some more. After that, I'll go outside with her, and we'll chat a little.

HANDOUT FOR PARENTS
HOW TO RELAX

1. Get comfortable in your chair. Close your eyes.

2. Become aware of your breathing.

3. As you breathe in and out, slow your breathing down.

4. As you slow down your breathing, with your next deep breath, slowly count from 1 to 10 as far as you are able to in that single breath.

5. Now exhale slowly, counting from 1 to 10 again until you are out of breath. (The stomach should expand and deflate with each breath.)

6. Repeat this deep, slow inhaling and exhaling while counting, until you are feeling relaxed.

7. Now gradually let your breathing return to normal and open your eyes.

THERAPIST AGENDA: SELF-CONTROL

Agenda	*Notes*

Beginning the Session

    Welcome the family and explain the agenda

Reviewing Past Efforts

    Review efforts at setting up for success

    Review the child's behaviors

    Draw out emotional/cognitive responses

    Link the prior discussion to today's agenda

Introducing the Concept of Self-control

    Explain the role emotions play

    Explain how thoughts determine emotions

    Teach procedures to modify self-talk

    Explain the physical tension/emotional self-control connection

    Teach relaxation procedures

Insuring Implementation

    Rehearse use of self-control procedures

    Problem solve potential difficulties

Giving the Assignment

    Explain the assignment

    Practice filling out the monitoring form

    Problem solve potential tracking difficulties

Closing

    Arrange for between-session phone calls

    Express confidence in the clients

Chapter Seven

DISCIPLINE

In this session, you will teach the parents how to respond more effectively when their child misbehaves. For many, this knowledge will be the single most important benefit they gain from treatment. Probably the most common reason parents with aggressive children seek help is that their children are literally "out of their control." The prior session, with its focus on teaching parents self-control techniques, should help. However, unless they also learn how to manage their youngster's behavior better, the overall situation is not likely to improve for long. When parents learn to apply the disciplinary procedures presented in this session, they will be taking a major step toward the permanent change they desire.

While the use of reinforcement is also an integral part of becoming an effective parent, there is a good reason for teaching disciplinary responses first. Both Wahler (1969) and Herbert, Pinkston, Hayden, Sajewaj, Pinkston, Cordua, and Jackson (1973) have found that, initially, behavior problem children are somewhat unresponsive to social reinforcement. It is not until the parents start becoming more effective disciplinarians that their children really respond consistently to other, more positive forms of social control. Incidentally, most children will tell you that they expect their parents to set and enforce limits. Furthermore, when discipline is carried out in a consistent, nonabusive, and rationale-giving manner, it directly contributes to the child's healthy development. There are ample studies in the child development literature (Baumrind, 1968; McCord & McCord, 1959) to substantiate this point. We feel that the procedures described in this section are in accord with such a supportive style of discipline.

During this session your major tasks are to:

- Review the prior week's assignment and family performance.

- Introduce some basic social learning procedures.

- Review with the parents the discipline procedure or set of procedures they should use to deal with the targeted problem behavior.

- Prepare the parents to use the chosen procedure(s) and include a careful discussion of anticipated problems.

- Outline the assignment for the coming week.

For this session, you may wish to have the children attend with the parents if they are able to understand what is prescribed, participate in discussions, and work to achieve some progress toward family goals. However, if you are seeing the entire family, you will need to exercise care regarding the issue of discipline when the children are present. Clearly, if the session were couched in terms of "this will 'teach' you not to...," the children probably would put up considerable resistance. Children are, in a very real sense, "victims" of their parents' frustrated efforts to deal with them. However, most children are willing to discuss and establish consequences for misbehaviors if they feel that the discussion does not single them out as the problem. Thus, by including the children in the session and by allowing them to contribute, you can gain their acceptance, if not actual cooperation. If the children refuse to cooperate, this should not prevent you from going ahead and laying out effective parental responses. Once children learn what will and will not happen under the new system, they usually see the advantages of operating within it.

One further consideration: you may find it particularly helpful to have the children present at this session to make sure that parents understand and can explain disciplinary procedures. When the family leaves, you can be more confident that everyone realizes what will happen during the week.

We will look first at the disciplinary techniques to be used in this session. You will learn what the techniques involve, how they can be used, and what problems clients may have in applying them.

Activities to be covered in this session are then described in detail. You will find appropriate parent handouts for each discipline technique at the end of the chapter. Finally, we outline issues to watch for when making between-session calls; we also suggest ways to handle some of the problems your clients may experience when using the new procedures.

UNDERSTANDING THE DISCIPLINARY TECHNIQUES

There are six disciplinary procedures we typically recommend, depending on the presenting problem, the child's age, and the parents' ability to deal with stress and confrontation. Those procedures are time-out, "Grandma's Law," natural consequences, withholding attention, removing privileges, and assigning extra work. Following is a brief discussion of each procedure. Additional information and points to consider are contained in a series of handouts for use in preparing the family to implement these techniques. The handouts appear at the end of this chapter.

Time-out

Time-out is a mild form of punishment, often used for dealing with noncompliance, defiance, and sibling rivalry. It involves isolating the child for a few minutes after each instance of the misbehavior. In the home, the bathroom or laundry room are the most frequently used places for time-out. A corner of the room does not work as well, since it still provides the opportunity of getting attention, and a child's bedroom provides access to toys and other forms of entertainment. In public, a bench, the car, or any place where the child is unlikely to get attention can be used. After the child has settled down and served the allotted time (3 minutes for children under 6 years old and 5 minutes for children 6 or older), the youngster can rejoin the parent. With younger children, should they refuse to go, we recommend that the child gently, but firmly, be put in time-out. Children 6 years and older who refuse to go to time-out should be given one warning. If the child still refuses to go, a privilege is removed.

Grandma's Law

"Grandma's Law," (also known as the Premack Principle) is a nonconfrontative but effective procedure for enforcing household rules, responsibilities, and routines. It takes its name from the legendary grandmother who told her grandchild, "First you eat your vegetables, then you can have some pie." Other examples of Grandma's Law are requiring a child to pick up toys before getting a snack, or to feed the cat before going out to play with friends. Basically, it involves parents insisting that children do whatever is expected before they get to do what they want. Youngsters who ignore their parents and do only what they want should be sent to time-out, lose a privilege, or be assigned extra work as a consequence.

Natural and Logical Consequences

"Natural consequences" (what would normally happen with no adult intervention) and "logical consequences" (letting the punishment fit the crime) are ways to deal with children who are often irresponsible or act helpless. Basically, using such consequences means that the parents will no longer act to protect their children from the negative consequences of their behavior. Examples include not joining the child in a frantic hunt for schoolbooks that have been misplaced, not rewarming a meal for a child who comes home late, or requiring a child who damages something to pay for its repair. These consequences work best for recurring problems where the parents can decide well beforehand how they will carry out the intended consequence.

Some parents, particularly those who are overly protective, will find it difficult to let their children suffer the consequences of their actions. The parents often feel sympathetic toward their children and guilty for not coming to their aid. For this reason, parents who are thinking about using natural or logical consequences should discuss the pros and cons of implementing this technique. If they decide to use these consequences, they may need to develop a list of positive self-statements to help them follow through and avoid feeling guilty.

Withholding Attention

This procedure works best with small children who whine, pout, pretend to cry, or pester their parents for attention. Parents who consistently ignore these behaviors usually see a dramatic decrease in their occurrence over time. However, parents need to be prepared to withstand the initial increase in annoying behavior that often results while their child "tests" the new discipline. Since these behaviors worked to get the parents' attention in the past, the child will probably increase using them when the parents first withhold attention. If the parents consistently ignore the negative behavior (while simultaneously reinforcing behaviors they would like to encourage), the negative behavior should decrease. Should the child's testing get too severe, the parent should be prepared to use time-out.

Taking Away Privileges

Removing privileges is a good consequence to use when a child tests the parents' use of time-out, Grandma's Law, or withholding attention. It also can be used when a family member fails to attempt or complete part of an agreement. Used this way, it's the most appropriate consequence for older children ("If you're home late, you can't watch TV after dinner"). Common privileges that can be removed are dessert or snacks, use of the telephone, bicycle, TV, or stereo, or the right to go out or have friends over. When using this method, most parents make the mistake of taking away too many privileges for too long (grounding a child for a week). In most cases it's more effective to withdraw fewer privileges for a shorter time, such as losing 1 hour of TV time or having to go to bed 30 minutes early. Except in special circumstances, the privilege should be lost for a *maximum* of 24 hours after the misbehavior has occurred. If the parents must withhold a privilege again that same day, they should choose a different one rather than extend the loss of the first privilege.

Assigning Extra Work

This procedure is most effective with more serious offenses including lying, stealing, damaging property, and causing problems at school. The amount of chores should be based on the seriousness of the behavior. White lies might earn 15 minutes of work; stealing, 1 to 2 hours. To discourage dawdling over the assigned task, the parents should identify the amount of work they expect to be done (clean the bathroom, including scouring the sink, tub, and toilet, and mopping the floor). They should also expect the work to be done well. Until the work is finished to the parents' satisfaction, they should deny the child access to any privileges.

Being able to deal with problem behaviors is only partly a question of knowing how to implement any or all of the suggested procedures. In fact, while the names for these disciplinary procedures may be new to some parents, the procedures themselves are probably familiar. Thus, it's equally important when teaching parents to use the procedures that you make sure they follow two other rules. First, for discipline to be effective, parents must use it *consistently*. Second, after the punishment has been dispensed, they should stop dwelling on the misbehavior and emphasize their child's positive responses. You will note that the instructions on the parent handout are designed to encourage these actions.

BEGINNING THE SESSION

Materials Needed

You should gather the following listed materials before starting the session. The handouts and Therapist Agenda are found at the end of this chapter. The blank Program Monitoring Form is provided at the end of Chapter Five.

- Therapist Agenda with notes
- Copy of last week's Program Monitoring Form
- Handouts for each of the disciplinary procedures you might be using
- Blank Program Monitoring Form

Welcome the Family and Explain the Agenda

After an initial period of informal talk, explain that you will be spending the first 10 to 15 minutes reviewing their Program Monitoring Form and discussing the family's use of the self-control techniques. Next, you will be teaching the parents some effective ways to discipline children when they misbehave.

Review Prior Week

Ask the family to share the Program Monitoring Form they have completed since the last session. Look over the form and ask the family members to describe some of the problem situations that occurred and how well they managed to maintain control of themselves. For example:

> TH: It shows here [on the monitoring form] that Will disobeyed you 10 times yesterday. Can you remember one of those times?
>
> CL: Sure. Once I told him to sit up and eat his corn, and he threw it across the kitchen floor instead.
>
> TH: How did you feel when that happened? What were you saying to yourself?
>
> CL: I started to get mad, then I told myself to go into the other room and calm down.
>
> TH: Good for you. How did you feel then?

Sometimes parents will report that on occasion they were unable to use the self-control techniques. Neither you nor they should be overly concerned if this happens occasionally. Even families who generally report success in maintaining composure find there are times that they lose it. Predicting such setbacks and minimizing their seriousness serves to give the parents permission to be honest about problems they are having in applying the program, and it minimizes the likelihood that setbacks will be viewed as a catastrophic signal that all progress has been in vain. If, on the other hand, the parents are still having considerable difficulty with either self-control or the setting-up tasks, take as much time as you need to review the problems, identify the specific difficulties, make the necessary changes, or reinstruct and prepare the family to go home and try the procedures again.

INTRODUCING SOCIAL LEARNING CONCEPTS

Explain the Basic Principles

Before turning to the heart of the session—teaching the parents how to respond to the first misbehavior they want to change—you need to introduce a few basic social learning principles. You don't need to concentrate on using the correct terminology, such as "modeling"; it's more important to make sure that the family clearly understands social learning concepts and principles. The basic principles are:

1. Children behave the way they do either because they have learned that behavior or because they have not learned alternative, often more positive, ways to behave.

2. There are three types of learning: (a) *Modeling*—Watching how others behave and copying what they do, (b) *Direct instruction*—Being formally taught, (c) *Consequences*—Doing something and seeing what the effect or consequence is. If children like the consequence of an action (get the parents' attention, earn a reward, or avoid something unpleasant), they will repeat that behavior and expect another desirable consequence. If children do not like the consequence (lose attention, fail to get a reward, or receive an unpleasant consequence), they will learn not to repeat the behavior.

3. Children rarely learn from only one cycle of doing and receiving a consequence. Many repeated cycles, occurring over many days and often weeks, are necessary before learning takes hold. This repeated trying or testing is a necessary part of learning.

4. If one time children receive a consequence they like and the next time receive one they don't like, they will find it harder to learn what to expect. Similarly, the longer the consequence is delayed, the harder it is to see its connection to a particular behavior. Thus, the more consistent parents are in delivering the consequence, and the more immediately it occurs after the behavior, the faster their children will learn.

5. Finally, viewing behavior in a social learning context suggests that in order to change how someone else behaves, we have to change the way we typically respond to that behavior. We want to make sure that the person's good behavior receives positive consequences and that bad behavior results in neutral or negative ones.

Present these principles to the family and follow-up with a few brief examples and a discussion. While this session provides a very simplified summary of social learning theory, you need to begin introducing certain key points and terms at this time. In effect, you are planting ideas that will be important throughout the program and providing new terminology for the family to use. Also, social learning theory promotes the concept that dealing with behaviors we don't like in others means changing ourselves as well.

Present Each Discipline Procedure, Highlighting Its Advantages

Based on the recommended procedures discussed previously, select the ones that you feel are the most appropriate for the problem behavior under discussion. You will need to be familiar with each of the disciplinary procedures and how they relate to each other, since some procedures require knowledge of others. Time-out, for example, requires that parents also know about withholding privileges. Give the family a brief description of what each procedure is and highlight its advantages for both the children and the parents.

From the children's perspective, these discipline techniques can mean that the parents will no longer be continually nagging them to mind, do chores, and the like. For instance, point out that both time-out and losing privileges can be more effective and less upsetting to them than being yelled at or spanked. In addition, doing extra chores is a way of handling a problem that can wipe the slate clean between themselves and their parents.

Parents benefit in several ways by using these techniques. They can discipline their children effectively without becoming angry, yelling, or resorting to physical punishment. For instance, time-out allows them a few minutes to cool off. These techniques are mild enough that parents don't usually feel guilty about using them, and yet effective enough that parents know they are really doing something to help correct their children's problem behavior.

Teach the Procedures

Having selected the disciplinary procedures for them to use, give a copy of the appropriate handouts to each participant. Carefully instruct them in the use of each procedure, going through the handout point by point. As previously discussed in Chapter Three, you should break each procedure down and cover one point at a time. Describe each task, skill, or step briefly and clearly. If necessary, explain why a particular step is important. Give examples relevant to the family, and model or demonstrate each step if possible. Make sure that the family understands your explanations either by questioning them or having them roleplay; proceed only after the family demonstrates that they understand.

The following example illustrates how one might teach the fifth point in time-out instructions: how to send the child to time-out.

> TH: (Explaining relevance) Now that we've decided where we will send Billy for time-out, let's talk about how to send him when he disobeys you. It may not seem important, but the way you tell him to go to

time-out makes a big difference. Usually when you're using time-out, he's just disobeyed you and it's easy to fall into the trap of staring him in the face and almost shouting at him, "You get into the time-out room right now!" However, we find that when you do that, the child gets angry. In other words, it's likely that he's going to test you to see who can win in a contest of wills. However, if you simply turn to him and in a matter-of-fact voice say (modeling in a matter-of-fact and rather calm voice), "Billy, I asked you to pick up your jacket and you didn't do it. That's disobeying. I want you to go to time-out now," he's likely to accept that tone of voice and quietly go to time-out. (Checking for comprehension with mother) Fran, why don't you pretend that you just asked Billy to wash his hands before coming to eat. He comes to the table and you notice his hands haven't been washed. How are you going to tell him to go to time-out?

MOTHER: Billy, I asked you to wash your hands and you didn't. Now go to time-out.

TH: Very good. Clear and right to the point, yet you said it in a calm, matter-of-fact way. Before we turn to the next point, there's something else worth mentioning. Sometimes when you'll need to send him to time-out, he'll be across the room or even in another part of the house. In that case, it's tempting to shout that he should go to time-out. But we've found that when you do that he may pretend he didn't hear you or the two of you could get into a shouting match, which we don't want. Let me give you a suggestion. If he's not close to you, either move closer to him or call him to you; when he's near you, tell him to go to time-out in the same calm, matter-of-fact way you did before. Any questions?

FATHER: No, I think I understand.

MOTHER: So do I.

TH: That's great. It may seem small, but one of the key factors in this technique is to set a tone that says to the child "This is no big deal, just go to time-out" in such a way that he knows you mean business. You're not pleading with him, and you're not asking him to go; you're simply telling him.

INSURING IMPLEMENTATION

Even after you carefully teach the key points in the procedures, the parents may still go home and fail to implement what they have learned. To reduce this possibility, we recommend that you follow what we call a "proper implementation sequence." In this sequence, you will:

1. Rehearse the use of disciplinary procedures (overtly and covertly).

2. Explain the specifics of the program (who, what, where, when, and how).

3. Problem solve potential difficulties.

4. Solicit concerns and predict problems, changes, or feelings.

5. Express confidence in the client.

The amount of time you allot to the sequence will depend on the family. With some clients, only a short session is needed. With others you may need to spend much more time going through all the steps until you are sure the family is prepared to carry out the instructions.

Rehearse Use of Disciplinary Procedures

Rehearsal is an excellent way to emphasize all the points previously covered and to assure yourself that the family is prepared to implement the procedures. In overt rehearsal, often called roleplaying, various members pretend they are the child or parents and go through each procedure step by step. In covert rehearsal, participants imagine they are going through the procedure. Usually their imagination is guided by your presentation. One advantage of covert rehearsal is that it also addresses the cognitive aspects of the intervention. The following example shows one way a covert rehearsal can be conducted.

TH: I'd like to try something now that I think you'll find interesting. Take a few moments to get relaxed; close your eyes and take a few deep breaths. (At this point, the therapist's voice becomes slower and more monotonous.) Imagine you've had a busy day. You tell Carla to set the table for dinner. She heads off and you compliment her for getting started so promptly. A few minutes later you notice that she's wandered off to play with her toys. Calmly but firmly, you call her name. She comes and you tell her, "I asked you to set the table and you aren't doing it. Go to time-out. I'll set the timer and tell you when you can come out." You remain very calm and say to yourself, "This will work, and it's a lot better than getting angry." After 5 minutes the bell rings and you tell Carla to come out. Then you tell her to go and set the table. You say to yourself, "I did that really well. I'll get the hang of this in no time."

In the following example, the same situation is rehearsed overtly.

TH: (To father) OK, Rick. Suppose I'm Carla, and instead of setting the table as you asked, I'm off playing with my toys. What would be your response?

FATHER: Let's see. Send her to time-out.

TH: How would you do that? What would you say?

FATHER: Carla, you're not setting the table as I asked. Go to time-out.

TH: Great. What if she sasses back?

FATHER: I'll tell her once that if she doesn't go to time-out now, she won't get to watch TV the rest of the night.

Work Out the Specifics of the Program

Make sure that all family members know exactly who will be responsible for implementing each part of every procedure. They should decide such things as when they will begin using the techniques, what they need to do to make the techniques work (perhaps "childproof" the time-out room), and who will get the time-out room ready. The therapist in this example helps the clients think through both the details of time-out and their individual responsibilities.

TH: Looks like you both understand how to send Carla to time-out. Now let's talk about the time-out room. When will you "childproof" it?

MOTHER: I can get that done tomorrow, during the day.

TH: Fine. Have you decided if you're going to take everything out? Or are you going to put everything in a box so you can carry it out when you have to?

MOTHER: Well, I'll take out the cosmetics and cleaning powders and such, but I think I can leave the toothpaste and plastic glass there.

TH: That seems reasonable. If that doesn't seem adequate, later on you can take more things out. When do you think you'll be starting time-out?

FATHER: Well, it's a little late this evening, but I suppose I could start tomorrow night when I get home from work.

MOTHER: I can start tomorrow after I get the bathroom ready.

Problem Solve Potential Difficulties

By identifying potential problems and brainstorming possible solutions, you can reduce the emotional impact of such difficulties should they occur. Also, parents will be better prepared to handle the problems and actually less able to claim ignorance as an excuse to avoid using the procedures.

While it may be tempting to tell parents how to deal with each problem that comes up, you need to give them the opportunity to suggest their own solutions. Doing so will help reinforce their initiative and give them greater confidence in their ability to carry out the program.

In addition to the concerns or problems the parents might raise, the following issues may also need to be considered.

- What to do if the child throws a tantrum or refuses to accept a correctional procedure and instead asks to be given a second chance. (The best solution is to follow through with the correctional procedure and tell the child that next time you will expect the child to do better. If the child continues to misbehave, remove a privilege for that day.)

- How to apply the procedure in the presence of guests or relatives. (Generally, the best course is to take the child aside, administer the consequence to avoid embarrassing the child in public, then return to the guests or relatives.)

- How to apply the procedure outside the home. (Most of the procedures can be adapted for use outside the home. This may, however, require some prior thought about possible time-out locations, privileges that can be removed, and other practical considerations.)

- What parents should do if they find themselves losing self-control. (They should step back from the situation for a moment, do the relaxation technique and/or think calming thoughts, then return to apply the correction procedure.)

For two-parent families, an additional set of concerns might include:

- How to insure that both parents use the correctional procedures in the same manner.

- How one parent can support the other in using the procedures.

- What to do if one parent thinks the other is doing something wrong. (Usually the first parent should attempt to speak to the other out of the child's presence. In some cases it is simply necessary to let the other parent proceed, then get together later to work out the disagreement and decide what to do differently in the future.)

For single parents, you may want to discuss the following issue:

- Since applying correctional procedures is often stressful, how can single parents get support from other people? (Do they have friends or extended family they can ask for support? You may also want to consider making extra phone calls or home visits to provide more encouragement and feedback during this usually stressful time.)

The therapist in the following example encourages two parents to preproblem solve how they will support each other when sending their child to time-out.

> TH: We mentioned earlier that the person who gives the command should be the one to send Carla to time-out

if she disobeys. What will you do, Walt, if Carla comes to you when Debra's sent her to time-out?

FATHER: Hmmm. Well, if she comes to me and tries to get me to take her side, I'll just tell her, "Your mom sent you to time-out and you should go."

TH: Great. That way you're backing up Debra's authority as well as sending Carla a consistent message. Another issue is how each of you will let the other one know if Carla's lost a particular privilege?

MOTHER: I'll just try telling him and he can try telling me in the same way. If that doesn't work, we can write down what privileges are lost on a blackboard.

TH: Great. That should work really well.

Solicit Concerns and Predict Problems, Changes, or Feelings

Before discussing the assignment for the upcoming week, spend a few minutes probing to find out whether the clients have any questions or concerns regarding their use of the chosen discipline techniques. Any points of confusion should be cleared up and any reservations brought out into the open and discussed.

In addition to soliciting and addressing their concerns, you should predict any problems, changes, or feelings you think they are likely to encounter in the upcoming week. This serves the same function as preproblem solving because it prepares parents for what may happen and lessens the emotional impact of subsequent events. Aside from any predictions you can make given the family's particular circumstances, two other common results warrant predicting. First, there is likely to be some increase in the child's undesirable behavior at the beginning. The youngster has had success in using the inappropriate behavior in the past and may try more of it to see if it will work in the future. The child will also be testing the parents' commitment to the new program. Second, if the parents use the procedure as directed, after a few days they will find that their child is becoming more loving and affectionate towards them.

GIVING THE ASSIGNMENT

Complete the Program Monitoring Form

Before sending the family home, you should help them complete a blank Program Monitoring Form. This form will serve as a record of how the discipline procedures were used and their impact on the behavior in question. As in previous weeks, the form also will remind the parents of what they are to do.

Parents should record (a) the occurrence of both the child's appropriate behavior and the targeted misbehavior; (b) the parents' attempts to set up for success; and (c) the parents' use of self-control techniques. In addition, during the upcoming week they should record each time they discipline their child with the predetermined discipline techniques and rate themselves daily on how well they implemented each of the discipline procedures. (See Figures 9 and 10.)

Practice Tracking

Once the Program Monitoring Form is filled out, have the parents practice tracking. Unless they had difficulty tracking any part of the

Figure 9. Fifth Sample Program Monitoring Form.

Day or Date	3/18	3/19	3/20	3/21	3/22	3/23	3/24
1. Complies	THL	THL III	THL I	THL I THL	THL IIII	THL II THL	THL
2. Does not comply	THL III	IIII	THL	III	III	III	THL I
3. Setting up for success	A	A	B	A	A	A	A
4. Self-control	B	B	C	A	A	A	B
5. # of time-outs	THL I	IIII	IIII	III	III	I	THL
6. Correct discipline	C	A	C	A	A	D	B
7.							
8.							

Things to Remember

Correct discipline:
1) send to time-out each
   time she does not comply
2) don't threaten or yell
3) no spanking
4) don't argue with her
   or defend myself
5) don't keep checking on her
   while she's in time-out
6) take away a privilege if
   she refuses to go to time-out

Setting up for success:
1) good commands
2) take all fun things and
   medicine out of bathroom

Figure 10. Sixth Sample Program Monitoring Form.

Day or Date	2/15	2/16	2/17	2/18	2/19		
1. *Makes bed in morning*	+	—	+	+	+		
2. *Sets table by 5:45 with no reminder*	—	+	+	+	—		
3. *Puts dirty clothes in hamper*	—	+	+	+	+		
4. *Setting up for success mom/dad*	B/B	A/B	A/A	A/A	A/A		
5. *John's self-control*	C	B	A	A	A		
6. *Parents' self-control mom/dad*	C/B	A/B	B/A	A/A	A/B		
7. *# of privileges lost*	2	1	0	0	0		
8. *Parents' discipline mom/dad*	C/NA	NA/B	NA/NA	NA/NA	C/NA		

Things to Remember

NA means either no discipline was needed or the parent wasn't responsible for the discipline that day.
Privileges to lose—
see list on Parent Handout

Correct discipline:
1) no arguing or debating
2) take away privilege for agreed-upon time
3) drop issue after punishment is given

previous assignments, this practice need only focus on tracking discipline. Make up several example scenarios pertaining to discipline and have them show you how they would track them. For example:

TH: Let's suppose that Michael did not get up to take a bath when you told him to. You send him to time-out by saying calmly, "You didn't get up and go take a bath as you were told. Go to time-out." Michael then says he'll take his bath as soon as he's through reading his story. After one warning to go to time-out, Michael is still reading, so you calmly tell him he must go to bed a half-hour early. Let's also say that the way you sent him to time-out was pretty reflective of the way you did it all day, with the exception of one time when you raised your voice. How would you track all that on your monitoring form?

CL: I wouldn't mark down a time-out, because he didn't go. But I would mark down that he lost a privilege.

TH: Very good. And how would you rate yourself for the day?

CL: Well, if I'd only blown it once, as you said, I guess I'd give myself a B+.

TH: Sounds reasonable.

Problem Solve Potential Tracking Difficulties

At this point in treatment, the parents are being asked to track several items each day. Therefore, be sure that the new assignment will not overburden them. If they feel the tracking assignment is too cumbersome, the most common response is to stop tracking altogether. If they express serious doubts about being able to track all of the requested information, you have two choices. First, have them track all of the areas discussed before but reduce the number of days that they must track. Second, drop any areas that the parents seem to have mastered and have them track only their child's appropriate and inappropriate behavior and how they used the discipline techniques. If the parents feel confident about their ability to track and their past performance substantiates this, they should be encouraged to monitor all aspects of the program to date.

Prepare Parents to Explain Discipline Techniques

If the child did not participate in the session, the parents should explain the discipline procedures to the child at home before using them. As with previous explanations, the parents should pick a neutral time to talk with their youngster. If they begin by saying something positive about their child's behavior, the child is less likely to be defensive when the issue of discipline is raised. Then they should matter-of-factly explain that they will be trying a new way of discipline when the youngster misbehaves, a way that will result in less arguing, yelling, and spanking. To help in their explanation, the parents may want to use the handouts describing the techniques as a reference.

If the parents will be using time-out, they should explain when the child will have to go, where time-out will be, how long it will last, what will happen if the child is extremely noisy while in time-out (time-out is extended), and what will happen if the child refuses to go (a privilege is taken away). If privilege losses are being used, the parents should share the list of potential privileges that may be taken away for a day. If work chores are to be used, they should also share the list of chores with the child and explain that, if assigned, they must be completed before the child will have access to regular privileges, such as watching TV, eating snacks, seeing friends, or using the phone. If the child is small, they should act out the process of time-out, because new routines can be frightening to younger children if they haven't experienced them before.

If their child becomes upset or argues with them during this discussion they should not debate, argue back, threaten, or be overly sympathetic. Rather, they should state that they are sorry that the child is upset but from now on they will be using the new discipline techniques.

CLOSING

Arrange for Between-session Phone Calls

Discuss with clients when you can contact them or they can contact you during the coming week to discuss their performance and/or any problems they are having. Once you have arranged specific times to call, write them down on your calendar and on top of the parents' Program Monitoring Form.

Express Confidence in the Clients

When family members feel confident that they can carry out the procedures and that the techniques will achieve the desired effect, they will be much more willing to implement them. The clients' self-confidence will be based in large part on the confidence you express in them. Such confidence can be conveyed through your tone of voice and your words. For example:

TH: Well, I think we've covered everything, and I feel really confident that this is going to go just great. You know what to do. You know how to handle yourself in the situation. I think by next week we will already be seeing some big improvements in your home. How do you feel about it?

MOTHER: I'm willing to try it.

TH: (To father) And you, Brad?

FATHER: I feel the same.

TH: Great! I'm looking forward to finding out how well you've done.

MAKING BETWEEN-SESSION CALLS

After talking briefly with the clients on the phone, ask them to discuss their weekly tracking form with you. Next, review the various situations that have occurred and the parents' responses to them. In particular, there are several issues to look for:

● Do they carry out the correction procedures with a sense of confidence that they will work? Specifically, if the child challenges or defies the parents, do they continue to use the procedure and apply the backup consequences as specified, or do they give in or resort to verbal or physical means to control their child?

- Do the parents apply the correction procedures consistently? Do they ever avoid using them when they think they should? Do they delay using them until the behavior is further out of control? Do the parents threaten to use the procedures instead of using them immediately? Some parents want to give their child one warning. If so, work out how they will do that. Beware of the parents resorting to multiple warnings.

- After the consequence has been enforced, can the parents "wipe the slate clean"? This is critical, since often the child may be *more* affectionate after having been corrected. The parents should be able to respond freely to this behavior. However, the display of affection should not prevent them from implementing the correction procedure again the next time the child misbehaves.

- Are the parents applying and carrying through with the backup consequences called for? Be particularly alert to this issue if the child is testing them when they use the initial consequence.

- What effect is the intervention having on the child's behavior? If it is improving, congratulate the parents on *their* effort and success. If, on the other hand, the parents report that they were unable to use the correction procedures properly or that they are having serious difficulties, probe for further details. Find out if the problems stem from one or more of the following: (a) a misunderstanding of the procedures; (b) the parents' inability to remain calm in the problem situation; (c) a reluctance to use the procedures; (d) environmental situations impairing the parents' ability to carry out the intervention (sick children, parental conflicts); or (e) a serious deterioration or escalation of the child's behavior.

If the main problem appears to stem from a misunderstanding of the procedures, spend some time reviewing the techniques with the parents. Include a review of each procedure to be used and how it will be implemented, and use extensive rehearsal and feedback. You should also reassure the parents that what they are learning is not easy and that you have confidence in their ability to apply these techniques.

If the parents are unable to remain calm when correcting their child, ask them to describe any negative thoughts they have had. Then have them imagine what positive self-statements they could say instead if a similar situation came up in the future. In some cases, the parents may have been able to say positive self-statements in certain situations but not in others. Have them explore the differences and determine how they can change their negative self-talk to positive self-statements.

If the parents resist using the correction procedures, find out what their specific concerns are and address each one. Often parents are afraid of losing their child's love if they set and enforce limits. You can point out that, on the contrary, once parents consistently use appropriate discipline, the child is likely to become much more affectionate and trusting.

When the problem involves outside pressures that are taxing the parents' energies and/or resources, determine whether those pressures will continue in the weeks ahead. If so, you may want to help relieve those pressures where possible, such as arranging day-care, or referring them to a marriage counselor. You might also consider postponing treatment a week or so until they are in a better position to benefit from your services.

If the child is escalating negative misbehavior, such as running out of the home when told to go to time-out or threatening to strike the parent, you must be prepared to help the parents assert their authority while reducing the risk of further escalation and possible harm. The following are recommendations for handling these situations.

Recognize that the parents will need all the support you can provide. Not only should this include your moral support and expression of confidence, but often your presence, either in person or by phone, at moments of crisis. At the same time, arrange for close support from other adults. If it is a two-parent family, review how they can support each other. With single parents, if possible, work with a relative or friend so that person can be an "ally" to the parent. If you are working in a group, you might arrange for another parent to be on call to offer support.

If conflict appears to be escalating, make sure that the parents are not trying to use physical force to control their child but instead are relying on backup consequences to enforce their authority. (The one exception is that it is permissible to take a child 5 years and under to time-out should the youngster refuse to go.) Removing privileges is particularly recommended because it avoids physical contact and the eye-to-eye type of confrontation. Help the parents avoid issuing ultimatums such as "Until you go to time-out, there will be no TV!" This sets up a conflict of wills and often prolongs the struggle. If the child refuses to go to time-out, the parents should remove the privilege and drop the matter. If, however, the child misbehaves again, another time-out should be issued; and should the child refuse to go, *another* privilege should be removed for that day. Eventually, the child will realize that the parents control enough privileges to make winning impossible. In cases where the child refuses to do an assigned work chore, the parents will need to remove all regular daily privileges until the task is completed. Enforcing this decision will require substantial support between the parents.

Once the parents have passed through the crisis, make sure that they do not back down in the next confrontation. The child will almost certainly test them again, and the parents must demonstrate that they are prepared to deal with each incident of misbehavior. In most cases, the child's successive tests aren't likely to be as extreme.

Finally, make certain that the parent who initiates the correction is the one to carry it through. If responsibility is transferred to another (either you or another adult), that parent will not have demonstrated an ability to manage the child. The role of others is to support, not to take over.

HANDOUT FOR PARENTS
TIME-OUT

Time-out is a mild but effective way to deal with noncompliance, defiance, and fights between brothers and sisters. It involves sending the child to a relatively isolated place for a few minutes immediately after each misbehavior. Time-out serves several purposes. It takes away the attention that may be encouraging your child's misbehavior; it stops the conflict; it reduces the likelihood that your child's behavior will get worse; and it gives your child a chance to settle down.

Directions

1. Describe the types of behavior that will be handled by using time-out. _____

_____

_____

2. Enter here where your child should go for time-out. A bathroom or laundry room works best. Avoid using either your child's room (too many distractions) or a chair in the corner (still in sight of other people).

_____

_____

3. For children under age 6, 3 minutes in time-out is recommended. For children over 6, time-out should last 5 minutes.

4. You will need to remove from the time-out location "fun" items (bath toys) or things that your child might get into or damage (pills, makeup). Enter the items you need to remove here. _____

_____

_____

5. Keys to the effective use of time-out are (a) telling your child that what he or she did is unacceptable; (b) telling the child in a firm, calm manner to go to time-out. Here's an example:

PARENT: Michael, I asked you to hang up your coat and you didn't. That's disobeying. Go to time-out now.

6. Once your youngster is in time-out, set a timer or check the clock and leave the child alone.

7. Your child needn't be absolutely quiet while in time-out. However, if your child yells or fusses loudly while in time-out, extend it until he or she has been quiet for the required time (3 or 5 minutes).

8. Expect your youngster to test you and the time-out procedure. If the child is under 6 years of age and refuses to go to time-out, gently but firmly take the youngster to the time-out place. A child 6 years old or older should be given one calm warning to go to time-out or lose a privilege for 24 hours. Later, if the child repeats the misbehavior and again refuses to go, remove another privilege. Enter here a list of privileges you can remove. _____

_____

_____

9. Should your child make a mess while in time-out, insist that it be cleaned up before the youngster comes out.

10. If your child is sent to time-out for not doing something he or she was told to do, tell your child to do what you wanted after coming out of time-out. Be prepared to back up this second command with another time-out.

11. Once the time-out is over, do not scold or lecture your child.

12. Don't be concerned if your child tells you time-out doesn't bother him or her; the child is bluffing. If you continue to use it, you'll find that the misbehavior happens less and less often.

HANDOUT FOR PARENTS
GRANDMA'S LAW

Grandma's Law is named for the white-haired lady of folk wisdom who told her grandchildren, "You can have some pie *after* you eat your vegetables." Essentially, it involves requiring children to do something they would rather avoid as a condition for doing something they like. For example, you can insist that your child put on a jacket before going outside or that homework be completed before turning on the TV. The key to Grandma's Law is that the privilege held back is something the child wants and was planning to do.

Directions

1. Think about the common problems you have with your youngster where Grandma's Law might work. List them in the column labeled *Do this first*. Next, think of activities that your child looks forward to that can be withheld until the required chore or activity is done. List those in the column labeled *Before you get to do this*.

Do this first: *Before you get to do this:*

_____   _____

_____   _____

_____   _____

2. Grandma's Law works best when you speak to your child in a friendly, positive, and enthusiastic way. Note the following examples:

Right way:

"Let's get those blocks picked up so we can read this story."

"Billy, your friends are outside. You can go out just as soon as you straighten up your room."

Wrong way:

"If you don't pick up those blocks, I won't read you this story."

"Billy, you can't go out until you straighten up your room."

3. If your child tries to go ahead with the desired activity without doing what you asked, call the youngster back and repeat what you said. If the child continues to ignore you, either use time-out or take away a privilege. List privileges you might take away here. _____

_____

_____

HANDOUT FOR PARENTS
NATURAL AND LOGICAL CONSEQUENCES

Natural consequences help correct irresponsible or immature behaviors. Your child must deal with the effects or consequences of an action. Another form of consequences is logical consequences, where we "let the punishment fit the crime."

Examples of natural and logical consequences:

Problem	Natural or logical consequence
Overslept and missed school bus	Walk to school
Child breaks toy	No replacement of toy
Damages neighbor's property	Make restitution by doing chores for neighbor
Wets bed	Must strip bed sheets and put in wash

Directions

1. Identify the specific situations or behaviors that can best be handled with natural or logical consequences. List those here. _____

_____

_____

_____

_____

2. Decide what the consequences for these behaviors might be and how they should be applied. List those here. _____

_____

_____

_____

_____

3. You may be concerned about letting your child face natural or logical consequences. What are the advantages and disadvantages of letting your child face those consequences?

Disadvantages	*Advantages*
_____	_____
_____	_____
_____	_____

Having weighed the advantages and disadvantages, make a list of appropriate thoughts you can say to yourself that will enable you to carry through with the use of natural or logical consequences. "_____"

" _____ "

" _____ "

" _____ "

4. Be prepared to deal with your child's testing. Often this takes the form of pleading helplessness. Such pleading should be ignored if the task is appropriate for the child's age. If your child refuses to accept the consequences, use time-out, loss of a privilege, or Grandma's Law—whichever best fits the situation. Describe here how you will handle these situations._____

_____

_____

_____

_____

5. You should not lecture your child nor offer sympathy after the consequence occurs. Treat the issue as closed.

HANDOUT FOR PARENTS
WITHHOLDING ATTENTION

This technique works particularly well with young children. Many annoying behaviors, such as whining, mock crying, and pouting, can be dealt with by withholding attention. By not attending to these behaviors, parents encourage their children to develop more appropriate methods of getting attention. On the other hand, there are other situations where this technique doesn't work. For example, some behaviors are too extreme or dangerous to ignore, such as hitting, defiance, verbal abuse, setting fires, running away, and damaging property. Other behaviors give the child immediate benefits while inconveniencing or harming others, for example, not doing chores, bullying, and stealing. Without a stronger consequence (time-out, loss of privilege, work chore), there would be little motivation to change. Finally, if you and your child do little together now, withholding your attention is not likely to affect your child's behavior.

Directions

1. List the types of behavior that will be handled by withholding your attention. _____

_____

_____

2. You can ignore your child by turning or walking away, talking to or looking at another person, or involving yourself in another activity. List things you can do when your child engages in the behaviors you listed in 1. _____

_____

_____

3. Pay attention to your child shortly after the misbehavior stops by smiling, praising, looking at, or talking to the youngster.

4. Be prepared: when you first start withholding attention, the child's annoying behavior will increase for a while. Usually, things get worse for several days before they improve.

5. If your child tries to get your attention by shouting, threatening to break something, or becoming defiant or verbally abusive, give one warning to stop. If the warning is ignored, send your child to time-out.

HANDOUT FOR PARENTS
TAKING AWAY PRIVILEGES

Removing privileges can be used if your child tests your use of time-out, Grandma's Law, or withholding attention. Loss of privileges is also an appropriate consequence by itself if your child fails to carry out an agreement made between you. Used in this way, it is probably the most appropriate method of discipline for older children and adolescents.

Directions

1. Decide which behaviors will be dealt with by removing a privilege. List them here. _____

_____

_____

2. The privilege must be something you can actually deny your child. For example, if you work and don't get home until after 5:00 p.m., you probably can't deny your youngster the privilege of watching TV in the afternoon. Ideally, the privilege taken away should not affect others. For example, if the child is to be denied TV, what effect will this have on other family members who wish to watch it? With these points in mind, list here those privileges your child would miss if they were taken away.

Behavior   *Time*

a. _____   _____

b. _____   _____

c. _____   _____

d. _____   _____

e. _____   _____

3. The number of privileges lost and the length of time for which they are removed should be matched to the age of the child and the seriousness of the particular behavior. Most parents make the mistake of taking away too many privileges for too long a time. This action turns what might have been a good learning experience into one of lingering hostility and resentment. We recommend that a privilege be removed for only 24 hours. In fact, parents often get better results if they use even briefer periods such as taking away a toy for a few hours or preventing the child from watching a favorite TV show for each episode of swearing or talking back. Next to each of the privileges you listed in 2, indicate the length of time that it will be removed.

4. When taking away a privilege, be calm but firm. If your child tries to ignore the restriction, remove an additional privilege. Finally, once the privilege has been lost, the punishment accepted, and the time spent, the privilege should be restored and the incident dropped. Avoid any further lectures or reminders.

HANDOUT FOR PARENTS
ASSIGNING EXTRA WORK

Having the child do extra work around the house can be an effective consequence, particularly for more serious misbehaviors such as lying, stealing, or damaging property. An added advantage of this technique is that it repays you for the time and effort spent dealing with the problem. In cases such as stealing or damaging property, doing extra work is one way for the youngster to repay the loss.

Directions

1. Describe here exactly which behaviors will be handled by assigning extra chores. _____

_____

_____

_____

_____

2. Decide how much work will be assigned. Take into account your child's age and the severity of the misbehavior. For example, a 9-year-old might be assigned a 15-minute chore for telling a lie, 30 minutes of work for stealing something worth less than $1, and 1 hour for items worth more than $1. A 12-year-old might receive double that amount of work. Next to the misbehaviors listed in 1, write in the amount of work to be assigned.

3. To discourage dawdling, explain to your child that the entire task assigned must be completed. This means assigning chores that your child can complete in the required time. For example, a 10-year-old child working steadily could probably straighten up and vacuum the living room in half an hour. If the child dawdles and delays, the job could take as much as 1½ hours. The choice is up to the child.

4. If you find out about a misdeed several days after it happened, you should still assign extra work. In some instances it is particularly important that you make it clear exactly why your child is being disciplined; otherwise the child will not link the punishment to the misbehavior.

5. Be prepared to handle testing (outright refusal, attempts to delay or dawdle). Refuse to argue or debate and avoid standing over your child while the work is being done. Until the chore is completed to your satisfaction, withhold *all* privileges, such as watching TV, using the phone, and having friends over. Once the chore is completed, the issue should be dropped.

THERAPIST AGENDA: DISCIPLINE

Agenda	Notes

Beginning the Session

Welcome the family and explain the agenda

Review prior week

Introducing Social Learning Concepts

Explain the basic principles:

Children behave certain ways because they learned them or did not learn alternative ways

Behavior is learned through:

Modeling

Direct instruction

Consequences

Learning takes repeated trials

Consistency and immediacy are important

Changing someone else's behavior means changing our own as well

Present each discipline procedure, highlighting its advantages

Options include:

Time-out

Grandma's Law

Natural and logical consequences

Withholding attention

Taking away privileges

Assigning extra work

Teach the procedures

Give out appropriate parents' handouts

Review each step with directions:

Describe step

Give brief rationale and relevance if necessary

Give relevant examples

Model or demonstrate if possible

Check by questioning or roleplay

Insuring Implementation

Rehearse use of disciplinary procedures:

Overt

Covert

Work out the specifics of the program

Who, what, where, when, and how for getting started

Problem solve potential difficulties:

Parent concerns

Other concerns:

Dealing with testing

Using procedure with guests present

Applying procedure outside the home

Regaining self-control

Insuring both parents are consistent

Supporting each other

Correcting the other parent

Supporting the single parent

Solicit concerns and predict problems, changes, or feelings:

Solicit and address client concerns or questions

Predict problems, changes, or feelings:

Expect testing (behavior may get worse)

Affection should increase

Giving the Assignment

Complete the Program Monitoring Form

Practice tracking

Problem solve potential tracking difficulties

Prepare parents to explain discipline techniques

Closing

Arrange for between-session phone calls

Express confidence in the clients

Chapter Eight

REINFORCEMENT

By now, the combination of setting up, better self-control, and changes in discipline should have resulted in improvement in the targeted concerns. The focus of treatment now shifts to reinforcement and the use of specific procedures for encouraging desirable behaviors. Hopefully, as parents rely more on this positive approach, they will have less need to turn to punishment-oriented procedures in managing their children. In addition, as the entire family becomes more sensitive to the use of social reinforcers, the overall level of positive interaction should increase. The major tasks to be accomplished in this session are:

- Review clients' performance during the previous week.
- Define reinforcement and explain its importance to the change process.
- Describe how people can inadvertently reinforce undesirable behaviors.
- Present social reinforcement techniques.
- Present a reinforcement system(s) based on the use of formal rewards.
- Prepare the family to implement the selected techniques.
- Develop the assignment.

While the primary focus of this session will be on rewarding the target child's appropriate behavior, you should not overlook the fact that reinforcement is something that everyone can use. Parents can reinforce parents, children can reinforce their parents, and children can reinforce each other. Pursued in this light, the session can leave everyone with an enthusiastic determination to make their home a positive and enjoyable place.

Before discussing in detail each of the tasks to be accomplished in this session, we will give an overview of the various reinforcement techniques to be used by families. These techniques are grouped into two general areas: social reinforcement and formal rewards.

Following this discussion, we cover session activities in detail, outlining how to present social and formal reinforcement principles and techniques to clients. They are then given a chance to practice implementing reinforcement using the handouts provided at the end of this chapter. Finally, we discuss issues you will need to cover when making between-session calls.

UNDERSTANDING REINFORCEMENT TECHNIQUES

Social Reinforcement

Social reinforcement includes any verbal message (praise, thanks, compliments), physical contact (hugs, smiles, kisses), or attention that strengthens or increases the behavior it follows. Generally, the more powerful forms of social reinforcement also communicate appreciation, affection, or concern, although technically they don't need to have that effect. The part of this session dealing with inadvertent reinforcement addresses that issue. For the most part, we adopt the common meaning of reinforcement as a synonym for a positive, rewarding behavior. The parent handout "Social Reinforcement" describes the three types of reinforcement in some detail. Each type has basic issues you will need to consider.

Verbal reinforcement. Families who learn to reinforce each other verbally build stronger, more trusting relationships. In addition, parents who are lavish in their use of verbal reinforcement help build their child's positive self-image and model for that child more socially approved styles of interacting with others outside the family.

Individuals will vary in their ability to use praise and compliments. For instance, while one father may feel quite comfortable in telling his son "I love you," another might view this statement as "unmanly." Verbal reinforcement does not necessarily need to be elaborate or said in an affectionate manner to be effective. Therefore, each family member should be encouraged to develop a variety of reinforcing statements they feel comfortable using. We have found that the more clients give and receive verbal reinforcement, particularly those who initially are guarded or reluctant, the more comfortable they become praising and complimenting others.

Physical affection. Physical affection is a powerful reinforcer, one that is often overlooked with older children. While the use of physical contact can be as pleasant to the giver as to the receiver, some parents report feeling silly, anxious, or afraid to show such affection. These feelings, as well as the fear of rejection, can be amplified if their child does not respond positively to their approaches. In these cases, parents may need to begin showing affection through less intense or close physical contact (sitting next to their child or tickling, rather than hugging or kissing). Once the parents and child become comfortable with these less intense forms of contact, they can usually graduate to more intensive demonstrations of affection with little difficulty.

Attention. Attention is also a powerful reinforcer, particularly with small children. Such behaviors as talking in a normal tone of voice (versus whining), using proper eating habits, playing nicely with other children, and independent play can be strengthened if regularly attended to by parents. As described in the "Social Reinforcement" handout, there are many ways of giving attention. In fact, most parents already are spending inordinate amounts of time attending to their child's misbehavior by arguing, spanking, pleading, and scolding. Your goal will be to help the parents redirect their attention and respond instead to their child's appropriate behavior.

Parents often report having one of three problems when attempting to use attention as a positive reinforcer. First, some parents have a hard time not attending to their child's misbehavior. To overcome this tendency, they should focus on using the self-control methods described in Chapter Six. In addition, consistently prompt them to analyze their actions from a social learning perspective, asking themselves such questions as "Is my attention reinforcing the behaviors I want or those I'd like to reduce?" Second, some parents find that at times it's inconvenient to attend to their child's positive behavior (while on the phone, cooking, working in the shop). However, parents who have learned the art of setting up for success can often find ways to take short breaks in their activities to give their child deserved attention. Finally, some parents will have gotten into the habit of "laying low" when their child is behaving well. As one mother put it, "I'm afraid if I go in while he's playing quietly, he'll want me to stay and play with him. Besides, he so rarely plays by himself that I cherish that little bit of quiet time it gives me." Again, it is best to get the parents to describe how they might be reinforcing their child's negative behavior and ignoring positive behavior. In the following example, the therapist helps a client understand the true nature of the parent-child interaction.

TH: You said Joe can't play quietly by himself for more than 5 minutes. What happens then?

CL: It varies. Sometimes he comes whining to me, and other times he gets overly excited and I have to go in and calm him.

TH: So he does something to get your attention.

CL: Yeah, I guess he does, doesn't he?

TH: Funny as it sounds, kids will resort to doing all sorts of things to get their parents' attention. If they can't get it one way, for instance, by playing quietly, they'll get it another way. Do you think that might be what Joe is doing?

CL: Oh, sure. And I'm reinforcing his whining and overactive play.

TH: Can you think of some ways you could attend to his quiet play that wouldn't disturb him or mean that you have to join him?

In teaching clients when and how to use social reinforcement, three general points should be stressed:

1. *Reinforcement should be given as soon after the desired behavior as possible.* However, the old adage "Better late than never"

is also applicable. If a person is unaware, forgets, or is not present when the desired behavior occurs, reinforcement should be given as soon after as possible.

2. *Appropriate behavior can be maintained with continued social reinforcement.* For example, a child initially complies with a request to stay by the parent in the store. By continuing to reinforce the child (talking to the youngster, engaging him in the shopping task, thanking him for staying close), the parent can increase the likelihood that the child will continue to stay close by. Behaviors should not be taken for granted once they've been initially performed.

3. *Social reinforcement alone may not be an adequate incentive to change.* In most cases, parents initially will want to combine social reinforcement with the use of more formal rewards. Formal rewards are discussed in the following section of this chapter. Once the desirable behavior is established, however, these rewards can be faded, or withdrawn gradually, and the new behavior maintained through social reinforcement.

Formal Rewards

Formal rewards include such items as food, toys, money, or special privileges. Generally, they are more powerful than social rewards since most people will work harder and longer for them than for social reinforcers. In addition, they are earned on the basis of some established agreement about a specific type of behavior and how often it will be performed. The systems chosen by families to disperse such rewards will vary depending upon the age of the child, the behaviors in question, the number of children being monitored, and, most importantly, the parents' ability to carry out the system. Families who are orderly and have a relatively stable daily routine can generally implement even relatively elaborate reward programs such as point or allowance systems with few problems. Other families, including those under considerable stress or that are relatively chaotic, will do best if they set up simple contracts such as agreeing that cleaning up one's room before school earns an extra half-hour of TV viewing. The steps to follow when setting up point systems, allowance systems, and simple contracts are described on the parent handouts at the end of the chapter. Here is a brief description of each, with further points for you to keep in mind.

Point systems. Point systems work as follows: each time a specific desirable behavior is done, the child is awarded a "point." Each point is tallied on a daily monitoring sheet. The child who earns a predetermined number of points within a specific time (a day, a week) is allowed to pick and receive a special treat or privilege. Some parents prefer to dispense tokens such as poker chips or beans, rather than marking points on a monitoring sheet. Then at specified times they collect and add up the tokens earned, record the total on a monitoring sheet, and provide the child with a formal reinforcer if earned.

Point systems seem to work best with children 10 years old and younger. Also, since point systems require regular monitoring, the parents should have demonstrated their ability to track behaviors and use the Program Monitoring Form consistently. Parents who have had problems tracking or who work irregular schedules or long hours may have problems staying on top of a point system.

In most cases, the behavior designated to earn points will be the behavior originally targeted for change. Therefore, a majority of clients will be issuing points when their children comply. Since parents differ in the number of commands they give, you'll need to consider both the parents' rates of commanding and the child's current level of compliance when determining how many points the child must earn. This criteria should be set at a level the child can reach to insure that the youngster realizes the connection between acting appropriately and receiving desirable outcomes.

If the behaviors that earn points are tasks or chores rather than compliance, the family should either assign points to several different tasks (2 points for doing homework, 3 points for making own lunch), or break down a single task into several components and assign each points (3 points for setting the table, 2 points for doing it with no reminders, 1 point for wiping off the table first). This system allows children to earn points for those aspects of a task they do well, and avoids putting them in an all-or-nothing situation in which they are rewarded only for completing the entire job.

The child should have the opportunity to earn a special privilege or treat at least once per day. This requires the parents to sit down with their child each day to review points. Parents should be taught through modeling and roleplaying to socially reinforce their child's positive efforts, even if the formal reward was not earned. In the latter case, parents must avoid feeling sorry for their child and giving the formal reward anyway. Also, they should not allow themselves to become upset or angry and turn the review into a lecture or a scolding.

Finally, in selecting privileges, the family should pick rewards that fit the behaviors in question, are appropriate to the child, and can be readily given. Parents also should choose rewards they won't feel guilty about withholding if not earned.

Allowance. An allowance, if given when the chore or task is completed, is actually just another type of point system. Allowances usually work best with older children, because they tend to value money more than do younger children. In addition, allowances are generally reserved for behaviors such as completing chores. In this way, giving an allowance conforms to the generally accepted notion of paying someone for work that is done rather than for social behaviors like minding and sharing.

The amount of money that a child can earn daily will depend on the family's financial means, the child's age, and the number of chores to be completed. However, most allowances fall into the range of 20¢ to 75¢ per day. Keep in mind that the daily amount chosen by the parents should provide their child with enough incentive to complete the designated chores.

We suggest that allowances be set up so that children can earn money for what they do accomplish, even if they do not complete all of the expected tasks. This means that each chore or task should be assigned a monetary value (10¢ for cleaning room, 5¢ for setting table).

As with other formal systems, parents should review their child's performance every day. In most cases, the parents should be prepared to pay their child on a daily basis. They will need to set up for success by having rolls of nickels, dimes, or quarters on hand. Once the allowance system is running well, a weekly payment can be instituted.

An allowance can be particularly useful when working with children who steal change from their parents, since it provides a legitimate means of obtaining money. However, the parents will still need to monitor their child carefully to make sure that the value of the child's purchases does not exceed the allowance earned.

Contracts. Contracts involve determining which behaviors one would like the other person to perform and then agreeing to do something pleasant for that person in return. Simple contracts work particularly well with chaotic or multi-problem families who are unable or unwilling to do the kind of detailed monitoring required by point and allowance systems. Also, since not all families can afford to give their older children an allowance, contracts provide an age-appropriate means for adolescents to earn special privileges.

Contracts can vary in detail; they may be very simple (if you do X, I'll do Y) or they may be more sophisticated (if you do X and Y in a specified time, at a specified rate, I will do A and B). Note that it is also possible for parents to write contracts between themselves that would cover basic child-management procedures. Listed here are some sample contracts.

Between parents and child:

1. If you pick up your room by 3:30, I'll play a game with you.

2. If you do your homework by 7:00, you may watch TV until 8:30.

3. When you do what I ask each day, and I don't have to remind you more than three times, I'll read you a bedtime story.

4. If your chores are all done, you may stay up late and have a nighttime snack. But if only part of your chores are done, you only get a snack and must go to bed at your regular time.

Between parents:

5. If you send Josh to time-out each time he disobeys you during the day, I'll do the dishes for you that night.

6. If we stay totally calm when disciplining Christine at least 5 out of 7 days, we'll treat ourselves to dinner out.

7. If you track his "minds" and "not-minds" during the day, I'll take responsibility for putting him to bed at night.

You will need to prepare yourself to deal with issues parents often raise about using point systems and especially allowances. In particular, parents often confuse formal rewards with bribery. If a child refuses to do something, the parent may say, "Ok, I'll pay you a quarter if you'll mow the lawn." In this case the parent, by offering the money only after the child refused, has rewarded the child for holding out for better terms. To keep allowance systems from becoming another form of bribery, tasks and rewards should be laid out in advance; also, parents should not try to "buy" compliance by increasing the rewards in the face of opposition.

Another concern parents often raise is their fear of being locked in forever to the use of formal reward systems as a way of motivating their children. Again, you can indicate the systems using formal rewards are mainly intended to turn behaviors around and that if performance is always accompanied with social reinforcement, the parent can expect to fade out the formal rewards in time.

If you raise and address these concerns first, parents are more likely to accept the procedures.

BEGINNING THE SESSION

Materials Needed

The following listed materials should be on hand when you start the session. You will find the Therapist Agenda and handouts at the end of this chapter. A blank Program Monitoring Form is available at the end of Chapter Five.

- Therapist Agenda with notes
- Copy of previous week's Program Monitoring Form
- Blank Program Monitoring Forms
- Handout for Parents: Social Reinforcement
- Handout for Parents: Point Systems
- Handout for Parents: Allowances
- Handout for Parents: Contracts

Welcome the Family and Explain the Agenda

As in previous sessions, after a few minutes of informal talk with the family, you should explain what you would like to accomplish during this session. First, you will review the previous week and determine how well they were able to implement the discipline procedures discussed at the last session. Given that they had no major problems using the discipline techniques, you will be teaching them some ways to encourage behaviors they would like to see happen more often.

Review Prior Week

Ask the family to share the prior week's monitoring form with you. Since you will have telephoned the parents at least once during the week, you should have some idea of how well they have been implementing their discipline procedures and a general idea about the child's level of performance. At this point, you should look over their monitoring form to see if the child's behavior has improved since your last contact and how consistently the parents have been using the techniques correctly. In particular, attend to any issues or problems that were discussed during the between-session phone calls. Review situations that appeared to go well and any that did not, asking clients to describe in detail how they attempted to set up for success, exactly what the child did, what the persons involved were feeling and saying to themselves, how consequences were used, and what the final results were. Have the family compare how they dealt with these situations versus their old way of doing things.

With the program in effect for several weeks, the parents should be reporting some reduction in their child's misbehavior. However, children who were out of their parents' control may continue to "test." If this is the case, and you are sure that the parents are correctly applying punishment, encourage the parents to continue, reassuring them that if they remain consistent, their child's testing will soon diminish.

If the testing is extreme (continued screaming or destroying property while in time-out), you should pay particular attention to the parents' use of self-control techniques during such episodes. These situations can be very upsetting to parents; at these times they are most likely to abandon the program by giving in or becoming angry or violent.

If the child's behavior has not improved and you suspect it is because the parents are not using the techniques as instructed, you will need to determine whether the difficulty is caused by inadequate comprehension, lack of motivation, or extenuating circumstances such as illness. Once this is determined, take the appropriate action. This could include:

- Reviewing the materials and better preparing the parents to use the techniques;
- Dealing with the parents' concerns;
- Revising the program
- Finding ways the family can reduce outside stresses or situations that make it difficult to conduct the program.

If the parents are having considerable trouble applying any of the techniques taught so far, you may need to spend the entire session reviewing problem areas and preparing your clients to carry out the techniques in the future. To keep up the momentum of treatment, we suggest you temporarily increase your between-session monitoring and reschedule the family for a session on reinforcement within a few days. If you are working with parents in groups, and only one family is experiencing difficulty, you may need to proceed with the material on reinforcement and schedule an individual session with the family having trouble implementing discipline.

PRESENTING REINFORCEMENT

Introduce Reinforcement

The primary goal of the session will be to teach the family ways to increase their level of positive interaction. In addition, you will be covering what parents can do to help their children learn desirable behavior through the use of reinforcement techniques. Since many clients will not know what the term "reinforcement" means, explain briefly that reinforcement is anything desirable following a given behavior that increases the likelihood the behavior will be repeated. Thus, reinforcing a behavior strengthens it and makes it more likely to occur in the future. Giving praise, recognition, affection, attention, privileges, and money are common ways of reinforcing people. Next explain that a reinforcer is more effective if:

1. It is something that the recipient desires;
2. It comes *after* the behavior;
3. The recipient is aware of the link between the behavior and the desired consequence;
4. At least initially, it *consistently* follows the desired behavior.

You should illustrate each of these points with brief examples.

Once the family understands the concept, have them discuss the reinforcers in their lives. If they are hesitant or cannot think of examples, you may want to disclose what reinforces you. In addition to using personal examples, you can also inquire about what reinforcement they receive in specific situations (for going to work, making the children cookies, keeping the house clean). It is particularly important for parents to realize how they are reinforced for behaving in certain ways. Once parents recognize how reinforcement affects their own behavior, they are less likely to hold such views as "reinforcement is just a bribe" or "he should do it because I told him to." It can also be helpful to point out that most of us, as we grow older, learn how to reinforce ourselves. As our self-confidence builds and as we acquire various interests, we develop self-esteem and learn to reward ourselves for a job well done (telling ourselves we did a good job, celebrating with a bottle of champagne). However, most children are not able to use self-reinforcement techniques as well as adults; as a result, they seek and require reinforcement from external sources, usually their parents.

Explain Inadvertent Reinforcement of Undesirable Behavior

After the family has demonstrated their understanding of reinforcement and how it can be used to strengthen desirable behaviors, you will want to explain that sometimes, without realizing it, people reinforce the *undesirable* behavior of others. This can be a difficult concept to teach and comprehend, and is best illustrated through examples such as the following:

A mother is having problems with her son's excessive whining. She tells him to pick up his toys, and he begins to whine. The mother comes over and tries to coax her son into picking them up.

While in the short run the mother may stop her son's whining, in the long run she is reinforcing his behavior by paying attention to him when he didn't pick up his toys.

Go over several such examples with the family. If the parents have a very young child, point out to them that young children in particular seek out their parents' attention, even when that attention involves being yelled at, scolded, or spanked. Next, have the parents explain how the people in the following examples are accidentally reinforcing behaviors they don't want. (You can also make up your own examples.)

Once a little girl is tucked into bed she calls to her parents, first for another kiss, then for another story, and finally for another glass of water. By the time she gets her water, her parents are really angry. They have been going through this routine for weeks.

A teenager stays out past curfew and gets home at 11:00. The following morning he is too tired to get up for school. To keep her child from being suspended from school, the boy's mother writes him an excuse for the day.

A young child throws a tantrum in the grocery store, saying she wants gum. Her father buys her the gum and she quiets down.

First, ask the parents to identify the negative behaviors in your examples and describe how they were unwittingly being reinforced. Second, have them think of ways in which they may have accidentally reinforced the behavior currently targeted for change. The most common ways are giving attention (coaxing, talking to, yelling at, threatening), giving in to children's demands, and protecting children from the consequences of their own behavior. When parents have identified how they have reinforced the undesirable behavior, have them discuss alternative responses that will not be reinforcing. Parents who consistently apply the discipline discussed during the previous week and who refrain from lectures, nagging, and scolding may already have stopped reinforcing the targeted misbehavior.

PRESENTING REINFORCEMENT TECHNIQUES

Before discussing in detail the various reinforcement techniques with the family, examine these techniques and choose those that are most likely to strengthen the child's desirable behavior and fit the needs and abilities of the parents. Although the parents should not be told exactly which reinforcers to use, this process should prepare you to address concerns, explain the implications of each technique, and help the family determine which ones are most likely to produce positive results. Things to consider include:

1. *How severe is the problem?* With all but some minor problems, social reinforcement alone will not be powerful enough to produce the desired change. Initially, the family should also use a point system, allowance system, or contracts.

2. *How old is the child?* As children approach adolescence, physical affection and attention from parents usually are not strong reinforcers. Money or special privileges should prove to be more effective reinforcers in such cases.

3. *What is the major goal of treatment at this point?* If the goal is to strengthen the parent-child relationship, you might focus on such techniques as giving attention, praise, or physical contact, or spending time in pleasant activities. If the goal is to build independence and responsibility in the child, you may want to emphasize using a point program or allowance system.

4. *How well do the parents use verbal and physical reinforcement with their child?* Parents who are not using these at all will tend to feel anxious or ridiculous and, at first, may sound a bit insincere. In such cases, two things can be done. First, you may discuss with them what they are saying to themselves in these situations and help them develop more positive statements around this issue ("We're going to get along better" versus "I feel silly"). Second, you may need to shape the parents' behavior by having them progress from less intense forms of reinforcement to stronger versions (first saying "Thank you," then "Good job," and finally "I love you") as they become more and more comfortable expressing their appreciation.

5. *When are the parents currently reinforcing their child?* Some parents feel very comfortable using verbal and physical reinforcement. Others may be regularly giving their child treats and special privileges. In these cases, the problem may not be *how* to reinforce socially or to use formal rewards, but rather *when* to use them. As discussed previously, these parents may be inadvertently reinforcing negative behaviors and/or not "catching" the positive behavior when it occurs.

Present Social Reinforcement

Give the family copies of the handout "Social Reinforcement," and have them spend a few minutes reading it over. Although most people will readily understand the concept, give a brief description of what you mean by social reinforcement. The following example illustrates one way to introduce it.

TH: The most common ways we socially reinforce each other include thanking other people, praising their efforts, complimenting them, being physically affectionate, and showing we're interested in what they're doing. Since I'm sure that you do some or all of these things already, we'll be talking about *when* to reinforce. Also, we're going to look at some ways to make your social reinforcement even more valuable to others.

Next, you should briefly cover the three types of social reinforcement listed on the handout: (a) verbal statements of thanks, praise, and appreciation; (b) physical contact; and (c) attention. When discussing verbal reinforcement, describe and roleplay both effective and poor ways of praising, focusing on each of the four points listed on the handout. After roleplaying poor ways to reinforce others verbally ("You made your bed, but you didn't hang up your clothes"), have the parents tell you what was wrong with your statement. Next, have them describe a more reinforcing way to communicate the message ("Thanks for making your bed. It looks nice. Now pick up your clothes and put them in the hamper"). Continue roleplaying until the clients have demonstrated they understand each of the four points listed on the handout.

When discussing physical contact, have the parents describe ways that they would feel comfortable being physically close to their child. The ways they choose need not be extremely affectionate (hugging, kissing) to be effective. Parents who feel uncomfortable showing physical affection should explore "safe" ways they can be reinforcing physically. This can be as simple as sitting next to the child, putting an arm on the child's shoulder, or tickling the child gently.

The previous discussion on accidental reinforcement should have shown the parents that attention can be a powerful reinforcer, even when it takes the form of yelling, scolding, or repeated commands to stop. At this point, you will be focusing on positive ways to give attention. Encourage the parents to imagine how they could give positive attention after their child does the targeted behavior and how they could use attention to maintain positive behavior.

Once you've covered the three types of social reinforcers, conclude by emphasizing the following three points:

1. The sooner they socially reinforce their child for desired behavior, the stronger the reinforcement will be.

2. They should not take their child's good behavior for granted. They must maintain positive behavior by continuing to reinforce it.

3. Social reinforcement alone doesn't usually produce a lot of change in children with behavior problems. Children will respond more quickly if their positive behavior results in a desirable treat or privilege.

Present the Use of Formal Rewards

The formal reward system you choose to present will vary from family to family. If the child is young and the parents have demonstrated their ability to monitor, you should present point systems. With organized families in which the target child is 9 years old or older, you may want to describe briefly both point and allowance systems, letting the family decide their preference. In multi-problem, chaotic, or overburdened families, it may be best to present only simple contracts.

Depending upon the system selected for the family, pass out the appropriate parent handout. Cover each of the steps listed on the handout; the family should decide how they will implement the steps at home and record this information on the handout. In most cases, family members will need to negotiate and compromise in order to set up a system that everyone thinks is fair and workable. Because of the potentially sensitive nature of this process, make sure that you structure the task well, that everyone's point of view is heard, and that final decisions are reasonable.

Close this part of the session with a reminder that formal rewards do not stand alone; they should always be paired with social reinforcement. Such a pairing not only makes the formal reward more powerful, but it increases positive feelings and helps make the fading of formal rewards easier later.

INSURING IMPLEMENTATION

Rehearse Use of Social Reinforcement and Rewards

If the child has been included in the session, prepare a roleplay in which the child pretends to do the desired behavior and the parents demonstrate how they would use social reinforcers and award points in response. Practice until the parents seem comfortable and skilled in their response. Make sure you give them positive feedback on their progress. If the child is not present, you may play that role. If a point or allowance system has been chosen, the family should also roleplay their daily review of the child's performance, including occasions when the child does and does not receive the reinforcer.

Work Out the Specifics of the Program

Spend a few minutes having the family work out the details of how they will implement the reinforcement techniques at home. Generally the following questions need to be settled:

Point systems

1. Who is responsible for awarding points and marking them on the point chart? Will both parents be sharing the responsibility?
2. When will they review the point chart with the child daily?
3. Who will do the daily review with the child? Will the parents do it together or take turns, or will one of them do it alone?
4. If formal rewards include special treats (small toys, candy, food), who will be responsible for making sure they are available? When will the child acquire them?

Allowance systems

1. By what time should chores or tasks be done?
2. Who will check to make sure that chores or tasks are completed satisfactorily and record allowance earned on the monitoring sheet?

3. Who will take responsibility for making sure that money is available if earned?

4. Who will review the allowance sheet with the child and pay the allowance earned?

Contracts

1. When must the child have fulfilled the contract (before school, by 4:00 p.m., before dinner)?

2. If the parents agree to do something in return when their child behaves as specified, when will they do it (how often, for how long)?

Problem Solve Potential Reinforcement Difficulties

Once the family has demonstrated that they understand how to implement the technique, take time to problem solve difficulties that might arise. Encourage them to identify potential problems they foresee. In addition, you can raise any of the following as issues to be discussed beforehand:

- What will they do if they forget to reinforce something at the time it happens or they are unable to give a formal reward at the agreed-upon time?

- How will they reinforce behaviors that occurred earlier when they were absent (things the child did before dad came home from work)?

- How will they use reinforcement when guests are around?

- If the family is using a simple contract, what will they do if either party lives up to only part of the bargain?

- What will they do if formal rewards aren't available?

- What can they do if the child consistently fails to earn the reinforcers?

- How will they deal with siblings who may not have been placed on a point or allowance system?

- What can they do on days that the child legitimately earns a privilege or allowance but also engages in serious problem behavior (stealing, violent temper tantrum)?

For two-parent families, additional concerns may include:

- How can they handle times when one parent thinks the other parent is reinforcing incorrectly?

- If one parent is conducting most or all of the program, how can the other parent support and reinforce him or her?

It helps if you write key decisions in the *Things to Remember* section of the monitoring form.

Solicit Concerns and Predict Problems, Changes, or Feelings

Common concerns that parents usually raise regarding the use of reinforcement include a belief that (a) formal rewards are bribes, (b) formal point systems can be cumbersome and require a lot of effort to run, and (c) they will feel "silly" or insincere using social reinforcement. When responding to these concerns, remain nondefensive and let the parents voice their feelings. After communicating that you understand their concern you should attempt to alleviate their misgivings by explaining the following:

1. Bribery in this context involves offering to reward others only after they first refuse to cooperate. Formal rewards operate in the opposite way. Earned through either point or allowance systems, they teach children to behave in a responsible manner. These rewards are given only when children have proven, without constant reminders, that they can behave appropriately.

2. Formal reward systems can usually be discontinued gradually after children have learned to perform as required and as long as parents keep socially reinforcing them. At first, however, stronger rewards are needed in order to give children the incentive to change.

3. It is not uncommon for parents to feel a little awkward when first using social reinforcement. Similarly, parents who have had major conflicts with their children in the recent past may feel a bit phony. Reassure them that social reinforcement need not be effusive to be effective. Suggest that they say only those things they really feel and believe. It is also useful, particularly with these parents, to predict that as they increase their use of thanks, praise, and physical affection, and as their child's behavior continues to improve, they will feel increasingly comfortable giving social reinforcement.

When working with parents who have had little positive interaction with their children in the past, it may be useful to make another prediction. Parents in this situation often find that their children do not respond immediately to social reinforcement. This can be very discouraging to parents, so reassure them that if they continue to praise their children the youngsters will soon learn to appreciate and desire it.

GIVING THE ASSIGNMENT

Establish a System for Recording Points or Allowance

Using a Program Monitoring Form, lay out the system for recording points or allowance. On the left side of the sheet, list the behaviors that can earn points or money. The available reinforcers and the number of points required to earn any of them should already be listed on the parents' handout for point systems. Instruct the parents to record each point earned in the box that corresponds to that day and the behavior performed. For allowance systems, they should check the appropriate box if their child satisfactorily completes the chore. These monitoring forms should be used when determining whether the child earned enough points to receive a formal reward or is entitled to money that day.

Have Parents Monitor Themselves and Their Child's Misbehavior

The parents should continue to track their child's misbehavior and the number of times each day the child received the appropriate discipline. The parents should also continue to monitor and rate their use of setting up, self-control, and discipline. Each of these tasks can be given one line on the monitoring form ("Time-out used consistently and correctly," "Used calming thoughts and relaxation when necessary," "Gave good commands"). If the parents are still reporting problems with any of the previously taught skills, they should list these problems separately, for example, "Did not argue or debate when taking away a privilege."

Finally, parents should track their use of social reinforcement and their avoidance of accidental or inadvertent reinforcement. The monitoring system should be simple, either recording the times social reinforcement is delivered or evaluating its quantity and quality. Also, encourage parents to record how well they avoided reinforcing undesirable behaviors. (See Figure 11.)

The parents may choose to complete two Program Monitoring Forms, one that tracks only the child's behavior, and a second that tracks their own behavior. It's often more convenient to use two forms at this stage because of the large number of items to be recorded. Also, older children often prefer to track their own behavior and like having a separate form of their own. (See Figures 12 and 13.)

Practice Tracking

Run through several hypothetical examples of situations in which the child earns a point or money and situations in which the child misbehaves. Have the parents show you how they would record those instances on the appropriate monitoring form. Also, roleplay various parental responses, including correct and incorrect ways to reinforce socially as well as situations in which you reinforce inappropriate behavior. The parents should be able to rate your responses correctly on their monitoring form.

Problem Solve Potential Tracking Difficulties

As mentioned in the last chapter, by this time the parents are being asked to do quite a bit of tracking. If the parents are clearly not able (or willing) to do so, you should simplify their monitoring assignment. However, at minimum, they should record points or allowance earned each day and monitor their use of social and formal reinforcement during the week.

Figure 11. Seventh Sample Program Monitoring Form.

Single Recording Form

Day or Date	3/25	3/26	3/27	3/28	3/29	3/30	3/31
1. *Complies*	THL III	THL THL	THL THL	THL II	THL THL I	THL III	THL IIII
2. *Does not comply*	THL	II	III	IIII	I	II	0
3. *Setting up for success*	A	A	A	B	A	A	A
4. *Self-control*	A	B	B	B	A	A	A
5. *# of time-outs*	IIII	II	III	II	I	II	0
6. *Correct discipline*	B	A	A	C	A	B	NA
7. *Formal reward given*	Yes	Yes	Yes	No	Yes	Yes	Yes
8. *Social reinforcement/ avoid reinforcing misbehavior*	A/B	A/A	A/A	B/B	A/A	B/C	A/NA

Things to Remember

Formal rewards—see Point
 Systems Handout
Social reinforcement—see
 Social Reinforcement Handout

Figure 12. Eighth Sample Program Monitoring Form.

Child's Form

Day or Date	2/22	2/23	2/24	2/25	2/26		
1. Makes bed in morning	+	+	—	+	+		
2. Sets table without reminders	+	+	+	+	+		
3. Puts clothes in hamper	—	+	+	+	+		
4. John's self-control	A	B	C	A	A		
5. # of privileges lost	1	0	1	0	0		
6. Allowance earned	40¢	60¢	40¢	60¢	60¢		
7.							
8.							

Things to Remember

Figure 13. Ninth Sample Program Monitoring Form.

Parents' Form

Day or Date	2/22	2/23	2/24	2/25	2/26		
1. *Setting up for success* *mom/dad*	A/A	A/A	B/A	A/A	A/B		
2. *Self-control* *mom/dad*	B/A	A/A	B/B	A/B	A/A		
3. *Discipline* *mom/dad*	B/NA	NA/NA	NA/A	NA/NA	NA/NA		
4. *Carrying out allowance* *system as agreed*	+	+	+	+	+		
5. *Social reinforcement* *mom/dad*	B/B	A/B	A/A	A/A	C/A		
6.							
7.							
8.							

Things to Remember

Prepare Parents to Explain Reward System

If the child is not present in the session, the parents will need to sit down with the child at home and explain what they will be doing. They should start by saying they will be making a greater effort to notice the nice things the child does and to give the child the feeling of being appreciated. Next, they should explain that in addition to telling the child what things they like, the parents will be giving him something special (special treats and privileges or an allowance) on the days when he acts especially responsible. At this point they should pull out the appropriate handout to use as a guide when explaining the program. If they are running a point program, they should cover exactly what the child must do to receive points, how many points must be earned to receive a special treat/privilege, how they will track points on the monitoring form, and when the points will be reviewed each day. The parents should then share the list of treats/privileges with the child and ask for any additions to the list.

If the parents are explaining an allowance system, they should cover how much money the child can earn each day, what tasks/chores can be done to earn the money, exactly what must be done for each task/chore to be completed satisfactorily, how much money each task/chore is worth, how the allowance will be tracked on the monitoring form, and finally how often the form will be reviewed and the allowance given.

The parents should roleplay this explanation with you during the session. This not only gives them practice describing the reinforcement system, but also helps you determine whether they understand how to run the program.

CLOSING

Arrange a time, early in the week, when you can call the parents, or they can call you, to check on how they are doing. Record the time at the bottom of the monitoring form. Also be sure to express confidence in the clients' ability to carry out the assignment.

MAKING BETWEEN-SESSION CALLS

As in the past weeks, you should make at least one phone call to the family early in the week. During the call, you will want to focus primarily on how the reinforcement system has progressed, touching on the following issues:

1. How was the child's performance? For instance, how many times did the child complete required tasks (chores, getting home on time)?

2. What did the parents do when their child behaved in the desirable way? Did they socially reinforce the child or did they forget to acknowledge the behavior? If they attempted to reinforce socially, did they make any reinforcement mistakes

(insincerity, tacking praise onto a negative statement about the child's past behavior)?

3. How did the child react to the social reinforcement and how did the parents feel when expressing appreciation or attending to the child?

4. Are the parents reinforcing the desirable behavior consistently?

5. Did the parents ever catch themselves reinforcing the undesirable behavior?

6. Is the child earning the formal rewards and actually receiving them?

7. If the child did not earn the reward on any given day, how did the family handle the situation? Did the parents briefly explain in a calm way that the child did not earn it; if so, how did the child react? Did the parents nag or scold the child for not behaving acceptably? How did the parents feel when the child did not earn a treat or allowance? Were they angry, calm, frustrated? Did they feel guilty about not giving their child a reinforcer or did they give in and award the privilege or money anyway?

The answers to these questions can be obtained by asking the parents to describe in detail several of the instances recorded on the child's tracking form as well as asking them to explain why they rated themselves as they did. If problems arose, determine exactly what they were and why they occurred (misunderstood an aspect of the point system, felt "silly" when saying nice things to their child). Depending on the reason, you may need to resolve the issue by either reviewing and/or rehearsing the techniques, providing relevant rationales to the parents, reassuring them that they will eventually feel comfortable reinforcing others but that it is quite natural to feel uneasy at first, or modifying the program to suit their needs and/or abilities. End by expressing confidence in their ability to carry out the program.

HANDOUT FOR PARENTS
SOCIAL REINFORCEMENT

There are three kinds of social reinforcement: statements of thanks, praise, or appreciation; physical contact that communicates affection; and attention.

Statements of thanks, praise, or appreciation

When you attempt to reinforce others by praising or complimenting them, it's good to keep the following things in mind:

1. *Be as sincere as possible.* Say only what you honestly feel. Otherwise, instead of being reinforcing, you'll sound phony or sarcastic.

2. *Don't mention how the person did poorly in the past.* For example, statements like "It's about time you learned to do it right" or "Good job; I don't know why you didn't do this well before" tend to remind others of what they did wrong in the past instead of reinforcing them for doing well now.

3. *Focus on what was done well.* If only part of a task was done well, reinforce the other person for what was accomplished; then pause and state what else needs to be done ("You did a nice job of washing the pans; now you need to dry them"). Stay away from "good, but" statements ("You did a nice job of washing the pans, *but* you didn't dry them"), since the other person will hear the criticism more than the compliment.

4. *Use praise that states exactly what behaviors you like and praise that is more general.* Examples of specific praise include "Thanks for *dusting the table*," "I like it when you *share your toys*," "You did a nice job *making your bed*." Examples of general praise include "You're a big help to me" and "I'm proud of you." Specific praise lets others know exactly which behaviors you appreciate, while general praise helps strengthen your relationships and makes other people feel good about themselves.

Physical contact

Physical contact can be a powerful reinforcer, particularly for a young child. There are many ways to show physical affection, including:

1. Sitting close to a person;
2. Sitting on another person's lap;
3. Hugging;
4. Kissing;
5. Tickling gently;
6. Playing physically, but gently (piggyback rides, etc.);
7. Rubbing a person's back;
8. Holding hands.

Pick ways of showing affection that you feel comfortable giving.

Attention

You don't need to completely stop what you're doing or give attention for long periods of time. You can give positive attention by:

1. Leaning toward and/or looking at another person;
2. Smiling;
3. Making a quick comment or asking a question;
4. Having a short conversation;
5. Joining in an activity.

HANDOUT FOR PARENTS
POINT SYSTEMS

To use a point system, you will give your child a "point" or some form of token (poker chips, beans) each time the youngster does the desired behavior. A child who earns a certain number of points or tokens over a period of time (for example, 10 points in 1 day) receives a special privilege or treat.

How to set up a point system

1. *Decide which behaviors earn points.* Remember, be very specific, so your child knows exactly what to do to earn a point. Also, pick behaviors that can occur often (daily chores, compliance, playing quietly for 15 minutes) so that your child has the chance to earn points and receive a reward each day. List each behavior in the *Behavior* column in 2.

2. *Determine how many points can be earned for each desirable behavior.* You may choose to:

   a.   Give a different number of points for different tasks (5 points for making the bed, 3 points for feeding pets);

   b.   Assign points to different parts of each task (cleaning the bedroom could be broken into three parts, such as 3 points for making the bed, 2 points for hanging up clothes, 2 points for sweeping the floor);

   c.   Award 1 point each time a particular behavior occurs (1 point for each time the child complies).

List the number of points that can be earned for each behavior in the *Points* column.

Behavior		*Points*
a. _____	=	_____
b. _____	=	_____
c. _____	=	_____
d. _____	=	_____
e. _____	=	_____

3. *Select a list of special treats or privileges.* Both you and your child should have some ideas about this. However, common treats and privileges include reading or telling your child a story, playing a game together, getting to pick a special meal or dessert, receiving a small toy, going to the park, staying up late, choosing the evening's TV programs, letting other children spend the night, or doing a special activity outside the home (movies, skating, a picnic).

List special treats and/or privileges here: _____

_____

_____

_____

_____

4. Decide how many points must be earned to receive a special privilege or treat, and how often it can be earned. Be realistic. Set the total number of points to be earned at a level your child can achieve. For example, if your child is only minding about half the time now, you might say the youngster must comply to 6 out of every 10 commands. This will help your child learn that behaving appropriately will get the things he or she likes. Later, once your child has made this connection and the behavior improves, you can gradually increase the number of points it will take to earn a treat.

Your child should have the opportunity to earn a special treat or privilege at least once a day. If your child is under 5 years old, you may want to give the youngster a chance to earn a privilege several times per day.

Total points necessary to earn reinforcer: _____

How often a reinforcer can be earned per day: _____

5. Monitor and award points. Each time your child does the behaviors that you listed previously, socially reinforce the youngster and award points or tokens. You should then mark this on the monitoring form. While points are usually indicated by checks or hatch marks, some children, particularly young children, prefer to have points represented by happy faces or stars.

Explain how you will track points: _____

_____

_____

6. Review points and either reward or withhold privileges. You need to go over the point chart with your child at the end of the prearranged time (or times) each day. If enough points are earned, you will socially reinforce the child and let him or her pick a special treat or privilege from the list. If the child does not have enough points, you will *briefly and matter-of-factly* tell him or her that no privilege was earned. (Remember: NO SCOLDING!)

HANDOUT FOR PARENTS
ALLOWANCES

Allowances are particularly effective with children aged 9 or older. Children at this age begin to value money and are usually eager to earn it. An allowance will give your child a good way to earn money and learn how to manage an income. Behaviors rewarded with an allowance usually involve chores or work tasks (doing homework, babysitting, doing dishes).

How to set up an allowance system

1. *Determine how much money your child can earn on a daily basis.* List the amount here: _____

2. *Select the chores/tasks your child will be responsible for completing.* Determine exactly what must be done for a task or chore to be considered satisfactorily completed (lawn mowed and trimmed around sidewalks).
   Describe the chores/tasks here: _____

_____

_____

_____

3. *Assign a dollar or cents value to each task.* If your child is expected to complete more than one task or chore daily, assign each one a monetary value (5¢ for taking out garbage, 10¢ for doing dishes). If any one task is (a) particularly difficult, (b) something your child really dislikes doing, or (c) very important to you, you may want to assign it a higher monetary value.
   Money earned for each chore/task: _____

_____

_____

_____

4. *Develop a system for tracking daily chores/tasks.* List each chore/task on a blank monitoring form. Every day, mark off each item on the form as it's completed.

5. *Determine how often your child will be paid.* It's usually best to pay each day, although some children aged 12 or older can be paid on a weekly basis. In either case, you should review your child's performance daily. During the review you should tally the allowance earned. If any or all tasks are not completed, you should refrain from scolding or lecturing.
   Write down how often you will pay the allowance earned: _____

_____

HANDOUT FOR PARENTS
CONTRACTS

A contract is an agreement to do something pleasant for someone when that person does something pleasing to you. Contracts should specify exactly what each person will do.

Example contracts

1. I'll wash your clothes if you put them in the clothes hamper.

2. If you get up and are dressed by 7:30, I'll cook your breakfast.

3. If you put your toys away when you're through playing with them, I'll read you a story before bed.

4. If you do what I ask with less than three reminders a day, I'll let you stay up a half-hour later than usual.

Write your contract here: _____

_____

_____

_____

_____

_____

_____

_____

_____

_____

_____

_____

_____

_____

_____

_____

_____

_____

_____

_____

_____

_____

_____

_____

THERAPIST AGENDA: REINFORCEMENT

| *Agenda* | *Notes* |

Beginning the Session

  Welcome the family and explain the agenda

  Review prior week:

    Review child's prosocial and negative behavior

    Review discipline

    Review self-control and setting up

Presenting Reinforcement

  Introduce reinforcement:

    It must be desirable to recipient

    It comes *after* the behavior

    The recipient must be aware of the link between behavior and reinforcement

    It must be used consistently, especially at first

  Explain inadvertent reinforcement of undesirable behavior

  Give examples

Presenting Reinforcement Techniques

  Present social reinforcement:

    Give out handout "Social Reinforcement"

    Remind them:

      Sooner the better

      Don't take good behavior for granted

      May need stronger rewards

  Present the use of formal rewards:

    Discuss point and allowance systems (with some families)

    Give out appropriate handouts ("Point Systems," "Allowances," or "Contracts")

    Work through handouts

    Remind to pair social reinforcement with formal rewards

Insuring Implementation

    Rehearse use of social reinforcement and rewards

    Work out the specifics of the program

    Problem solve potential reinforcement difficulties

    Solicit concerns and predict problems, changes, or feelings:

        Bribery issue

        Eventual fading of formal rewards

        Feeling awkward

Giving the Assignment

    Establish a system for recording points or allowance

    Have parents monitor themselves and their child's misbehavior:

        Record child's misbehavior and discipline given

        Continue to monitor setting up, self-control, and discipline

        Track their use of social reinforcement and avoidance of inadvertent reinforcement

    Practice tracking

    Problem solve potential tracking difficulties

    Prepare parents to explain reward system

Closing

    Arrange for between-session phone call

    Express confidence in the clients

Chapter Nine

COMMUNICATION

Conflicts within the family that have no clear and agreed-upon solutions require problem solving. Parents who lack positive communication skills are apt to be ineffective in their attempts to resolve conflicts. On the other hand, parents who learn to communicate well have a much better chance of finding appropriate and satisfactory solutions to problem situations.

While family therapists and researchers agree that good communication is essential, there is no universally accepted list of exactly what communication skills are. Indeed, one could look at each of the earlier chapters in this book as ways to modify patterns of communication. For instance, in the session on goal setting and setting up for success, clients were taught to communicate the behaviors they desire. The chapters on discipline and reinforcement taught parents how to communicate their pleasure and displeasure regarding their children's behaviors. The format of this chapter will provide a more formal review of communication skills, focusing on those pertinent to problem solving and conflict resolution.

There are two reasons for formally teaching the communication skills discussed in this chapter. First, several studies have found differences in the communication of distressed and nondistressed families. For example, Gottman, Notarius, Gonso, and Markman (1976) found that 57% of the communication of nondistressed couples was positive versus 37% for distressed couples. Horne and Fuelle (1981) noted that compared with mothers of non-clinic-referred children, mothers of impulsive and socially aggressive children were more critical, had difficulty staying on a topic, and failed to resolve conflicts. Barton and Alexander (1979) have noted that communication in families with delinquent children is marked by greater defensiveness than in normal families. Significantly, Alexander and Parsons (1973) found that after treatment the communication patterns in the two groups were similar. At this point, we don't know whether distressed families communicate poorly because they are distressed or whether families become distressed because they communicate poorly. However, we believe that if families are to become happier, they must first become more effective communicators.

The second reason for teaching families communication skills is that, beginning with the next session, the initiative for addressing problems and developing solutions will shift from you to the family. Unless family members have the tools to discuss problems—getting their points across without evoking anger or defensiveness and listening to each other's points of view—their attempts at problem solving will fail.

Knowledge of communication skills is essential; but, as with child-management skills, that knowledge is only useful if acted upon. It is here that self-control skills are particularly needed. If family members can enter a problem-solving situation in a calm, composed, and controlled manner, they are more likely to use their communication skills. Excessive anger, anxiety, depression, and/or guilt get in the way of effective problem solving. As a result, families must learn to use their self-control skills in any problem-solving discussion.

To teach both effective communication skills and how to stay calm when problem solving, you will need to complete the following tasks:

- Review the previous week's assignment.
- Provide clients with a rationale for learning communication skills.
- Discuss the use of self-control procedures when problem solving.
- Introduce nonverbal communication skills.
- Introduce verbal communication skills.
- Help family members identify personal strengths and weaknesses as communicators.
- Develop assignment.

Before presenting the session outline, we describe communication skills in some detail in the following section. The discussion provides a list of communication dos and don'ts we have found useful in helping clients identify their strengths and weaknesses as communicators.

We then describe the treatment session, going through activities that will help clients improve their communication skills. This session should assist family members in understanding how they communicate, catching their own negative patterns, and working to improve the general level of family communication.

UNDERSTANDING COMMUNICATION SKILLS

We have broken communication techniques into three areas: nonverbal communication, effective verbal communication, and negative communication patterns to avoid.

Nonverbal Communication

Numerous studies have found that the nonverbal component of communication carries the greatest weight (McCroskey, Larson, & Knapp, 1971). Nonverbal messages are particularly powerful for communicating feelings and preferences, and either confirming or contradicting the verbal message. When nonverbal communication confirms the verbal message, then both sender and receiver can trust the message. When the verbal and nonverbal messages are inconsistent, however, the receiver does not know whether to believe the verbal or the nonverbal messages. For example, a child who is told "I love you" in a cold tone of voice hears the words but does not *feel* loved. Similarly, the parent who says to her child, "I always have time for you" and immediately picks up the phone to call a friend is sending a double message. People tend to believe the message that is hardest to fake—the nonverbal. When family members deliver inconsistent messages, the receivers are likely to become cautious and suspicious—characteristics that undermine good relations among family members. The following is a list of nonverbal cues that signal either concern, interest, and involvement, or hostility, passivity, and avoidance. Family members intuitively know the meaning of these signals. Your objective is to make them more aware of how they use these signals and how they might change their nonverbal behavior to get more desired responses from others.

Nonverbal cue	Desire to communicate, interested, concerned	Hostile, passive, uninvolved
Distance	Near, unobstructed, undivided attention	Far, obstructed, distracted
Posture	Leaning toward, relaxed	Leaning away, stiff, rigid
Eye contact	Directed toward other person	Looking away, glancing, distracted, leering
Facial expressions	Smiles, relaxed, puzzled	Frowns, exasperated, tense
Gestures	Open, spontaneous	Closed, tense, uninvolved
Touching	Gentle, frequent	Rough, avoided
Voice quality	Warm, soft, involved	Cold, hard, distant

Effective Verbal Communication

We have identified a set of nine verbal behaviors that facilitate clear, open, and effective communication.

Speak your piece. This applies primarily to people who seldom speak or voice their opinions during discussions of problems. There are several reasons why these people need to speak up. First, other people need to know how problems affect the person and what it is they want. If they don't express their feelings and desires, other people will make decisions and act on assumptions about what the person desires. Since others' assumptions are often incorrect, they may actually be acting against those people's best wishes. Second, some quiet people sit on problems for a long time, then explode in a fit of anger or hysteria.

Talking about conflicts as they come up reduces or eliminates the potential for such explosions.

From a social learning perspective, many family members who do not speak out have been shaped to behave this way. They may have been punished for their efforts to speak out in the past, perhaps by being criticized or not taken seriously. Thus, it is your duty to create a "safe" environment for these people to talk by encouraging their expression, using active listening skills (paraphrasing, empathizing), reinforcing them for contributing to the discussion, and prompting other family members to use good communication skills (letting the person finish speaking, listening attentively).

Use "I" messages instead of "you" messages. "I" messages are a way of confronting other people without having a destructive effect. "I" messages communicate what the speaker is feeling and why. "You" messages focus on the receiver and emphasize blame, criticism, or judgment. "You" messages generate defensiveness, anger, or humiliation, whereas "I" messages promote clear communication of behaviors, emotions, and rationales. Here are some examples of "I" versus "you" messages.

"I" messages	*"You" messages*
"I worry when you come in so late."	"You're never in on time."
"When I first get home from work I need a few minutes to relax."	"You're on my back as soon as I walk in the door."
"I want you to get to school on time."	"Why can't you ever get to school on time?"

Be specific. The exercise of setting goals and defining desirable behaviors was the family's first lesson in being specific about what they do and don't want. They should avoid using labels to describe problem behavior (inconsiderate, stupid, disrespectful, pigheaded), since this tends to alienate the other person and block effective problem solving. Instead, they should use behavioral descriptions of what they want. If they have a problem, they should cite a specific instance as an example of what they mean. This lets the other person know exactly what the problem is. Also, they should be encouraged to give examples of the specific type of behavior they'd like the other person to do more often.

Be brief. Many people are longwinded, bringing up episode after episode and point after point. When this happens, others become confused or inattentive and, in some cases, even hostile. These people must be taught (a) to give only one or two examples, (b) not to repeat points, and (c) to monitor how long they've "had the floor." Sometimes people go on and on because they get little or no acknowledgment from others that indicates they're being understood. To remedy this, you must prompt others to paraphrase, empathize, and summarize.

Check to see that others are listening. People who are not sure that others have understood their point need to learn to stop and ask their listeners if they understand what is being said ("What do you think about that?" "Do you agree?" "Am I making sense?"). This technique is far more effective than simply talking on and on. Asking questions involves the listener and checks for comprehension. The communication is no longer a monologue but has become more of a dialogue.

Find out what others are thinking. Generally, people are reluctant to accept solutions they didn't help develop. One way of making this point with clients is to have them think of a situation in which another person (boss, friend, spouse) did all of the talking and problem solving; how committed were they to make the *other person's* solution work? To insure that a solution belongs to the entire family, members (particularly the most talkative) must get everyone involved. There are two ways they can encourage others to express their ideas. First, they can ask quiet members for their viewpoints or suggestions ("What do you think?" "How would you like to do it?"). They should remain silent even if the other person says nothing at first. Though an extended silence can be uncomfortable, the quiet member will eventually say something. Second, they should allow others to finish speaking without interruption and show interest in the other person's point of view.

Show that you're listening. Family members can let others know they are listening by maintaining good eye contact and indicating that they understand what others say and how they are feeling, in other words, reflecting the speaker's words and the emotions behind them. The following are examples of reflecting feelings and content.

Feeling reflection

> SPEAKER: I get ticked off when people at work tell me how to do my job.
>
> LISTENER: You sound pretty angry.
>
> SPEAKER: I'm mad because Monty won't come out and play with me.
>
> LISTENER: It hurts when that happens.

Content reflection

> SPEAKER: I get ticked off when people at work tell me how to do my job.
>
> LISTENER: People at work tell you how to do your job.
>
> SPEAKER: I'm mad because Monty won't come out and play with me.
>
> LISTENER: You'd like Monty to come play with you.

Feeling and content reflection

> SPEAKER: I get ticked off when people at work tell me how to do my job.

LISTENER: You get angry when people at work try to tell you how to do your job.

SPEAKER: I'm mad because Monty won't come out and play.

LISTENER: It hurts when you want Monty to come play and he won't.

When letting others know their problems or points of view are understood, it's best not to offer solutions or communicate judgment immediately. In the following examples, the mother heard what her son said but was judging or giving solutions rather than just listening.

CHILD: Monty won't let me play with him.

MOTHER: If you didn't mess up his toys, he'd like you better. (judging)

or

MOTHER: Why don't you play with your train set instead? (giving solution).

A better way to let her child know she was listening would be:

MOTHER: You'd like to play with Monty, but he won't and that hurt your feelings.

Ask questions if you're confused. While we don't advocate that families continually interrupt each other, it's better to interrupt or interject and get clarification than to be confused or later act on a false assumption. In fact, Alexander et al. (1976) noted that normal families commonly interrupt each other to clarify and request elaboration of points. For those people who are embarrassed to ask for clarification, reassure them that the speaker usually appreciates questions; it means that you are listening and trying to understand.

Stop and let others know when communication is breaking down. When families get into arguments, each individual has a particular position and may try to force it on other family members. When this happens, communication can break down, and the discussion may need to be stopped temporarily.

To facilitate calling a temporary "truce," the family members should determine in advance exactly what they will say as a signal to the others that the discussion needs to be stopped; for example, they could say, "I need to stop talking about this right now" or "I'm getting upset; could we talk about this when I calm down?" (note the emphasis on using "I" messages). Family members should also agree in advance that if even one person gives the appropriate signal the discussion will be ended temporarily. Finally, they need to set a time for continuing the discussion. If members signal each other before they get overly upset, they can usually resume the conversation within a few minutes. The sooner they can calmly talk about the problem the better. As a result, we recommend that the longest "cooling off" period be no more than a day. This last point is particularly important, since otherwise some people may use the call to stop a discussion as a way of avoiding the problem altogether.

Communication Patterns to Avoid

There are eight negative communication patterns that family members should attempt to avoid when talking to each other. While most of the items listed here are often communicated verbally, many can be communicated nonverbally as well.

Putdowns. Putdowns include name-calling, insults, inappropriate laughter, rude remarks, and belittling the ideas or efforts of others. The way people put down others can be quite blatant, such as statements like "How the hell would you know?" and "So now you're the expert, huh?" or by laughing at a person who is upset. Putdowns also can be communicated subtly, such as rolling the eyes after someone's statement or inferring that the other person will be unable to handle or cope with a situation ("I better handle it. You know how upset you get"). Putdowns can evoke anger, defensiveness, resentment, guilt, or depression—emotions that undermine effective communication and problem solving.

Blaming. Blaming means to say or imply that a problem is the other person's fault. People may blame by directly accusing others of creating or maintaining the problem, as in the statements "You just spoil him" or "If only you'd spend more time with him...." People can also transfer blame to the other person by acquitting themselves of any fault, such as saying, "Lord knows I've done everything *I* can" (implying the other person has not).

Blaming sets people against each other rather than putting them on the same team to solve a problem. You will need to stress with your clients that it's not important to fix the *blame* but to fix the *problem*, to determine how they will solve it and who will be involved. This technique shifts the focus from the individuals involved to the problem situation.

Denial. It is not uncommon that someone in the family brings up an issue that others dismiss. Other people may see personal benefits in maintaining the status quo (if dad got some time by himself after work, mother would then have to watch the kids while getting dinner ready), or they may find it easier to cope with a situation than the person expressing the problem (a messy living room may bother mom but have little or no impact on the rest of the family). Although some people may not see the issue as a problem for themselves, they should recognize that it is a problem for the other person. Therefore, in the interest of good family relations, they need to address the situation and help the person resolve it.

Defensiveness. People become defensive when they feel they are being blamed (whether or not they are actually being accused) or misunderstood. People display defensiveness in a variety of ways.

Some people become angry or argumentative, while others make excuses, become distraught and cry, or fall silent and refuse to participate in the discussion.

People's self-talk plays an important part in how defensive they become. Someone who thinks, "I suppose she'll say I'm too lenient," is likely to lash out at the other person. Another person may say, "There's no use trying to defend myself" and stop all communication. On the other hand, those who think, "I need to help find a solution to this problem" are more apt to remain calm and nondefensive.

Communicating hopelessness. The types of behaviors that communicate hopelessness include statements such as "Nothing works," "What's the point," "I'll try, but it won't do any good," "He'll never change." Hopelessness can also be communicated nonverbally by gestures such as heavy sighs and rolling of the eyes. A third way of implying hopelessness is through a series of subtle cues such as always needing to be prompted, giving short one- or two-word replies ("I don't know," "I guess," "Whatever"), and using a passive, depressed tone of voice.

Realistically, not all problems can be solved, certainly not the first time family members sit down and talk about them. However, clients do need to focus on what changes they can make. They may need to lower their sights and tackle problems one step at a time. When a problem cannot be resolved at the time (they can't come up with possible solutions, they're too emotionally charged, they can't find a reasonable compromise), they should put the discussion aside for a while and decide to deal with it later rather than to say the problem can never be resolved.

Finally, there will be times when a problem cannot be solved or when the solution isn't within a family's control (their child's teacher refuses to cooperate, dad's drinking heavily and won't participate in treatment). In these circumstances, you will need to help them find ways to cope with the situation as best they can.

Mind reading. When people engage in mind reading they are saying or implying that they know what the other person's motives or opinions are. "He won't agree with me on this," "You care more about your mother than me," and "He doesn't care what the kids do after school" are all forms of mind reading. Family members should ask each other what they're thinking—not tell them.

Talking for others. People can fall into the conversational habit of talking both for themselves and other people. They may do it for benevolent reasons, interpreting the other person's silence as an inability to formulate or articulate thoughts and feelings. In the short run, the silent person may even feel "let off the hook." However, in the long run families usually suffer from such an imbalance of viewpoints. As stated earlier, for problem resolution to occur, everyone needs to say how they are affected and what they feel, and commit themselves to working on a solution everyone can accept.

Sidetracking. Sidetracking is talking about anything that isn't immediately relevant to the task or subject at hand. People often sidetrack by taking a long time to come to the point, giving example after example, and telling stories. They may also bring up new problems before the one under discussion is resolved. Sidetracking derails the discussion and prevents or impedes resolution of the problem.

BEGINNING THE SESSION

Materials Needed

Have the following listed materials on hand to begin the session. The Therapist Agenda and handouts can be found at the end of the chapter. A blank Program Monitoring Form is provided at the end of Chapter Five.

- Therapist Agenda with notes
- Copy of previous week's Program Monitoring Forms
- Handout for Parents: Self-control and Communication
- Handout for Parents: Communication Skills
- Blank Program Monitoring Forms

Welcome the Family and Explain the Agenda

Spend the first few minutes chatting with the family, making sure you attend to each family member. Next, explain that today you will begin by reviewing how they were able to implement the reinforcement techniques. In addition, you will be discussing their use of all the skills learned thus far and taking a closer look at any changes that have occurred in the targeted behavior.

Finally, at the end of the review you will be discussing some effective and ineffective ways to communicate. Reassure them that although you will be covering new information, you won't be asking them to take on any new tasks during the upcoming week. Since most families have worked hard up to this point, they appreciate this "mini-vacation" from having to add another new component to their program.

If the child is present for this session, you may want to consider excusing her after the review. The approach we use with communication skills is aimed mainly at parents, though children 10 and older may benefit from this information. If it is not possible to have the child leave the meeting room, give the youngster something to play with should she become bored. Periodically reinforcing her patience should permit you to work with the parents for the last half of the session.

Review the Use of Reinforcement Techniques

With the previous week's Program Monitoring Forms in hand, ask the parents to describe a few situations when they socially reinforced their child. Probe to find out how they felt when they reinforced their child and what their child's response was. Next, if the family is using a formal reward system, look at the child's monitoring form to determine whether or not the child earned the reward or allowance each day. Determine if formal rewards were given on days when the child met criteria and were withheld on days when the youngster did not. Praise everyone for their efforts and success. Encourage family members to describe *to each other* how well they are doing and prompt them to give examples of times they behaved in desirable ways.

If the child did not earn a formal reward consistently, you should determine whether (a) the parents were inaccurately monitoring the child's behavior or neglecting to award points, (b) the parents were not using social reinforcement appropriately, or (c) the criteria set during the previous week were unreasonably high. The clients' answers to these questions will indicate whether the difficulty involves a comprehension, motivation, or practical problem.

Review Remaining Aspects of the Program

Once you have reviewed the parents' use of reinforcement techniques and taken action to remedy any problems that may have surfaced, you should extend the review to touch upon their continued use of all aspects of the program. You should cover:

1. Overall changes in the target behavior;
2. Current use of discipline procedures;
3. Current use of self-control procedures;
4. Current use of setting-up procedures.

The family should be reporting a decrease in the targeted concern and an increase in more desired behavior. If this has not occurred, probe carefully to determine whether the parents are correctly using the techniques they have learned. If not, determine the reason and either reinstruct them or have them problem solve how they could use the techniques in the future.

INTRODUCING COMMUNICATION SKILLS

Explain Importance of Communication Skills

Before talking in detail about ways to communicate effectively, it's useful to spend a few minutes talking about why it's important to focus on communication skills. The key points to make during this discussion include the following.

1. Even though all families have problems, some families can deal with them more smoothly, calmly, and effortlessly than others. The families that do better generally have good communication

skills. Learning to use effective communication skills helps the family resolve future problems on their own.

2. People who are effective communicators tend to feel more appreciated and understood than individuals who do not communicate effectively.

Link Self-Control to the Use of Communication Skills

In your discussion of good communication, point out to clients that we all have some skills in dealing with each other and with our problems. However, when we get very upset we are less apt to use these skills effectively, particularly when we try to sit down and talk about problems. Thus, we need to use the same self-control procedures taught earlier to help us be more composed during problem-solving discussions.

Distribute the handout "Self-Control and Communication." Give the family time to look it over and to share some of the things they typically tell themselves either prior to, during, or after they have discussed a problem with other family members. Point out the relationship between what they say to themselves and their ability, or lack of ability, to stay composed. Have them write at the bottom of the handout some upsetting thoughts and some calming thoughts. Encourage clients to include among their calming thoughts some self-reinforcement ("I'm doing well," "Keep it up," "See, I don't have to let this upset me"). Have them keep this handout, and make a copy to put in their folder so you'll have it on hand during the next session.

Present Nonverbal Communication Skills

Give clients the handout titled "Communication Skills" and have them look it over. Explain that for the remainder of the session you will be going over each of the items and are interested in finding the areas where clients do well and where they could improve.

Explain that you would like to start by covering the nonverbal communication skills list at the top of the form. In reviewing each technique, we recommend that you do an exaggerated demonstration of each of the unhelpful ways and ask the family to describe what you were communicating. Then ask them to show you how to do it better. Praise their attempts to demonstrate more effective skills and help them develop better skills if they seem unable to do so on their own. The following are ways you can demonstrate unhelpful nonverbal communication.

1. Distance
   a. Move across or out of the room.
   b. Hold a book in front of your face.
   c. Turn your chair away.
   d. Do a second task (write, sort through your drawers).

2. Posture
   a. Slump or slouch.

b. Cross your arms tightly.
c. Be stiff and rigid.

3. Eye Contact
   a. Let your eyes wander.
   b. Look down at the floor or at your desk.
   c. Stare at someone's shoulder or just above someone's head, but do not make eye contact.
   d. Leer at them.

4. Facial Expression
   a. Look exasperated (frown, sigh, roll eyes).
   b. Look skeptical.
   c. Look angry (glare, clench teeth).

5. Gestures
   a. Point your finger at people.
   b. Look jittery, tap your fingers, bounce your leg.

6. Touching
   a. Poke someone.
   b. Grasp someone's arm tightly.

7. Voice Quality
   a. Be loud.
   b. Sound depressed.

Present Verbal Communication Skills

Explain that the next set of items on the handout is verbal skills that improve communication. Briefly cover the nine skills by describing what they are and why they are useful communication tools (see the "Understanding Communication Skills" section earlier in this chapter for complete definitions and relevant points to cover with clients). Throughout this discussion, provide "right" way and "wrong" way examples to illustrate each skill; you should be able to cover each one within a few minutes. However, in cases where family members do not understand the communication skill or where they need definite improvement (the use of "I" messages with a family that blames each other), you may want to spend additional time discussing and roleplaying.

Present Communication Patterns to Avoid

Next, briefly cover and roleplay each of the items listed on the handout under the heading *Avoid*. We suggest two ways to reduce clients' potential defensiveness as you cover these items. First, repeat that, to some degree, we all do the things listed in this section and we can all improve in certain areas. The purpose of covering these items today is to help the family identify areas in which they would personally like to improve. This makes the behaviors seem more normal and sets the expectation that everyone can improve. Second, when modeling each negative pattern, use impersonal examples that are exaggerated and/or humorous. This puts clients at ease and alleviates any fear that you will bring up ways they have communicated poorly in the past. After modeling each pattern, have the family roleplay a more effective way of saying the same thing.

Have Family Identify Their Communication Strengths/Weaknesses

After presenting each of the points on the handout, ask family members to identify what they do well when communicating with each other. Have them mark these skills on the handout with a plus sign. Whenever possible, confirm their evaluation by indicating you have noticed them using some of these skills and by citing specific instances. If appropriate, also identify other skills that they may have overlooked. If other family members can do the same in a positive manner, encourage them to share examples of how the person used the skills well in past discussions.

Next, have each individual identify one or two areas within each of the sections listed on the handout that needs to be improved. Generally, we have found that people accurately pinpoint both their strengths and their weaknesses. By this time in treatment, you should have enough credibility with your clients to point out, if they do not, one or two areas where greater effort would be to their advantage. Have them indicate these areas on the handout with a minus sign. After making a copy for yourself, have them put the completed form in their folder for use next week.

GIVING THE ASSIGNMENT

Since this week is a "vacation," the family will not be asked to track any new tasks. However, they should continue to use the program they have built over the last several sessions. Give the parents a new set of Program Monitoring Forms and fill in the areas to be tracked (including both child and parent behaviors). Mention that the coming week's data on the child's behavior will be especially important, because at the next session you will again be reviewing their overall progress to date.

While you will not be asking them to do anything specific regarding the communication skills during the next week, suggest that they think about what was covered.

CLOSING

Schedule your next appointment. Unless there have been problems, it is not necessary to schedule a between-session phone call. Compliment clients on their current progress and express confidence that they will continue to improve.

HANDOUT FOR PARENTS
SELF-CONTROL AND COMMUNICATION

When we are calm and relaxed we are likely to communicate effectively; when we are upset our communication is likely to become distorted by our emotions, and we often fail to say what we really mean.

Here is an example of how our emotions and thoughts can have either a positive or negative effect on how we communicate.

Upsetting thoughts	Emotion	Communication
"I'm sick of being his private maid. Things are gonna change around here or else!"	Anger	"Michael, get in here and pick up this junk right now! You've been a real slob lately and I'm sick and tired of looking at your stuff strung out all over this house!"

Calming thoughts	Emotion	Communication
"I need to talk to Michael about leaving his clothes lying around. If we sit and discuss this calmly we should reach a good solution."	Determination Composure	"Michael, we have a problem. I get upset when I find your clothes all over the house. We need to talk about this and work out a solution."

Now, think about situations in your family in which your goal was to make things better but, in fact, they got worse. List here some upsetting thoughts that contributed to your communication breakdown. Then list some thoughts that would be calming and lead to more effective communication.

Upsetting thoughts   *Calming thoughts*

HANDOUT FOR PARENTS
COMMUNICATION SKILLS

Communication skills

Be aware of your nonverbal communications:

_____ Distance between you and others

_____ Posture

_____ Eye contact

_____ Facial expression

_____ Gestures

_____ Touching

_____ Voice quality

Do:

_____ Speak your piece.

_____ Use "I" messages instead of "you" messages.

_____ Be clear about what you want.

_____ Be brief.

_____ Check to see that others are listening.

_____ Find out what others are thinking.

_____ Show that you're listening.

_____ Ask if you're confused.

_____ Let others know when communication is breaking down.

Avoid:

_____ Putdowns

_____ Blaming ("It's your fault!")

_____ Denial ("It's not a problem!")

_____ Defensiveness ("Don't blame me!")

_____ Communicating hopelessness ("What's the use?")

_____ Mind reading

_____ Talking for others

_____ Sidetracking, getting off the topic

THERAPIST AGENDA: COMMUNICATION

Agenda   *Notes*

Beginning the Session

    Welcome the family and explain the agenda

    Review the use of reinforcement techniques:

        Parents' use of social reinforcement

        Parents' use of formal rewards

        Identification of source of problems:

            Inaccurate monitoring or awarding of points

            Inappropriate use of social reinforcement

            Unreasonably high criteria

    Review remaining aspects of the program:

        Overall changes in target behavior

        Parental use of disciplinary procedures

        Parental use of self-control methods

        Current use of setting up for success

Introducing Communication Skills

    Explain importance of communication skills:

        Help them resolve future problems without major conflict

        Help people appreciate each other more

        Result in happier families

    Link self-control to the use of communication skills:

        Explain we communicate more effectively when calm

        Provide handout titled "Self-control and Communication"

        Write both upsetting and calming thoughts on handout

Present nonverbal communication skills:

    Distribute handout titled "Communication Skills"

    Focus first on nonverbal communication

    Demonstrate poor nonverbal communication and have family demonstrate positive nonverbal communication

Present verbal communication skills

    Cover each skill:

        What it is

        Why it's important

        Model "right" way, "wrong" way examples

Present communication patterns to avoid:

    Reassure clients that we all do these behaviors at times

    Explain purpose today is to identify areas to improve

    Briefly cover and roleplay each item, using exaggerated and/or humorous examples

    Have family demonstrate appropriate way to communicate

Have family identify their communication strengths/weaknesses:

    Mark areas they do well with a plus

    Mark areas they need to improve with a minus

Giving the Assignment

    Add no new components this week

    Continue to monitor as they did the previous week

    Have them think about communication skills discussed during upcoming week

Closing

    Arrange next appointment

    Express confidence in the clients

Chapter Ten

GENERALIZATION

The sequence of sessions described in Chapters Four through Nine is designed to provide the family with basic skills for resolving one of the problems initially presented. While some improvement in other behaviors is often noted, it is usually necessary to apply the basic intervention to other identified concerns if a general resolution of all the presenting problems is to occur. The generalization phase of treatment described in this chapter provides a basic format for achieving this objective.

UNDERSTANDING GENERALIZATION

The term generalization refers to more than extending improvement across behaviors, however. It also includes extending it across time. In other words, improvements should persist and future problems should be resolved without your aid. To encourage this process, one of your major objectives during this phase is to help the family develop their knowledge and skills so they can successfully carry on after discontinuing treatment. Consequently, you will need to incorporate some of the following strategies into your remaining work with the family.

1. Use the process of addressing the remaining problems as a vehicle for the family to practice their new skills. Thus, a family that initially targeted their son's noncompliance may now turn its attention to getting the same child to do his chores or to getting their daughter to go to bed without a fuss. Fortunately, once the parents have become familiar with the basic social learning principles, less time is usually required to apply these principles to other problems. Further, as the more pressing problems are resolved, others usually come under control much more easily.

2. To help insure that the family will be able to apply what they've learned without your assistance, steadily reduce the amount of direction you offer. During the previous phase, your job was to teach the family new skills and techniques. Now you will want to shift away from that role and instead encourage your clients to take the initiative. For the most part, reserve your comments except to guide the direction

of the session ("What I'd like you to begin doing now is..."), to offer prompts and ask leading questions ("Suppose she stays in bed after you close the bedroom door; how do you plan on reinforcing her for going to sleep as you wanted?"), and to reinforce clients' efforts.

3. Because the ability to analyze problems and generate solutions is dependent on understanding certain basic principles about behavior, you should help the family broaden its grasp of the basic social learning concepts. Significantly, McMahon, Forehand, and Griest (1981) found that parents who were taught social learning principles in addition to behavioral techniques perceived their children as better adjusted and continued to reward their children more frequently than did parents who received training only in basic behavioral techniques.

You can insure that parents grasp these principles by pointing out how setting up, self-control, discipline, and reinforcement come into play in their daily interactions with their children. For example, a father who reported that his son had a tantrum might be told the following:

> TH: John, when Jerry threw a fit when you told him it was time for a bath, you said he stopped when you told him just to wash his hands and face. In the short run that was reinforcing for you, because you were able to shut off his temper tantrum. However, Jerry is learning that if he throws a tantrum, he's more likely to get what he wants.

Another way to emphasize basic social learning principles is to ask the client to analyze problems in terms of the relevant principles and then propose solutions based on that interpretation. Most clients will need considerable assistance and prompting at first ("What has been the result of remembering to thank Joan when she volunteers to do things for you?" or "What were you teaching Joan when you took away that privilege?"). With practice, they will learn to relate to everyday situations in this manner.

4. While knowing how to implement the various skills and procedures is important for generalization, the family must also be comfortable using the various communication skills and problem-solving procedures essential in developing new programs. Without those abilities, the family will likely falter when future concerns arise. Thus, in the course of dealing with the remaining concerns, you need to place great emphasis on the communication skills presented in the last session, as well as the problem-solving sequence described in this chapter. There are several ways this can be done.

First, before the family moves to tackle a new problem, or review progress on an old one, ask them to review the handout titled, "Communication Skills" that was completed during the session described in Chapter Nine. You should also have them review the handout titled "Problem Solving" that is described later in this chapter. When working with a single parent or with a group of single parents whose children are under 8 years old, you may want to use only the parent handout "Problem Solving."

Second, when working with two-parent families or whenever the child is present, encourage participants to talk to each other rather than to you. For example, if the family is establishing expectations about coming home in the evening, you might say the following:

TH: (To mother) Helen, can you tell your son Steve when you would like him to be home in the evening?

MOTHER: (To the therapist) Well, I would like Steve to...

TH: (Taps mother gently) Tell Steve.

MOTHER: Steve, I would like...

Third, interject positive comments about the communication skills you observe them using. Continuing the previous example:

MOTHER: Steve, I would like you to be in the house by 7:30 on school nights and 9:00 on other evenings. That way I won't worry about your safety.

TH: Nice. You did several good things. You were brief and to the point, you said how you felt, and you said it in a way that didn't put Steve off.

Fourth, if communications start to break down, intervene and redirect. You are likely to have more success if you couch this in terms of helping speakers achieve their objectives. Continuing the prior example:

SON: (Referring to his mother's previous request) But Mom, that's not fair! You never...

TH: (Interrupting) Excuse me, Steve, I'd like to check something out with you. From that last statement you made, it sounds like you disagree with your mom's suggestion. What I'd like you to do is tell her how you feel in a way that will let her hear what you're saying without getting upset or angry.

While interruptions are sometimes essential, wait, if possible, for natural pauses or breaks to step in. If you notice communication problems, however, you should not wait until the process has broken down completely before intervening.

BEGINNING THE SESSION

Materials Needed

When starting the session, be sure to have the materials listed here on hand. The Therapist Agenda, Treatment Plan, and handout are at the end of the chapter. A blank Program Monitoring Form is provided at the end of Chapter Five.

- Therapist Agenda with notes
- Copy of previous week's Program Monitoring Forms
- Copy of the most current Treatment Plan (if one has been developed in previous generalization sessions)
- Copy of the completed Communication Skills handout
- Handout for Parents: Problem Solving
- Copy of the completed Goal Setting Form
- Blank Treatment Plan
- Blank Program Monitoring Form

Note: It is useful to have copies of the previous handouts available as well, such as "Setting Up for Success," "Time-Out," and the like.

Welcome the Family and Review the Previous Week

After greeting the family and making them comfortable, shift the conversation to their use of the program during the prior week. In the course of the discussion, be sure to inquire about each component of their treatment (setting up, self-control, discipline, reinforcement, communication), examine their recorded frequency of appropriate and inappropriate target behavior, and gain each participant's evaluation on how well things are going in general. Based on this discussion, you must decide whether to (a) continue working on the current targeted behavior, (b) shift the focus to a new target behavior, or (c) move toward termination.

If the last option is most appropriate, you should follow the procedures described in the next chapter. Should you decide that the family needs to continue focusing on the current targeted behavior, you can use the format described in this chapter to review and make necessary modifications. If you feel that the family is progressing well and is able to carry out two programs simultaneously, review the current program and then have them begin developing a second program. If you choose either to revise an old program or develop a new one, follow the suggested steps outlined in this chapter.

Distribute Handouts on Communication Skills and Problem Solving

Have the parents take out their copies of the handout called "Communication Skills" that they discussed in the previous session. After giving them time to look over the handout, ask participants to review the items they felt they did well and those items they felt needed improvement.

Next, distribute copies of the handout "Problem Solving" and mention that if they follow the steps listed when solving problems, everyone should be satisfied with the results. Explain that while today you will be spending about 30 minutes on this process, in the future they should be able to go through the entire sequence in half that time. It often helps if you select one person as coordinator and secretary to mark off the steps as they are covered, keep track of ideas, and tactfully let people know when they are getting off task. If this is your first generalization session, you may want to assume that type of role.

REVISING CURRENT PROGRAM AND ADDRESSING NEW CONCERNS

Select a Problem or Concern

If the parents decide to begin working on a new problem, we suggest that you have the family review the Goal Setting Form they previously completed and select a concern that has not shown much, if any, improvement. In many cases, however, once treatment is under way, new problems will become apparent. In this case you may want to focus on one of these concerns. If the concern is not already listed on the Goal Setting Form, the clients should enter it in the box labeled *Concerns*.

Clarify and Negotiate Positive Behavioral Expectations

Having selected the concern, the next step is to clarify and target exactly the behavior or behaviors that the family wants to occur more often. If you are working on a concern already listed on the Goal Setting Form, the targeted behavior may already be listed in the box labeled *Desired Behavior*, though the family may decide to change the description. If the concern is not listed on the Goal Setting Form, you should help the family decide what behavior they desire and add it to the form.

In helping the family define the desired behavior, there are several issues you should keep in mind. First, make sure that the targeted behavior is realistic in terms of the child's age (wanting a 4-year-old to keep a bedroom in perfect order would not be appropriate), the child's current level of performance (parents shouldn't expect A's and B's from a child who is failing all subjects), or general standards of acceptable conduct (a 10-year-old should not be allowed to stay out late at night without supervision). Whatever the case, you should provide the necessary "expert" advice on what is appropriate and help people revise their expectations.

In those instances where parents' expectations are unreasonable in light of the child's current level of performance, you may first want to stress the concept of successive improvements or shaping as the most effective way for parents to achieve their ultimate objective. "Successive improvement" or "shaping" means to break a task into a series of steps that build upon each other. For example, making a bed can be broken down into pulling up the sheet and blanket, tucking them in, putting on the bedspread evenly, placing the pillow at the head of the bed, and bringing the spread over it.

The parents should explain and model one step at a time, then have their child do it, and finally praise the child's accomplishment. Each step should be mastered by the child before the next step is taught.

Second, be sure that the targeted behavior is stated positively, that is, in terms of a behavior parents want to see happen more frequently. Often the family will need some prompting to think in such terms. Useful prompts include:

TH: What would you like to see happen instead of (the misbehavior)?

TH: Can you give any examples of when Julie did what you like?

In one case, for example, the parents complained that their daughter was acting like a "guest" in their house. After some discussion of what constituted "member" as opposed to "guest" behaviors, they decided to target "doing things for the household or other family members without being asked."

Third, make sure that the targeted behavior is clear so that everyone understands *what* is expected, *when* it is expected, and *how* it should be done. A helpful exercise is to present various personalized hypothetical examples and have each family member indicate how each would be handled. If the targeted behavior was not listed previously on the Goal Setting Form, spend a few minutes completing the remaining boxes for this concern.

Brainstorm Solutions

The next step is to brainstorm solutions for revising the current program or developing a comprehensive treatment plan regarding the newly targeted concern. This means generating a list of ideas drawing from each of the major treatment components—setting up, self-control, reinforcement, and discipline. Covering one component at a time, have the family generate possible solutions with the "secretary" writing down all suggestions. Discourage debate until the family has exhausted all ideas regarding a given component. Be prepared to step in and cut off any debate.

Once they have generated a list of possible solutions, have them discuss each idea, pointing out both the advantages and disadvantages of each. You might need to prompt individuals who see only the positive side of an idea to consider how it may create problems. Conversely, if they see only the negative side, ask them how the solution might also resolve a conflict. Being able to evaluate solutions, particularly those proposed by someone else, will provide a good test of the clients' communication skills. After discussing all the proposed solutions, have the family choose a solution or combination of solutions they can accept and follow. Agreements reached should be entered in the appropriate space on the Treatment Plan, provided at the end of this chapter.

The issue of power or status within the family should be taken into account when negotiating solutions. It is our contention that a family is not a group of equals. Parents should be in charge and have the ultimate say regarding what solutions will be accepted. However, you should encourage the youngsters to have some input and the parents to listen and consider that input.

In the next sections we describe how to cover each of the treatment components.

Setting up for success. If you are simply revising an existing program, you should review what had been previously decided and how well it was carried out. If problems in setting up for success did exist, you should lead the family in discussing among themselves what the problems were and how they might be resolved. All suggestions should be written down.

If you and the family are addressing an entirely new problem, you may want to review the material on the parent handout titled "Setting Up for Success." (This handout is located at the end of Chapter Five.) Examine each of the possible categories of setting up and select the one or two most applicable to the target behavior. Briefly, those categories are as follows:

1.   The physical setting in the home

2.   Routines and consistency

3.   Clarity of commands

4.   Teaching of new skills

5.   Expression of mutual care, respect, and love

6.   Strengthening of marital ties

7.   Parenting coordination and communication

8.   Parental growth and well-being

After writing down all proposed solutions, have the family negotiate which ones they will implement. Record the agreed-upon setting up for success procedures on the Treatment Plan form.

Self-control procedure. If you are reviewing and revising an existing self-control procedure, the steps are similar to those described for setting up for success. Again, if there were problems, you should first check for comprehension and then for practical and/or motivational obstacles.

If you are developing a new Treatment Plan, have the family members identify those situations related to the targeted behavior that upset them and describe how they behave. Next have them propose solutions that can help them maintain or regain their composure. You might want to prompt them to consider ways of modifying their self-talk, focusing on "What is my goal?" and/or using relaxation. As ideas are generated, write them down. Enter those that are chosen on the Treatment Plan.

Discipline. The procedure for revising the discipline component of the Treatment Plan is identical to revising the previously discussed components. Don't be too willing to abandon a possibly sound procedure simply because the problem behaviors still occur. Infrequent or erratic misbehavior is as likely to result from continued testing as it is from a deficiency in the planned response. It is therefore important to examine the frequency, duration, average grade earned, or other measure of the problem behavior to see if the behavior is moving in the desired direction. Plotting how often the behavior occurs each day is a useful way to spot the direction of any trends. If it seems that the discipline technique is not having any effect, you may need to revise it or select an alternative technique. If you are developing a new program, you will find it helpful to review the possible discipline options presented on the parent handouts at the end of Chapter Seven.

Whatever solutions are proposed, make sure that the parents will not be working at cross-purposes. This problem can be avoided if the disciplinary procedures are selected through the process of discussion and negotiation. Nonetheless, it is also helpful to talk over what role each parent wishes the other to take when they are administering discipline. Good prompting questions are:

- How can you support (spouse) at the time when (he or she) is disciplining the child?

- If one of you decides it's necessary to discipline your child, how can you let the other person know so the youngster can't get between you or play one of you off against the other?

- What would you like (spouse) to do when you decide your child needs disciplining?

Administering discipline successfully often hinges on parents navigating various "what if" pitfalls; we recommend that you discuss and write down their "what if" responses on the form. For example, if they are concerned about their youngster completing homework, they may choose to use a logical consequence of waking the child an hour earlier if the work is not completed the previous evening. They should also think about what their response will be if the child won't get out of bed (remove the blankets and turn on the lights).

Again, once the family has evaluated each of the discipline methods suggested, have them write the preferred method on their Treatment Plan.

Reinforcement. If you are revising an existing program, review the reinforcement component and revise as necessary, as you did for the other program components. If you are developing a new program, we suggest you look at two different aspects of reinforcement. First, what can be said or done to reinforce the desired behavior? Second, how might the parents be inadvertently reinforcing the undesirable behavior and how could they stop doing so? In laying out the plan, these two issues are probably best reviewed separately.

In dealing with the first concern, you might want to begin by briefly reviewing several of the reinforcement options discussed in

Chapter Eight. You should then turn the matter over to the family to brainstorm the various options. Useful prompts to facilitate the discussion are:

- Is the reinforcer "strong enough" to make a difference?
- Is the reinforcer practical or realistic to provide?
- Is it likely that the child will grow tired of the reinforcer? If so, how can they prevent that?

To address the issue of inadvertent reinforcement, ask the family to think of any instances where they may have accidentally reinforced the undesirable behavior. This often involves giving in or in some way giving attention to the behavior. If family members find they have done so, prompt them to think of ways to avoid continuing this behavior in the future. With two-parent families, or where relatives or other adults are involved, investigate the possibility that the adults, or even older siblings, are unknowingly working against each other in reinforcing or not reinforcing behavior. Again, have them discuss what they can do to be more consistent among themselves.

Finally, have them write down on their Treatment Plan the solutions they have chosen for reinforcing the desired behavior and withholding inadvertent reinforcement when the child does the targeted misbehavior.

FINALIZING THE TREATMENT PLAN AND ASSIGNMENT

Review the entire program, checking that everyone understands what is to be done. Discipline procedures should be reviewed and backup consequences determined. If the program involves a point system, details for that system should be settled, including what the daily or weekly criteria for earning rewards will be, when the day's points will be totaled, and what the possible rewards will be. Help the family think of potential problems they may encounter and how they will handle them. Your role should be to prompt the family to resolve areas that are unclear or unworkable. Once a plan is established, you should enter the behavior or behaviors to be tracked during the upcoming week on a blank Program Monitoring Form. This should include both the child's behavior and those things the parents will do to carry out the program (use self-control, praise the child's efforts). Make sure you have a copy of their treatment plan and their Program Monitoring Form to refer to during between-session phone calls. Families in the latter stage of the generalization phase who are gradually discontinuing the use of formal tracking will not need to fill out a Program Monitoring Form.

CLOSING

The final step is to establish a trial period for the Treatment Plan. The period should be long enough to give the plan a fair trial yet not so long that clients feel locked in to the program forever. The most typical period is 1 or 2 weeks. Schedule the next appointment to coincide with the end of the trial phase. You should arrange to call the family early in the period to make sure things are off to a good start. Before the family leaves, reinforce their work with the program and express optimism about their continued success.

TREATMENT PLAN FOR _____

(concern)

1. *Clarification of Expectations*
   The specific behavior(s) I/we would like to see _____
   do more often are _____

   _____

   _____

2. *Setting Up for Success*
   To help _____ do these behaviors more often I/we will _____

   _____

   _____

   _____

3. *Self-control*
   To control my/our own behavior so that I/we contribute to a positive
   atmosphere and respond more effectively, I/we will _____

   _____

   _____

   _____

4. *Discipline*
   When _____ does the following misbehavior _____

   _____

   _____

   I/we will _____

   _____

   I/we will also avoid reinforcing that behavior by _____

   _____

   _____

5. *Reinforcement*
   To reinforce _____ for doing the appropriate behavior, I/we will

   _____

   _____

   _____

   Trial Dates _____ to _____

HANDOUT FOR PARENTS
PROBLEM SOLVING

Check off as you go through the steps.

——1. Pick a time when there is enough time to talk.

——2. Identify and work on one problem at a time.

——3. Clarify what you do and don't want.

——4. Brainstorm as many solutions as possible for each area:
   — Setting up for success
   — Maintaining self-control
   — Reinforcing
   — Disciplining

——5. Evaluate each solution.

——6. Negotiate and agree on solutions; be willing to compromise.

——7. Finalize exactly how the solution will be implemented, making sure everyone understands and agrees.

——8. Set a trial period and check back.

THERAPIST AGENDA: GENERALIZATION

Agenda   *Notes*

Beginning the Session

    Welcome the family and review the previous week:

        Review each component of current treatment

        Determine course of treatment:

            Continue working on currently targeted behavior

            Focus on new target behavior

            Move toward termination (see Chapter Eleven)

    Distribute handouts on communication skills and problem solving:

        Have clients identify those communication skills done well and those that need improvement

        Explain that problem-solving steps will be used in developing the new or revised program

Revising Current Program and Addressing New Concerns

    Select a problem or concern

        Add to Goal Setting Form if necessary

    Clarify and negotiate positive behavioral expectations:

        Make sure that it is:

            Reasonable

            Stated positively

            Clear to everyone (what, when, how)

        Complete Goal Setting Form if necessary

    Brainstorm solutions:

        Setting up for success

        Self-control procedure

        Discipline

        Reinforcement

    Negotiate and agree upon solutions

Finalizing the Treatment Plan and Assignment

    Complete Treatment Plan form

    Review entire program

    Anticipate concerns and problem solve potential difficulties:

        Child behaviors

        Parental behaviors

    Fill out Program Monitoring Form if necessary

Closing

    Determine trial period and schedule next appointment

    Arrange for between-session phone call

    Express confidence in the clients

Chapter Eleven

TERMINATION

This chapter addresses the issue of terminating treatment. While there are many reasons to keep treatment as brief as possible, it is not clear how brief the program can be and still have the desired effect. Patterson (1974) reported that the first major outcome study of the predecessor of this treatment model averaged 31.5 hours of professional contact. Yet treatment in The Family Center and Helena Family Teaching Center replication was approximately half that length (Fleischman & Szykula, 1981), with roughly comparable degrees of maintenance.

Nonetheless, maintenance of treatment effects can be a problem. As mentioned in Chapter Two, therapists at a recent multi-site replication effort were not able to maintain improvements in their clients past the first 6 weeks of treatment. While there were many problems with the implementation of the program at these sites, one particular difficulty was the lack of time spent insuring that earlier benefits would persist.

To avoid this situation in the future, therapists will need clear directions on preparing clients to maintain their improvements and on knowing when a family is ready to terminate. The remainder of this chapter will address these issues.

ENHANCING CLIENT MAINTENANCE

The following section describes five strategies you can use to prepare clients for treatment termination and to strengthen their ability to maintain positive changes.

Fade Formal Tracking and Encourage Informal Monitoring

While some families will want to maintain the use of formal tracking systems after treatment termination, the majority will not. To insure a smoother transition for parents who appear unlikely to continue formal monitoring after termination, we have several suggestions.

First, responsibility for tracking can be shifted from the parents to the child. This increases the child's sense of maturity and trust while lessening the burden on the parents. Posting of the tracking form serves as a prompt for the child and a reminder to the parents to attend to their youngster's continued positive performance. Of course, parents will need to monitor the child to verify that the behavior (chores done, home on time) actually did occur. In the evening, reviewing the form can be the focus of a brief family meeting.

A second suggestion is to have the behavior ratings become more general as treatment progresses (an overall rating of the child's daily minding versus exact counts of minds and not-minds; a general rating of self-control versus ratings for relaxation and positive self-talk). Families using this global tracking system should be asked during reviews of weekly tracking to give specific examples to justify their ratings. For example, "Julie, you gave yourself a B on reinforcing Joey's minding. Can you think of some examples of your use of reinforcement?" Parents who are able to back up their general ratings with concrete examples are more likely to track and reinforce or discipline behaviors in the future when all formal tracking is dropped.

Third, the amount of tracking can be decreased. For example, a parent who has been tracking 5 days a week may be asked to track only 2 or 3 days weekly.

Formal tracking should end when the family members demonstrate two skills. First, they should be able to monitor, reinforce, and discipline consistently using one or more of the reduced tracking schedules previously suggested. Second, they should be able to describe instances where they applied techniques to problems not being formally tracked. Some examples of the latter include giving their child increased social praise for a task done well; making a daughter finish her homework before going to a football game; buying a son gum at the end of a shopping trip because he was well behaved; taking quiet toys along for a child to play with during a doctor's appointment; and, while eating dinner, casually negotiating a system for getting the nightly dishes done.

Fade the Amount of Treatment Contacts

As a family becomes proficient at designing and successfully implementing interventions, you should begin to decrease the amount of contact you have with them. For example, you might move from weekly sessions to semimonthly to monthly appointments; from several phone calls a week, to one a week, to no scheduled calls. This procedure allows you to serve as a resource for the family while testing their ability to maintain the use of treatment techniques without your constant encouragement. Families who are unable to maintain progress in the face of reduced treatment contacts may need one or more of the following:

- Additional instruction in particular areas (more training in problem solving, communication skills, or self-control).

- More practice designing programs independently during sessions. The family may still be relying on you for the answers to their problems. The family will need to be coached to problem solve on their own. Your input should be limited primarily to reinforcing their independent efforts.

- To be connected into a broader support network. This is particularly important for single parents who are socially isolated. In such cases, you may have been the parent's primary source of reinforcement for continuing the program. Encouraging single parents to make new contacts can help alleviate this situation. To help your clients make and maintain these contacts you may need to help them strengthen their social skills by providing training in assertiveness, initiating social contacts, controlling social anxiety, and the like.

- Referrals to other services to help them deal with problems and/or stresses other than those related to family conflict.

Once the reason for the family's failure to maintain treatment improvements is pinpointed and addressed, you should once again begin to decrease your contacts while assessing the clients' ability to maintain positive changes.

Have the Family Develop a Preventive Program

We have repeatedly observed that many parents who seek help for their child-management problems often are simply "reacting" to their environment rather than using forethought to influence and direct situations. To help remedy this situation, once family members have applied their new skills successfully to several existing problems, they should be taught to use them in a preventive way. They should be encouraged to identify upcoming situations that may be potentially disruptive and to design strategies for coping with them. These situations may be either small (a small child's first visit to the doctor's office) or large, (a grandparent coming to live with the family), and include both immediate events (company coming over for dinner at the children's bedtime) and those in the future (when the baby is born, when the child changes schools, when mom goes back to work).

You may need to prompt your clients by asking leading questions based on information received earlier in treatment. For example:

> TH: Sara, I remember a while back you told me that John is going to visit his brother for a week next month. Can you think of any potential problems that might arise for you and the kids while he's gone?

Another way to help clients anticipate problems is to ask if they foresee any major changes in their routine in the coming months, for example, a vacation, moving, birth of a baby, visitors, children starting school, or hospitalization. Finally, ask them to anticipate the different parent-child problems they will face as their children grow older.

Once the family has identified situations that may become troublesome, they should brainstorm ways to deal with them by applying the principles and techniques learned in treatment. Many families have found that by setting up for success and immediately reinforcing desired behaviors, they rarely need to use the prearranged punishment. In addition, people who anticipate problems are better prepared to cope with them should they arise.

Teaching families to anticipate and handle problems is an important step in the treatment process. The goal is not only to reduce the number and severity of family problems but also to prevent future ones and to maintain an improved level of family functioning.

Predict Relapses and Prepare Clients to Reinstate the Program

Many, if not most, families will experience a period when they do not use the skills they have learned in treatment. This "relapse" is often triggered by some type of crisis or change in the individual's or family's life (illness, financial stress, death in the family, vacation) and generally results in an increase in negative behaviors. In the face of such relapses, many clients become discouraged and frustrated. Often they believe that increases in negative interactions are out of their control and rationalize that treatment did not really work. To help prevent such discouragement, you should predict that some relapses will occur. When clients realize that relapses are normal, they tend to view them as less of a catastrophe.

Once a crisis subsides, you must help clients "get back on their feet" by having them reinstate their use of social learning and cognitive interventions. For this part of treatment, you may need to increase your amount of contact and encouragement temporarily. By encouraging the family to reinstate the program, you will once again be demonstrating to them that it is within *their* ability to correct problems. Clients who see how their behavior can impact the behavior of those around them (both positively and negatively) are more likely to prevent relapses in the future and to reimplement techniques in the wake of a relapse.

Link the Family to Other Community Resources

This step can be particularly fruitful when working with either socially isolated parents or families who are experiencing many forms of stress in addition to parent-child conflict. Introducing isolated parents to community groups and programs can provide them with a natural support group. Connecting multi-problem families with pertinent community resources can help families decrease the stress in their lives and teach them how to seek appropriate help for their problems. The type of resources needed by families will vary, but typical referrals include the following:

- Agencies that provide assistance with food, housing, clothing, or home heating
- Organizations that provide relief child-care or day-care
- Organizations for youth such as a big-brother or big-sister program, Head Start, 4-H, and the like
- Local self-help groups (Weight Watchers, Alcoholics Anonymous, Al-anon, single-mothers groups, special interest groups)
- Organizations that provide or assist a person in academic or skills training (CETA, applying for a scholarship, programs that teach job interviewing skills)

- Medical referrals
- Psychological referrals for problems other than parent-child conflict (marital problems, depression)

DETECTING INDICATORS THAT PREDICT CLIENT MAINTENANCE

While there is no one indicator that will predict how well clients can maintain treatment gains, several client variables have been identified that we believe contribute to successful maintenance. They are (a) consistent implementation of techniques learned in treatment, (b) increased prosocial and decreased aversive behaviors on the part of all children in the family, (c) parents' ability to conceptualize and discuss situations from a social learning perspective, (d) an overall increase in the family's level of positive interactions, and finally, (e) the absence of major stresses on the family.

Family Consistently Implements the Techniques

While it's important that families use the program, it's even more important that they use it without constant prodding from you. Clients should have reached a point where they are being reinforced for their new behaviors by other family members and by the positive outcomes of their own actions.

With two-parent families, the parents should be able to demonstrate that they can work together to deal with problems. Such parent teamwork includes agreeing on which behaviors need to be targeted for change and what reasonable expectations are, developing mutually agreed-upon interventions based on social learning principles, and supporting each other when carrying out interventions. Parents should be able to work together without becoming unduly defensive, argumentative, or critical.

Siblings' Behavior Improves

At termination, most or all of the goals initially identified for the target child on the Goal Setting Form should have been achieved, and there should not be any serious new behavior problems. In addition, the parents should be noting favorable behavior changes in their other children. This is particularly important in light of Horne's (1981) finding that siblings from families with a deviant target child demonstrate higher rates of aggressive behavior than children from a sample of families with a normal target child. Parents who are able to generalize their new skills to change the aversive behaviors of all their children are more likely to maintain treatment gains.

Clients View Behavior from a Social Learning Perspective

There are several ways clients can demonstrate that they have adopted a social learning perspective. First, in talking about problems, they speak in terms of behavioral rather than personality traits. Examples include:

"He can't play by himself for over 2 minutes" versus "He's hyperactive."

"She talks on the phone for hours at a time" versus "She's inconsiderate."

Second, in talking about their children's behavior, they indicate in various ways that they see a connection between their own behavior and that of the child. ("Now that I'm not getting so upset, he's more relaxed" or "After I sent her to time-out, she was much better.")

Third, they interpret events with the concepts drawn from social learning training. ("When my friend gave her son the candy, I said to myself, 'She's just reinforced his whining' and sure enough, within 10 minutes he started up again.")

Fourth, clients should be adept at using the cognitively based self-control skills in positive and constructive ways. They should be able to describe how they are using rational and positive self-talk (particularly how they have used these cognitive skills during conflict situations). Clients who have not replaced negative labeling and self-talk ("He's a brat," "I can't handle him") with more productive thoughts are not likely to continue applying social learning techniques to their family problems.

Family's Level of Positive Interaction is Higher

The family not only should have succeeded in reducing the negative behaviors targeted but also should have successfully replaced them with appropriate positive behaviors. For example, a child taught not to fight with other children is also taught to share toys and take turns when playing games. Additional signs that suggest a family is functioning in a more positive way include an increased rate of social reinforcement among members; displays of affection, empathy, and concern for each other; a greater number of pleasant family activities; and an increase in pleasant conversations and expressed interest in the activities of other family members.

Family has No Major Stresses or Can Deal With Those That Exist

Families who are faced with major stresses are less able to focus on strengthening the parent-child relationship. The more stressors that families experience simultaneously, the more detrimental the effects on children's behavior. This clinical observation is congruent with Rutter's (1979) finding that the negative effects on a child's behavior in families with four or more major stressors was *three times* the effect of three or fewer stressors. Common family stresses that have been associated with behavioral disturbance in children include marital distress and parental conflict, parental unemployment, overcrowded living conditions, and low socio-economic status.

The existence of any one problem or even any combination of these stresses does not necessarily mean that a family will not maintain treatment improvements. However, it seems clear that families with the fewest stressors at termination or who are taking constructive steps to curtail those stress factors (receiving marital therapy, joining a group activity to make social contacts, going to school to learn a skill) are more likely to do better at maintaining treatment gains.

MAKING FOLLOW-UP CONTACTS

After terminating, we strongly urge that you periodically telephone the family for at least 6 months. These calls serve several purposes. First, if the family is functioning well, the calls provide opportunities to reinforce their success. Second, if problems are beginning to recur, the calls can prompt the family to take some immediate action. Finally, if you find that the family has seriously reverted to old patterns of behavior, you can offer some brief assistance or "booster shots" to turn the situation around.

Aside from inquiring about the target child's behavior, you can take this opportunity to assess several other areas. They include:

1. The parents' ability to monitor their child's appropriate and inappropriate behavior consistently;

2. The parents' use of appropriate reinforcers and punishers to manage their child;

3. The ability of family members, particularly the parents, to maintain their composure in the face of problems;

4. The parents' ability to intervene constructively when confronted with new problems;

5. The family's use of problem-solving and communication skills;

6. The family's overall level of positive interaction and activities.

To gain this information, you will need to ask them for specific descriptions and examples ("Bedtime used to be a problem; why don't you describe how John's bedtime went last night" or "So John's been a pretty nice boy to be around. That's great. What are some of the nice things he did for you this past week?"). If setbacks have occurred, or you suspect that they have, you should reassure the client that some "slippage" is normal. This is particularly important since many clients regard setbacks as failures and thus hesitate to reveal their problems.

In the following dialogue, notice how the therapist encourages the client to look at the problem more objectively.

TH: So John's been minding you most of the time with the exception of a day here and there. That's pretty normal and nothing to worry too much about. Let's spend just a few minutes talking about what's happening on those days that he repeatedly disobeys you.

CL: Well, I know that he often has a bad day when I do.

TH: What do you make of that?

CL: Well, I suppose he's reacting to my yelling and being upset. Also, on those days that I feel upset, I'm not very consistent with him.

TH: Those things are probably having an effect on John's behavior. I was thinking, from what you said earlier, that it sounds like you're under a lot of pressure at work right now. That must make it hard to relax when you come home to your family. Can you think of some ways to relax when you're tense?

CL: I suppose I could use the relaxation technique you taught me or perhaps lie down for 15 minutes when I first get home.

TH: Either of those are good ideas. They should make you relax and help you stay calm when you talk to John.

Making follow-up contacts in addition to handling active cases can place a heavy demand on your time and energy. However, we feel the benefits far outweigh the costs. When one considers the hard-won gains attained during treatment, and the individual, societal, and financial costs that can result from relapses, the time allotted for follow-up contacts seems a prudent investment.

USING THE CLIENT INDICATORS OF TREATMENT GAINS FORM

While treatment averages 3 to 4 months, the decision to terminate should be based on your assessment of the family's ability to maintain treatment gains and resolve future problems independently. In this chapter we have described both client behaviors and situations that must be considered when determining whether to discontinue regular treatment contacts. We have summarized the client maintenance indicators in a checklist, Client Indicators of Treatment Gains, which appears at the end of this chapter. We strongly recommend that throughout the generalization phase of treatment you periodically rate the family's ability in each of the areas listed on this form. You may choose to rate with a plus-or-minus system or a grading system. If the family is having considerable difficulty in any of the areas listed, you will need to address the problems before terminating treatment. The checklist should also be consulted during follow-up contacts to help determine whether a family's treatment gains have persisted.

CLIENT INDICATORS OF TREATMENT GAINS

Family _____

Date _____ _____ _____

Consistent Use of Techniques	Rating	Rating	Rating
1. Ability to set up for success			
a. Dealing with existing problems	____	____	____
b. Preventing future problems	____	____	____
2. Use of self-control techniques			
a. Self-talk	____	____	____
b. Relaxation	____	____	____
3. Use of punishment			
a. Correct implementation	____	____	____
b. Consistent use	____	____	____
4. Use of reinforcement			
a. Social reinforcement	____	____	____
b. Material rewards	____	____	____
5. Communication skills			
a. Nonverbal communication	____	____	____
b. Verbal communication	____	____	____
c. Communication patterns to avoid	____	____	____
Siblings' Behavior Improves			
1. Favorable changes in other children in family	____	____	____
2. Parents generalize their skills to all their children	____	____	____
Comprehension of Social Learning Principles			
1. Describe problems and desired outcome in behavioral terms	____	____	____
2. Understand how their behavior affects others	____	____	____
3. Use social learning interpretations	____	____	____
Positive Interactions			
1. Increased prosocial behaviors	____	____	____
2. Pleasant family activities	____	____	____
Absence of Stresses			
1. Lack of major stressors and/or ability to cope with and alleviate stressors	____	____	____
2. Social support	____	____	____

Chapter Twelve

SCHOOL INTERVENTION

This chapter describes how to extend the treatment to deal with school-related problems. It is intended for elementary school-aged children, but also may be used with some junior-high or middle-school students. Problems appropriate for treatment include noncompliance in following classroom and school rules, lack of attention to tasks, inappropriate social behavior, and poor social interaction skills.

Many youngsters with school behavior problems also have serious academic difficulties. While treatment should be aimed primarily at improving the child's classroom behaviors, it's important not to overlook a possible need for individualized or small-group instruction and other special services such as speech therapy. Providing these services is usually outside your specific province as a therapist, but you should be alert to such needs and recommend any extra help children may require.

The school intervention program presented in this chapter has four components: (a) building a good working relationship with school personnel, (b) developing an intervention based on a Daily Report Card procedure, (c) conducting the intervention, and (d) fading. An essential feature of this program is that it is based on a set of goals agreed upon by both parents and school personnel. These goals serve as the anchor for developing the intervention and the basis for evaluating the program.

In addition to working to improve the youngster's in-school behavior, the school intervention program also aims to foster positive interaction between the parents and the school system. Your role will be to initiate that interaction and to take the lead in designing the program for changing the child's in-school behavior. Once that is under way, you should transfer responsibility for maintaining the program to the parents and school personnel.

UNDERSTANDING THE DAILY REPORT CARD PROCEDURE

At the heart of most home-school interventions is the Daily Report Card. Sample report cards are shown in Figure 14. On this card are listed the child's behaviors that both parents and teachers agree need

Figure 14. Sample Daily Report Cards.

Tommy Sullivan		Date	4/7	
Desired Behaviors	Reading	Social Studies	Math	Science
Attends to and stays on task	1	0	1	1
Works independently	1	0	0	1
Completes and turns in assignments	1	0	1	1

Total points __8__   Teacher's signature ___Marsha Hill___
Comments:

Cheryl James		Date	2/11
Desired Behaviors	8–10 a.m.	10 a.m.–Noon	Noon–2 p.m.
Complies with classroom teacher's commands	Yes	No	Yes
Accepts teacher's judgment	Yes	Yes	Yes
Speaks appropriately to other children	No	No	Yes

Total yeses __6__   Teacher's signature ___Tom Brown___
Comments:

improvement. Each day the teacher completes the card by noting which behaviors were satisfactory and sends it home with the student. At home the parents deliver prearranged consequences, either positive or negative depending on the child's performance.

Such a system serves several purposes. It brings the parents and school together regarding what changes they would like to see. It sets forth clear behavioral expectations for the child and gives both child and parents daily feedback on how the youngster is doing. The program starts at the child's current level and gradually shapes behavior to more generally accepted standards. Finally, once the child's behavior is satisfactory, the card can be faded.

The actual format of the card will vary depending on the presenting problems, the child's age, and whether the child spends the entire day with one teacher or shifts from teacher to teacher. Typically, the three or four behaviors the child is to work on are listed down the left side of the card. These should be stated positively ("Follows teacher's directions quickly") rather than negatively ("No refusals, arguments, or dawdling"). They should be written in words the child can understand.

Across the card will be a row of boxes that designates the time periods that each behavior is to be scored. With preschoolers and children in the early primary grades, ratings should be frequent when first starting a program, perhaps every 30 minutes. Older children should be rated after each period or every couple of hours at first. Later, daily ratings can be used.

Behaviors listed on the Daily Report Card are strengthened with social reinforcers and access to privileges at home such as using the telephone, watching TV, riding a bicycle, having special snacks, and inviting friends over. If the child is already on a point system at home, you must decide either to set aside certain privileges that can be earned only on the basis of in-school behavior or to add the points received at school to those earned at home as part of one large point system.

Whichever is chosen, the criteria or minimum number of points or "yeses" on the Daily Report Card should be high enough to challenge the child while still allowing reasonable chances for success. Some therapists prefer an all-or-nothing system (10 or more points earn the privilege). Others suggest a privilege menu where more points earn more desirable privileges. The advantage of this method is that it encourages even greater performance; the drawback is its increased complexity. A compromise suggested by Schumaker, Hovell, and Sherman (1977) is to develop separate lists of basic and special privileges. Basic privileges such as use of the television, telephone, and radio can be earned each day by reaching a minimum percentage of the total number of points available. Special privileges include activities such as visiting friends, skating, getting an allowance, or giving a party, and can be earned by accumulating points beyond the minimum criterion.

IMPLEMENTING THE SCHOOL INTERVENTION

Gaining the School's Cooperation

The effectiveness of a home-school program depends on everyone's cooperation. As you have already established a relationship with the family, you must now do so with the child's teacher or teachers and principal. In working with school personnel, approach them as fellow professionals who share your concern for the youngster's education and well-being.

If you have not had previous contact with the school, you will need to gain proper entry by learning the appropriate school protocol. First, be certain that you have the parents' written permission to contact the school. Second, the principal is generally the first person to contact, either by phone or by appointment. In general, you will be cordially welcomed after you explain your purpose. In all likelihood, the principal is aware of the child's school problems and will appreciate your initiative. This is also a good time to ask about any prior interventions or special services the school may have tried or is currently providing the child.

Finally, ask the principal who else you should speak to besides the child's teacher or teachers. This can include special education teachers, counselors, school psychologists, and teachers' aides. Such information not only lets you know whom to include in your intervention program, but also serves as an introduction to other people in the school system.

Initial Contact with the Teacher

The next step is to contact the child's teacher and anyone else recommended by the principal. At the first meeting, avoid launching into the program right away. Rather, explain your role as a family therapist and ask about their experiences with the child and the family. Next discuss any efforts they have made to work on the child's problems. It is quite possible that either the teacher or someone else has already developed a program to deal with many of the same concerns you have. In that case, you may simply need to get the family involved in the school program. Doing so will accomplish your original aims without duplicating the teacher's efforts. It is important to be an empathic listener with teachers. The greater concern you demonstrate for their point of view, the greater chance you have for obtaining their cooperation. You should also describe the work you have been doing with the family and ask whether they have noticed any recent changes at school. Finally, outline the basic intervention you wish to set up. Briefly describe the Daily Report Card system to teachers, outlining the projected demands on them, and ask if they would be willing to cooperate. If they indicate their willingness, ask permission to observe the child in the classroom and/or on the playground and inquire about the best time to visit. At the end, arrange a meeting between them, yourself, and the parents.

Occasionally you may work with school personnel who have had previous difficulties with the parents. You can alleviate the staff's reservations by showing them evidence of the family's cooperation and success in the home-based treatment program. In effect, you may find yourself acting as an advocate for the family in helping school personnel overcome their prejudices. They should recognize that parents have valuable input that will make the school intervention more successful and will enable the school to function more smoothly.

In talking with school personnel, watch for any signs indicating that they are reluctant to cooperate. Signs of resistance include complaints about limited time and excessive teaching loads, objections that what you are proposing conflicts with existing school policies, and ideological disputes about the best way to help the youngster. We suggest you exercise patience and flexibility when handling these problems. After school personnel have had the opportunity to work with you for a while, their cooperation should increase naturally.

On occasion, you will encounter a teacher who has exhausted her resources for dealing with a particular child. Bringing that teacher, the principal, and yourself together to discuss the situation sometimes can help motivate the teacher to try further. In other cases, it may be worth raising your concern tactfully with the principal to arrange the child's transfer to another class. School principals can be very helpful in selecting the teachers who are likely to be the most supportive and effective with difficult children.

You may also be aware of the parents' hesitation to work more closely with the school. Their past experience with schools may have been unfavorable or they may feel that the school is not providing their child with a good education. You can begin to bridge the gap in communication and understanding by talking to the parents about the school personnel and their concern for helping the child.

School Observation

The purpose of this observation is twofold: (a) to watch the child in the setting in which the intervention will take place and (b) to provide you with information that you can directly relate to the teachers ("After watching Mel in class, I understand what you mean about him spending lots of time out of his seat"). Explain that you would rather not be introduced to the class, but that you will sit quietly in the back of the classroom and remain as unobtrusive as possible.

Make sure you explain to the child in advance that you will be attending class and that you will remain anonymous. If the child wishes to acknowledge you and explain who you are, he may do so; but the youngster shouldn't be surprised or embarrassed by your presence.

During your observation, note the occurrence of any behaviors listed on the School Behavior Checklist at the end of this chapter, as well as any other behavior problems specified by the teacher. Also note the type and quality of the teacher's interaction with the child and any contact the child has with peers.

Goal Setting Meeting

The purpose of this meeting is to bring together all involved school personnel, the parents, and yourself to establish the goals of the school intervention. The child may be invited to attend if you feel the child's presence will be a positive experience; otherwise, the youngster should be excluded. Following are the specific steps to be covered in this meeting. For this session you will need to have copies of the School Behavior Checklist and a blank Goal Setting Form (at the end of Chapter Five).

Introduce everyone. In meeting with everyone, your first step will be to introduce each person present, explaining how or why each one is involved with the child. This may seem unnecessary, but we've found parents frequently don't know the school personnel actually involved with their children.

Review work to date. Next, provide a brief overview of the steps that have been taken by the family in working with you over the past months. Emphasize the positive changes that have occurred, giving the family credit for their youngster's improvement. Mention the family's cooperation to date and their willingness to extend treatment to problems in school. Also mention the school personnel's eagerness to work on improving the child's behavior.

Present agenda. Before turning to the major tasks to be covered, share your agenda for what you hope to accomplish during the meeting. Objectives would include:

1. Discussing the child's in-school behavior and identifying the few key behaviors to be worked on.

2. Setting goals for improving each of those behaviors.

3. Setting up a Daily Report Card system so that parents will know how the child behaves each day.

4. Outlining a list of privileges the child will receive at home based on school behavior. If the child is not present, this list may need to be modified when the parents explain the program to the child.

5. Outlining negative consequences the child will receive at home for inadequate or inappropriate in-school behavior.

6. Ironing out any remaining details necessary to implement the system and adjust it as necessary.

Discuss positive behaviors and prioritize concerns. Start the discussion of the child's school-related behavior by giving everyone a copy of the School Behavior Checklist, provided at the end of this chapter. This checklist will keep the discussion focused on specific behaviors and can be used for identifying strengths and prioritizing key concerns. We recommend that you have everyone review those behaviors the child does well before moving to identify those in need of improvement. Of course, participants may want to add specific behaviors that are not included on the checklist. All told, no more than four behaviors should be targeted for change at any one time. If you try to work on too many things at once, progress will be slower.

Complete the Goal Setting Form. The process of setting school-related behavioral goals is similar to that used previously for the in-home program. The steps in completing this form are as follows.

1. Enter each of the selected behaviors in one of the boxes in the row labeled *Concerns*.

2. In the first box in the row labeled *Desired behavior*, describe exactly what the child should do to meet the first concern. Expectations should be in terms of what the average child does and not some exemplary level of performance. As much as possible, state expectations positively rather than as behaviors to be avoided. Consult the

School Behavior Checklist for possible definitions. When the first desired behavior has been described, repeat the process for the remaining concerns.

3. Moving to the row labeled *Current level*, have the teacher estimate how frequently the child currently performs the desired behavior. Estimates should be entered for each concern. These estimates or measures of frequency will depend on the type of behavior listed as a concern ("Stays on task for approximately half of the social studies period" or "Initiates conversations with at least two different children during each recess").

4. In the row labeled *Change expected*, describe the outcome for each concern using the measure of frequency noted in *Current level*. Remember that the expected change should be appropriate to the child's current behavior, minimal levels of acceptability, and how the youngster's average classmates behave. Expected change should not call for perfect behavior.

5. Finally, repeat this process for the row *More than expected change*. Again, avoid calling for perfection.

An example of a section of a Goal Setting Form completed for one target behavior would look like Figure 15.

Figure 15. Sample Section of Completed Goal Setting Form.

CONCERNS	*Disturbs others*
DESIRED BEHAVIOR	*Pays attention to her own work during seatwork and group instruction*
CURRENT LEVEL	*1 work period daily out of 17*
CHANGE EXPECTED	*4 work periods daily*
MORE THAN EXPECTED CHANGE	*5+ work periods daily*

A copy of the Goal Setting Form should be given to the teacher and parents; retain the original for yourself.

Remember that in addition to helping complete this form, your role throughout the process is to facilitate communication between teachers and parents. They need to practice solving problems together, independent of your mediation. While it's natural for them to want you to select the behaviors and set the goals, when possible turn the responsibility back to them. You can do so with such comments as "What problems cause you the most concern, Mrs. Smith?"

Introduce the Daily Report Card. Explain that having set goals, the next step is to set up a system to keep the parents closely informed of their child's behavior so they can deliver appropriate consequences at home for good and bad days.

The card, or piece of paper, should be layed out so that the desired behaviors on the goal sheet can be listed down the left side of the paper and appropriate spaces drawn on the right side for marking yes/no, +/–, or number of points earned. Again, spaces may be set out for each period or activity, or for various blocks of time (8–10 a.m., 10 a.m.–Noon, Noon–2 p.m.). (See Figure 14.)

Next, discuss with the parents (and child if present) the privileges that can be awarded *at home* for scoring well on the card. Define the standards or criteria for earning those privileges and whether an (a) all-or-nothing system, (b) privilege menu, or (c) a system of basic and special privileges will be used. Reread the section "Understanding the Daily Report Card Procedure" for details about how to award privileges.

Also decide what the discipline for inappropriate behavior will be and when the consequence will be delivered. There are four circumstances under which the child receives discipline. The first is when the child does not earn enough points or yeses to meet a minimum number set by her parents that is below the number needed to earn a reward. The second is when privileges are denied or extra work chores at home are added following the occurrence of one or two specific negative behaviors. Penalties should also be enacted when the child does not bring the card home or when portions of the card are blank without a legitimate explanation.

Decide which teacher or teachers will monitor the Daily Report Card at school and where the child can obtain a blank card at the start of each day. Make sure that the child understands that she is responsible for having all necessary teachers sign the card. Write down both the privileges and penalties and give a copy to the family.

Rehearse. So that everyone understands what to do, ask them to go through how they will carry out their end of the program. Have the teacher complete a Daily Report Card for the child for the day just completed or for the previous day. Ask the teacher to explain the particular ratings given. Listen for clear, behaviorally specific statements that are consistent with the definitions of desired behaviors listed on the card. Next, have the teacher give the card to the parents, and ask the parents what they would do if the child brought home this report card today. Go through the consequences the parents would provide and have them explain their answers.

Arrange for all parties to stay in contact. To minimize problems, it is helpful if the parents, teachers, and you agree to stay in close contact, especially for the next 2 weeks. Youngsters may try to sabotage the program by claiming the teacher was absent or that she forgot to hand out the card, or by altering the teacher's markings. Parents should be able to call the teacher to clear up any questions they may have about the report card.

Prepare parents to explain the program to the child. If the child was not present when the Daily Report Card system was set up, the parents should be prepared to explain it and to get the child's input regarding the privileges to be earned. Since the youngster has probably been exposed to an in-home point system, this report card should not be unfamiliar. The parents will also need to mention the penalty for not bringing the card home.

Emphasize the importance of social reinforcement. A problem with some school report cards is that parents and teachers come to rely too heavily on the formal consequences and overlook the importance of frequent and immediate social reinforcement. Emphasize to both parties that the card should also be a signal to them to praise the child and to express their pleasure in the effort being made. Make sure they understand that if the card is paired with social reinforcers, they will be able to fade the card sooner.

Close. Thank everyone for their effort. Let both the parents and teacher know when you will be contacting them or how they can reach you. We suggest you try to talk with everyone at least twice in the first week to make sure everything is going as planned.

MONITORING THE INTERVENTION

With the Daily Report Card in place, your job is largely to step back and let the parents and teacher run the program. You should stay in contact, more to support and reinforce the others, and to point out when a problem may be developing or when changes may be needed rather than to solve the difficulty or propose specific changes yourself. Here are some problems you should watch for:

- The child has difficulties in picking up the card or getting it signed at the end of the day.
- The child may be altering the ratings.
- The teacher is not issuing cards consistently.
- Parents are not asking for the card and/or are not delivering consequences consistently.
- The card needs to be revised. This can include dropping some behaviors and adding others or altering the frequency with which markings are entered.
- The privileges or the criteria for earning them need to be revised.
- The child is not being socially reinforced either by the parents or the teacher for in-school behavior.

From the very beginning of the school program, you should have periodic meetings with the parents and teacher to develop a cooperative relationship, define problem areas, review progress, and assess change. You should consider taking responsibility for coordinating these meetings. At the beginning, it may be a good idea to meet every week for 3 or 4 weeks. This schedule can be followed by weekly phone calls and meetings every 3 weeks. After terminating the school program, you should be responsible for having phone contact with the parents and teacher once every 3 to 4 weeks.

FADING

The goal of fading is to reduce the structure of the program gradually while still maintaining the child's progress. Fading should not be undertaken until the child has been earning the privileges fairly consistently for at least 2 weeks. When you feel the child is ready for this step, arrange a meeting with the parents and teachers. Begin this meeting by reviewing the Goal Setting Form. If the child's behavior approximates the *Change expected* levels set forth on that form, move to a discussion of fading. However, if one or more of the concerns is still below the expected level, determine the problem and revise the program accordingly. In such cases fading probably should be postponed. A general rule in fading is not to move to the next less structured phase until the child meets criteria in the current phase. If the child cannot maintain the desired behavior in a less structured program, return to the previous phase to retrieve earlier gains. When the child's behavior meets expected levels, you can initiate the following steps in fading the card.

Step 1

The first step is to increase the interval of time for which each rating is made. Thus, a child who is currently being rated for each activity or period should now be rated for the entire morning or even the entire day. Reducing the number of ratings will reduce the number of points or yeses that can be awarded, so the criteria for earning rewards will need to be adjusted.

Step 2

The second step in fading is to move to a semiweekly card. We recommend that the card be issued on Tuesdays and Fridays and that ratings be for behaviors over the prior 2 to 3 days. Thus, the student would need to behave appropriately for all of Monday and Tuesday to be rated positively on the card sent home on Tuesday. Because the child will still be earning privileges daily despite the fact that cards will be coming home only twice a week, it should be explained that Tuesday's card will cover privileges for Tuesday, Wednesday, and Thursday, and Friday's card will cover Friday and Monday. After 2 satisfactory weeks with the system in this phase, move to the next stage.

Step 3

This step is a weekly card which reflects the student's behavior for the entire week. Privileges are still provided daily, but whether they are earned will depend on a general assessment of the child's behavior over the previous week. This card is usually completed by the teacher on Friday. Again, if the student fails to meet criteria for 2 consecutive weeks, return to the semiweekly card.

Step 4

The final stage of fading is simply a merit system. Now the child will automatically receive privileges unless given three warnings within a 1-month period about any of the behaviors previously listed on the card. Teachers will need to contact the parents when the child has had three such warnings. If the child has consistent problems with this system, there should be a return to the weekly card.

CONDUCTING AN END-OF-PROGRAM REVIEW

Once the program has been discontinued, schedule a meeting with the parents and the school personnel who have been involved to review progress and thank everyone for their cooperation. Use this meeting to review the original Goal Setting Form and indicate what level of change was accomplished for each behavior. This goal form can then be included in the child's school record.

SCHOOL BEHAVIOR CHECKLIST

Mark *Y* for *Yes* if the child does these behaviors.
Mark *N* for *No* if the child does not do these behaviors.

Classroom behavior

____ 1. *Complies with classroom teacher's commands* quickly and pleasantly.

____ 2. *Complies with classroom rules and routines* without being reminded.

____ 3. *Stays in seat* except with permission to leave.

____ 4. *Raises hand* before speaking out.

____ 5. *Accepts teacher's judgment* without complaints. If questions a decision, does so politely.

____ 6. *Is prompt* in completing work or in changing activities.

Outside classroom behavior

____ 7. *Obeys teacher's commands* in playground, lunchroom, or hallway promptly and pleasantly.

____ 8. *On playground,* plays according to rules and is a "good sport."

____ 9. *In hallways,* goes only where he or she is supposed to be without disturbing others.

____ 10. *On bus,* stays in seat and obeys bus driver.

____ 11. *In cafeteria,* waits in line, stays in seat, eats properly, and disposes of garbage according to rules.

Academic behaviors

____ 12. *Approaches new tasks and material willingly.* Acts interested and curious in class discussions.

____ 13. *Attends to and stays on task* during independent and small-group work. Interrupts work only to seek teacher's help.

____ 14. *Works independently.* Tries to solve problems alone.

____ 15. *Requests help* when needed. If he or she cannot solve problem, gets assistance.

____ 16. *Doesn't disturb others.* Pays attention to his or her own work.

____ 17. *Completes and turns in assignments* on time without complaints or excuses.

____ 18. *Listens and pays attention.* Follows directions.

Peer interaction

____ 19. *Responds well to teasing.* Either tells them to stop or ignores it. Seeks adult interventions only as last resort.

____ 20. *Initiates conversations* and activities with peers. Responds positively when others initiate conversations or activities with him or her.

____ 21. *Shares equipment and materials* when asked. Asks others to share without demanding, grabbing, or threatening.

___ 22. *Speaks appropriately to other children.* Avoids swearing, name-calling, and ridiculing.

___ 23. *Plays and interacts appropriately* with others. Avoids using physical aggression, picking fights, or rising to challenges to fight. Attempts to work out disputes.

___ 24. *Takes a leadership role* at times. Thinks of ideas, initiates activities, and organizes peers without being bossy.

___ 25. *Develops friendships.* Has a special friend or friends with whom he or she frequently plays and shares.

Other social behaviors

___ 26. *Stealing.* Doesn't take things that aren't his or hers. Does not claim items are "borrowed," "found," or "traded."

___ 27. *Honesty.* Does not lie or leave out part of a story. Admits to wrongdoing.

___ 28. *Takes care of own and others' property.* Does not destroy things or treat them so they are likely to wear out or break. Does not waste materials.

___ 29. *Self-stimulation.* Does not engage in inappropriate body rocking, masturbation, hand or facial gestures.

___ 30. *Toileting.* Remains dry and clean. Uses the bathroom when necessary.

___ 31. *Controls "nervous" behaviors* such as nail biting, picking, handwringing, tics.

___ 32. *No smoking.* Doesn't bring cigarettes or matches to school.

___ 33. *Eye contact.* Looks others in the eye when talking to them.

___ 34. *Dresses appropriately.* Conforms to school dress code. Wears clothing that is appropriate for weather, activity, or body build.

___ 35. *Personal cleanliness and grooming.* Is clean and reasonably neat.

Chapter Thirteen

TREATMENT IN GROUPS

The model described in this book for working with individual families can also be applied effectively to groups of parents. Working with groups offers several advantages. A primary one is that therapists can use their time more efficiently since they can see more families. Second, groups can supply individuals with social support. Parents experiencing difficulty with their children often feel isolated, angry, incompetent, or defeated. In groups, parents can share their frustrations and get encouragement from people who are experiencing similar difficulties. Groups can be particularly therapeutic for single parents who are isolated from other types of emotional support. Finally, seeing some members of the group learn, apply, and succeed with the treatment procedures can encourage other group members to carry out the program. Group members who support the efforts of others can share in their successes.

However, conducting the program in groups also has some liabilities. Perhaps the greatest disadvantage is that this form of treatment restricts the involvement of the children. This is not a particular concern when working with parents of very young children; but when the targeted children are 8 years old or older, we believe they can often make valuable contributions to their family's treatment plan. Second, you will have fewer opportunities to learn how the members in each family interact with one another, thus making it more difficult to tailor the program to individual family needs. In addition, parents may have specific fears, concerns, or problems that do not get addressed. They may be unwilling to share personal information with the group or simply not have enough individual time with you. A final problem in conducting groups is that they place somewhat different demands on the therapist. You must not only be familiar with the content of each session but also be able to address the needs of parents and make sure they understand and can apply what you are teaching. You must do all this, stay on task, and still move ahead! While over time this process becomes easier, if you have limited experience working with groups, we recommend that you conduct your first few groups with a cotherapist.

There are several steps you can take to help the group get off to a good start. First, to the extent possible, see that parents share many of the same presenting problems. You can then focus on certain pre-selected procedures that all parents can use. For example, if defiance and not minding are problems for all the parents, everyone would benefit from learning to give good commands, use time-out, and set up a point system. Also, parents with similar problems are in a better position to empathize with and act as a resource for each other.

Second, select people who would be reasonably compatible. Thus, you would avoid putting a younger, single parent on welfare in with a group of more middle-aged, professional couples. Nor would a two-parent family be likely to feel comfortable in a group of single mothers.

Third, for the groups to function effectively, the participants must be able to attend regularly. Some parents, because of jobs or other commitments, are forced to schedule appointments on a week-by-week basis. These families should not be seen in a group. Otherwise you will find yourself squeezing in makeup sessions to keep them abreast of the group; also, they are less likely to feel part of the group when they do attend.

The size of the group is also an important consideration. We recommend that you select between 6 and 10 members (3 to 5 couples for each group). Cohesiveness becomes more difficult if the group is larger, and participants may not have enough opportunities to talk, let alone get your personal attention.

The setting for group meetings does not have to be elaborate, but it should be comfortable, pleasant, and conducive to work. It should be large enough to seat everyone comfortably and still leave room for roleplaying. Since group meetings usually take 1½ to 2 hours, we recommend you have refreshments available and schedule a short break in the middle of the session. We have found that providing pastries or cookies makes the meeting more relaxed. After the first meeting, you may want to suggest that parents rotate responsibility for providing food.

In the remainder of this chapter, we discuss modifications in the treatment format and issues concerning the clinical skills used to conduct this program with groups. These two topics will be covered as they relate to each of the four treatment phases: pretreatment, intervention, generalization, and maintenance.

CONDUCTING A PRETREATMENT INTERVIEW

Even though you will be working with the parents in groups, you still need to meet each family individually to conduct an initial interview. During this interview you should follow the agenda provided in Chapter Four. When you reach the point where you describe the treatment, explain that you would like to work with them in a group of four to eight other parents. Emphasize that working this way will give them an opportunity to meet other parents who share many of their concerns. Also, other parents will benefit from their experiences, and, hopefully, they will find out from others what works and doesn't work in child management.

You will need to allay their anxieties about what the group will and will not be. You should explain that unlike typical group therapy, no one will be put on the spot or asked to discuss their "innermost thoughts or feelings." Rather, it will be task oriented; they will be learning new skills to help their children and themselves. You should mention that if you or they feel they need to meet with you individually, private sessions will be arranged. Finally, discuss when the group will start, how long sessions will last (1½ to 2 hours), what the schedule will be, and how many meetings are involved (usually 10 to 12). While weekly sessions are most common, groups have been scheduled to meet twice weekly. Whatever you propose, be sure to stress the importance of regular attendance.

It is important not to wait too long after the initial interview to start the group. If after 2 weeks there are not enough families to form a group, we strongly suggest that you either begin individual treatment immediately or proceed with a smaller group.

DEVELOPING THE INTERVENTION

During the initial interview, you should have begun building a positive relationship with each of the parents. In the first group session your goal should also be to facilitate the development of such a relationship among group members. Most people will hesitate to share their concerns and suggestions unless they feel comfortable with and accepted by other group members. One simple way of beginning the group is to have each parent introduce and say something unique about him or herself. We often start this process by disclosing something humorous about ourselves. This technique can be a good ice breaker and set people at ease. There are several other techniques that build group cohesiveness and promote interactions.

1. *Encourage group members to direct their comments to the group rather than to you.* This may require active directing, as in this example:

TH: Just a second, Julie, let me stop you for a moment. I'd like to encourage you to tell the group rather than me what's been going on in your family and what you and your husband will be working on, OK?

2. *Draw connections between different group members.* In the following example, the therapist relates one parent's experiences to those of another couple.

TH: Thanks, Julie, for sharing that. You know, I believe Bill and Carol have had some similar experiences in their family. Bill or Carol, maybe you'd like to respond to what Julie just said with some of the things you've been experiencing.

3. *Refrain from giving all the answers; instead encourage others to offer suggestions.* This point is a variation on several of the points for promoting independence made earlier in the clinical skills chapter.

This technique also serves to bring the group closer. In the following example, the therapist calls on the group to answer a parent's question.

CL: (To therapist) I don't know what to do when Billy refuses to go to time-out. How should I handle it?

TH: A good question. Well, parents, what should she do? What do you suggest?

4. *Reinforce participants for sharing or acting as a resource.* Many parents will wait for signals from you regarding how active a role to take; therefore, you should acknowledge and thank those individuals who are willing to share their experiences openly, listen attentively to others, and offer relevant solutions to problems.

5. *Develop a phone network.* In a phone network, each person (or couple) is assigned one or two other people (or couples) to call during the week. In the case of two-parent families, each spouse makes one call. In turn, each person or couple receives two calls during the week. This process is called "Check in, Check up, Check out." *Check in* refers to checking in with other parents and reinforcing them to stay on task with weekly assignments or work. *Check up* means checking up on how the family has been following the program during the week, while *check out* refers to checking out any problems or concerns that have arisen and then helping the family problem solve them when necessary.

In addition to the network calls families receive, you should phone each family twice a week to review their monitoring forms and provide assistance or coaching. Your first call should take place within 2 days of the group meeting to make sure that parents have started off well. The second call should come just prior to the next meeting. You can collect information from their monitoring forms for the past week and address any personal concerns they may have. This procedure will save valuable time during the review part of the next group meeting. Also, during calls, check to be sure parents have been calling the other parents in the group, as assigned. As weeks go by, it may be good to rotate phone call assignments so that all group members have an opportunity to work with each other during the course of treatment.

For the most part, when conducting each of the intervention sessions, you should follow the agendas provided in Chapters Five through Nine. However, instead of presenting a variety of techniques from which each parent can choose (time-out, Grandma's Law, work chores), you will select and teach only those techniques that seem most appropriate for the presenting concerns of the entire group. For example, with a group of parents whose major problem is their children's thefts, you might teach them to (a) set up for success by increasing adult supervision, (b) require their children to do extra chores whenever they're caught stealing or possessing something for which they can't prove ownership, or (c) set up an allowance system if the children have no legitimate way to purchase items.

Although all of the parents in the group will share some common concerns and be taught the same techniques, each parent may be particularly deficient in certain skills. For example, one parent may not know how to give clear commands, while another may not be able to provide effective consequences. As a result, you will need to note each person's strengths and weaknesses, making sure you give adequate instruction and supervision to individuals in their area of greatest need. You may have to provide additional clarification, roleplaying, phone contacts, and, in some cases, a home visit for personalized instruction and feedback. In addition, since most people will enter treatment with some effective parenting skills and others will readily pick up on certain techniques, you will want to tap these people as group resources whenever possible. For example, during roleplays, you can pair a person who seems competent in a given area with one who is having a problem grasping the skill. You may also link these people in the phone network for that week.

As stated earlier, when covering setting up for success, self-control, discipline, and reinforcement with groups, we recommend that you focus on only one or two of the techniques described in each chapter. However, when conducting the session on communication skills, you should cover all the skills mentioned in Chapter Nine. Both single parent and two-parent family groups can benefit from learning these skills, as they will use them when talking with their children. In addition, in two-parent families, spouses will need these skills when solving future family problems together.

TEACHING GENERALIZATION

Once the group has been taught to apply the basic techniques described in Chapters Five through Nine, they should have experienced a reduction in targeted behaviors and an increase in other, more desirable behaviors. The parents are ready to begin applying these skills to other child or family problems. In this phase of treatment, parents are taught to use problem-solving steps to develop a complete intervention around a novel problem.

Give each person a copy of the handout titled "Problem Solving." Review the steps for problem solving with the entire group before they begin to develop a new intervention. In the case of two-parent families, also briefly review the communication skills, since they will be asked to concentrate on these while problem solving and negotiating solutions with their spouses. In addition, have each parent identify at least one communication skill from each of the three areas (nonverbal, verbal, and patterns to avoid) to be focused on during that session.

To decide which problem to tackle next, parents should refer back to their original Goal Setting Form. If any of the concerns listed on that form are still problems, they should choose one for the next intervention. If they decide to work on a new problem that was not listed previously, they should add it to the form.

Once the parents have chosen a problem, they should follow the problem-solving steps on the handout and begin to develop an intervention. When working with two-parent groups, it's best to have each couple develop their own intervention and proposed plan of action. In single-parent groups, parents can work either individually or work in pairs.

As the parents are developing their interventions, you and your cotherapist, if one is available, should circulate from person to person or from couple to couple to make sure each one understands the task and is applying the techniques appropriately. Answer any questions that arise. In the case of two-parent groups, monitor each couple's use of the communication skills, paying particular attention to those skills they have chosen to focus on. Remember, your objective is to encourage each pair in turn and give the two of them feedback on how *they* are developing the intervention; if they're stuck, don't fall into the trap of doing the work for them. Rather, guide them through the steps of problem solving, prompting *them* to generate ideas.

If time allows at the end of the session, ask one or two individuals to share their planned interventions with the group. Sharing interventions can be extremely valuable. It exposes parents to a variety of ways the techniques can be applied to problems, and it provides them with feedback regarding their plans and encouragement to carry the plans out. While some parents at first may be nervous about sharing their plans with the group, they will relax if they see that the group is supportive.

In order to monitor each family's progress over the phone, you will need to have a copy of each person's proposed intervention plan. When setting up the weekly phone network for single parents, you may want to assign those who were paired off during the session to call each other. In this way, the callers will be familiar with the other person's program, enabling them to ask specific and pertinent questions. Rearrange the phone network each week so that parents have a chance to work with everyone in the group.

While parents will often use generalization sessions to develop new interventions, these sessions can also be used to revise previous programs. Revisions may be necessary either because a program is not working or because it *is* working and the parents want to increase their child's criterion performance level or begin to fade out the formal program. In either case, the parents should spend session time problem solving effective ways to accomplish their goals.

Finally, after the parents have had practice developing several interventions on their own during sessions, they should pick a new problem to work on. Their assignment should be to problem solve and develop an intervention at home. These interventions can be critiqued by the group at the next meeting.

INITIATING TERMINATION AND FOLLOW-UP

As mentioned previously, we recommend that the group meet for 10 to 12 sessions. This allows 5 sessions to teach the basic social learning concepts and 5 to 7 generalization sessions. Most families will have reached their treatment goals by this time. However, some families may need to continue meeting with you individually to solidify and maintain treatment gains.

We also strongly urge you to make several follow-up phone calls to each family, and, if group members seem amenable, to continue the group phone network for a few months (although calls can be scheduled less frequently). This can give parents added support and incentive to continue using the skills they learned in the group. In addition, as when working with parents and children in a nongroup setting, it is advisable to have a follow-up session. You should plan to reconvene the group in 3 to 6 months for a booster session.

Chapter Fourteen

SPECIAL PRESENTING PROBLEMS

The program described in this book is flexible and comprehensive enough to be applied across a wide range of presenting problems. Nonetheless, there are certain problems that present particular difficulties. In this chapter, we discuss how the program can be modified to help treat the following problems:

1. Children engaging in covert behaviors: setting fires, stealing, lying.
2. Children who are impulsive or hyperactive.

SETTING FIRES, STEALING, AND LYING

Setting fires and stealing are particularly frustrating behaviors for parents, not only because of their relative seriousness, but because they usually occur in secret. Thus consequences cannot be applied immediately. Lying also falls into this category because it is rarely obvious that a child is not telling the truth. Despite these obstacles, however, covert behaviors can be addressed within the general approach described.

The treatment of setting fires, stealing, and lying follows the same format used for other misbehaviors:

1. Specify the child's inappropriate behavior.
2. Alter the environment to reduce the likelihood the misbehavior will occur.
3. Increase parental self-control skills to help parents manage the behavior effectively.
4. Select negative consequences for specific misdeeds.
5. Provide positive reinforcement of competing or alternative pro-social behaviors.
6. Improve communication skills and positive interaction among all family members.

We have found that the following modifications in the basic treatment program have helped reduce or eliminate instances of setting fires, stealing, and lying.

Clear Identification of the Problem

When stealing, lying, or setting fires is the concern of the parents or the referring agent, take time to assess the extent of the problem. If the child is quite young or if there have been only one or two incidents, you will probably not want to follow the program described here. For example, children referred for lying who have not yet learned to tell fact from fiction or who tell big stories just to get their parents' attention would not be appropriate candidates for this intervention. In these cases, parents should be taught to help the children learn the difference between truth and fantasy by giving them clear explanations, paying little attention to fanciful stories, and attending to and praising telling the truth. A similar approach would be used for young children who have had only one or two stealing incidents. The parents should explain that stealing is wrong; the children should then return the item to its rightful owner.

If the problem is more serious, the first step is to specify exactly what will be considered as stealing, setting fires, or lying. We strongly recommend that these definitions include not only the specific misbehavior but also behaviors or events that would be likely to raise parental suspicions as well. Without such an all-inclusive definition, parents often find themselves suspecting their child of something they can't prove. They are then put in the position of playing detective and inquisitor. Likewise, the child is left under a lingering cloud of suspicion, often with no alternative but to lie. While the exact wording will depend on each family's need, typical definitions include:

Stealing

1. Taking anything, regardless of its value, that is not theirs.
2. Possessing any item for which they cannot prove ownership. This would include things that are "borrowed" and "found."
3. Being present when someone else steals anything.
4. Being accused of stealing something and not being able to have their presence elsewhere verified by a trustworthy person.

Setting fires

1. Setting fires, no matter how small.
2. Playing with matches.
3. Having matches or a lighter.
4. Being present when someone else lights a fire or plays with matches.
5. Not being able to account for their presence and have their location verified by a trustworthy person during a time when a fire was set.

Lying

1. Outright lying.
2. Telling a half-truth or leaving out an important part of the story.
3. Telling a highly improbable story.

Once a definition is established, it should be made clear that the parents are the sole judges of whether the behavior in question meets the criteria described in the definition. Remind parents that if they *suspect* something, they should not put the child in a position where lying is the only way out (don't ask "Did you steal this?" or "How did you get this?"). Rather, they should present their suspicions and proceed to act on them. If the child protests innocence, parents should attempt to verify the youngster's account (ask for a receipt, call the school to see why the child was "let out early"). If that is not possible, or the parents still are not satisfied, they should carry through with the consequence. Though the parents may be wrong at times, the important point is that the burden of proof rests with the child, and not with the adult.

Setting Up for Success

Many children who steal or set fires are unsupervised for long periods of time. If this is the case, the amount of free time should be decreased while simultaneously requiring that children check in more frequently in the afternoon or weekends. Perhaps the children can be enrolled in some organized activities like scouting, Little League, or an after-school recreation program. If the parents work, arrangements should be made for the children to check in after school with a relative or neighbor, leave notes as to their whereabouts, or call their parents at work if possible.

Some children steal because it's the only way they can get the things they need. In these cases, enabling them to earn desired items by providing jobs or an allowance can help.

Finally, some children who steal or set fires appear to be socially withdrawn. Here a program to reinforce social interaction within and outside the home, coupled with participation in some structured group activities, can help children learn more appropriate forms of getting attention and recognition. Two programs you may wish to consult for teaching social skills to children are the PEERS program (Hops, 1982; Hops, Fleischman, Guild, Paine, Walker, & Greenwood, 1978) and the Structured Learning Approach described by Goldstein, Sprafkin, Gershaw, and Klein (1979).

Self-control

Teaching parents self-control skills should have a central place in this program. For specific procedures, review Chapter Six. While parents will differ in their internal dialogues, typical self-statements often include "catastrophizing" ("If this doesn't stop, he'll end up in jail"), worrying ("I just can't be sure if he took it"), and anger ("He's doing this out of pure hate"). Once these self-statements have been identified, help the parents develop alternative comments that affirm (a) they don't approve of the behaviors, (b) they are learning to deal effectively with the behaviors, and (c) the child will change.

Discipline

The usual consequence for stealing, setting fires, or lying is 1 or 2 hours of extra chores per incident, as described in Chapter Seven. For suspicious behavior, thefts of negligible value (under $1), or playing with matches, 1 hour is recommended; for more serious events, 2 hours. Until the child completes the work to the parents' satisfaction, *no* privileges should be given (friends, phone, food, TV). Once the work is done, privileges should be restored and the issue dropped.

Aside from the extra work, two other consequences should be applied after serious episodes. First, if someone (a neighbor, another family member, a storekeeper) is victimized by the event, the child should be made to meet that person, return what was taken, and apologize. Second, if the item is damaged or lost, the child should be prepared to make whole or partial restitution. Children who are not able to repay the entire cost can pay back a portion of the loss by working for pay or having money deducted from an allowance.

Reinforcement

Stealing, setting fires, and lying all raise certain difficulties regarding reinforcement. Because there is no assurance that all thefts, fires set, or lies will be detected, it is not recommended that the child be reinforced for not stealing, setting fires, or lying. Nonetheless, some form of reinforcement is important. Many families whose children steal, set fires, or lie have low levels of interaction, warmth, and closeness. To improve this picture and to give the parents something positive to attend to while conducting the program on stealing, setting fires, or lying, you will need to develop parallel programs to address other problems. Depending on the child and the parents' concerns, these additional programs can focus on doing more around the house (chores, getting along with siblings or peers), improving school performance (attendance, classroom behavior, homework), developing social behaviors (making friends, being more independent), or enhancing communication skills. While these programs probably will contain disciplinary procedures, they should also have elements that insure positive parental attention and reinforcement. If family members rarely do anything together, they should be helped to plan family activities. However, beware of overplanning or requiring that they conform to some idealized example of family life. Older children in particular are likely to prefer having more time with their peers. One or two brief weekday events or one weekend activity may be sufficient.

When working with families whose presenting problem is covert behavior, you will need to keep in close touch with the parents for at least 2 months. Without careful monitoring, parents may become less vigilant and overlook the recurrence of suspicious behaviors. Before terminating treatment for these families, there should be no reports of the suspicious behavior for at least 2 months. In addition, you should be confident that the parents will carry out the appropriate consequences should the misbehavior recur.

The following case involves a 9-year-old boy who was reported for three episodes of setting fires in 6 months. The boy was quiet, relatively timid, and had little self-confidence. He lived with his mother, a rather depressed and passive woman, and his two siblings, one of whom was handicapped. The mother was very concerned for all her children and overly protective and restrictive of her son in particular. Aside from setting fires and some problems in getting chores done, her son was relatively well behaved.

After an initial meeting with the parent and then the child, a simple treatment program was drawn up that included a definition of what constituted setting fires and the designation of extra chores as a consequence. Simultaneously, a chore program with an evening activity as reinforcement and an extra chore for not doing the assigned work was developed. Both programs ran smoothly with only one subsequent misbehavior—playing with matches. The mother, after first telephoning the therapist to seek direction and reassurance, provided the appropriate consequence.

With these components of the program in place, 6 more sessions were devoted to fostering positive interaction in the family and increasing the amount of responsibility placed on the boy. The mother's concerns about her son's safety outside her presence were dealt with by reviewing her self-talk and substituting thoughts that affirmed he was safe and that being allowed to play outside unsupervised was appropriate for a 9-year-old. To address the boy's shyness and lack of self-confidence, a program was set up whereby he reported daily to his mother something he had done that showed "courage," such as raising his hand to volunteer in class, jumping off the diving board in swimming class, and not running away from dogs. The mother was taught to reinforce these behaviors and to award points for the daily report. The points were then redeemable for time with the mother after the other children went to sleep. After 3 weeks the boy was given responsibility for filling out the point chart. Later, the formal chart was eliminated. There were no further instances of setting fires and the boy continued to show increased confidence. The mother reported she was satisfied with the child's new behavior and felt she could handle further problems.

TREATING IMPULSIVE AND HYPERACTIVE BEHAVIOR

In contrast to the delinquent behaviors of stealing, setting fires, and lying and the aggressive or oppositional behaviors of disobedience, defiance, and fighting are the behaviors grouped under the labels "impulsive" or "hyperactive." Whether youngsters exhibiting these behaviors are truly a distinct group from their more antisocial or aggressive peers is unclear (Achenbach, 1978; Achenbach & Edelbrock, 1978). While many so-called hyperactive and impulsive children are also control problems, their behavior is less characterized by the defiance and struggle for control typical of their more aggressive peers. Rather, the presenting problems of these children often include one or more of the following patterns.

The first includes children who find it hard to amuse themselves and instead constantly seek their parents' attention. While much of their interaction with parents may be relatively appropriate play or talk, the parents soon find even that disturbing since they have little relief from the constant demands on their time.

A second behavior pattern concerns children who frequently become overly upset when frustrated. We are not speaking of the angry or defiant outbursts some children exhibit when told to do something. Rather, we are concerned here with children who destroy property, cry, or scream in rage when little things do not go their way.

A third pattern relates to children who are extremely active, continually on the move, and invasive in their interactions with others. These are the children who "never sit still" and have unlimited amounts of energy.

A fourth pattern concerns children who are highly impulsive. They talk rapidly, act before thinking, and attempt to be at the center of activities. These children frequently are considered major problems by classroom teachers.

Again, we are not claiming that children with these problems are or are not different from others. We do want to emphasize that children exhibiting these conditions, including those formally diagnosed as "minimally brain damaged," "attention deficit," or "hyperactive," *may* benefit from the combination of parent training and family therapy set forth in this book.

In particular, this model is designed to treat children using methods other than the prescription of psychostimulant drugs. Drug treatment currently is the most widely used intervention for hyperactive children. This is not to say that medication is not helpful. Rather, we take the position that nonmedical approaches should be explored first, with medication used as a final resort and then as a supplement to family treatment. It has been our experience that once parents learn to manage their child's behavior more effectively, they report how much calmer and relaxed their youngster has become. The remainder of this chapter will discuss specific points to keep in mind when applying the basic program to this population.

Information-gathering for the Selection of Target Behaviors

Selection of the target behaviors for change should be based on the information gathered from the parents and child in the initial interview. If the parents describe their child as impulsive, attention seeking, or hyperactive, you should ask for specific descriptions of problem episodes to determine the exact behavior underlying the label. In discussing compliance-related behavior, pay particular attention not only to whether the child actually complies, but to the manner in which the youngster does so. It may appear that compliance occurs after a period of argument, or the child complies but does so in a begrudging or hostile manner. If so, you will want to target compliance, focusing on *how* the child complies as one of the behaviors for change. Thus, an appropriate expectation would be that the child "complies without arguing, whining, or complaining." Any resistance would be considered a noncompliance.

Besides investigating whether and how the child obeys direct commands, you should check the degree to which the child can play or work alone for reasonable periods of time. If the parents report this is a problem, find out if the child demands attention constantly or seeks attention at particular times, such as right after a parent comes home from work or when the parent is involved in another task (preparing dinner, tending an infant). If attention seeking or demanding is indeed a problem, you should establish the expectation that the child will learn to play or work independently for 15 to 30 minutes, depending on the child's age. This "solitary play" can occur either upon request or at a specific time during the day, for example, when the mother is preparing dinner.

Finally, you should investigate impulsive or explosive behaviors that are not related to compliance. Ask parents how the child handles frustration, and whether it results from coping with difficult tasks, delays, or disappointments. If this is an area of concern, useful expectations for a treatment program might include (a) the child's remaining calm when frustrated or under pressure, and (b) the child's working to solve whatever problem arises or (c) managing to cope so the situation doesn't become worse.

After you and the parents discuss the child's behavior, it's important to spend time with the child. You might have the child sit in with the parents during the intake interview. This would enable you to observe the child in a situation the youngster would probably find boring. You can then see how the child and the parents handle the situation.

In addition to observing the child in the interview, we also recommend that you watch the youngster play alone. Make sure toys are available so you can observe how the child spends the playtime. If a teacher referred the child for treatment, visit the classroom to observe how the youngster acts when with the teacher and others and when doing individual, in-class work.

In summary, based on careful gathering of information, you will want to design a program either to (a) improve compliance, (b) increase independent play, (c) increase skill in coping with frustration, or (d) any combination of these behaviors. It should be noted that a program combining components to improve compliance and increase independent play was reported by Wahler and Fox (1980) to be highly effective with aggressive, oppositional children ages 5 to 8.

Setting Up for Success

If increased compliance is one of the target behaviors, then teaching the parents how to give better commands will increase the likelihood that the child will obey them. See Chapter Five for a review of the steps in giving good commands.

To increase independent play, you might want to make sure the child has a variety of age-appropriate toys and activities to play with alone. Building sets, crayons, paper, Play Doh, children's records, and books are all popular. You should also determine whether there is a place the child can play and still keep the parents in sight. A child who seeks a lot of attention will probably have a harder time playing independently if it involves going to a separate room.

Much is made these days about the role diet plays in our behavior. Scientific evidence is still equivocal here, particularly regarding the effect of certain additives on hyperactivity in children. Until more is known, we suggest that you be guided by common sense. Children should receive balanced meals, consume sugar only in moderation, and avoid caffeine, which is found in many soft drinks and in chocolate. Checkups with physicians are encouraged and their suggestions regarding diet are to be followed.

Finally, when considering steps for setting up for success, you should be aware that children who do not tolerate frustration well usually benefit if their lives can be made more regular and predictable. You might want to discuss with the parents establishing routines and schedules for waking, eating meals, bathing, going to bed, and the like. Often we find that the internal chaos a child experiences is a reflection of the entire family's situation. Regulating the lives of all family members can help them take great strides toward a more harmonious lifestyle. It's difficult to have a calm child when the child's world lacks structure.

Parental Self-control

In our experience, even the most reasonable parents become frustrated, angry, and tense when faced with the daily chores of coping with a demanding, impulsive, or hyperactive child. For these parents, and those who are less emotionally stable, learning the self-control procedures described in Chapter Six is extremely valuable. It not only enables them to apply other components of the program more effectively, but it provides immediate benefits for the parents' own mental health. Teaching self-control methods to impulsive children is also crucial. Procedures for working directly with the children are presented later in the chapter.

Discipline

The disciplinary responses of withholding attention and time-out are particularly effective for dealing with impulsiveness, demanding or seeking attention, and hyperactivity. Withholding attention is beneficial since the parents often unknowingly reinforce frequent but minor behaviors that can be extinguished if ignored. You will need to demonstrate this procedure carefully and closely supervise the parents' performance. Effective training almost always requires some in-home teaching. If this is not possible, the child should be brought to the treatment facility, given some toys, and instructed to play alone. You can then coach the parents as to when to attend to and when to ignore what the child is doing.

Time-out is valuable not only because it stops the behavior immediately, but also because it gives both the parents and the child a few minutes to settle down. Be certain to monitor both the frequency with which time-outs are given and their duration, as some parents may use extended time-outs as a way of gaining peace and quiet. Should this appear to be happening, it is also important to develop a program to increase the child's independent play.

Reinforcement

One of the features of this program is to redefine problems in terms of a lack of certain prosocial behaviors such as complying appropriately, playing independently, and demonstrating self-control. This approach plays down the negative and emphasizes a positive, skill-building view while pointing to a set of behaviors that can be reinforced. Reinforcement can be provided by any of the procedures or combinations of procedures described in Chapter Eight.

You should bear in mind that children exhibiting impulsive behaviors tend to be fairly immature regardless of age. For this reason, make sure that backup reinforcers are delivered soon after they are earned. These children will respond better if rewards or privileges are not delayed too long.

Self-control for Impulsive Children

A variety of procedures are available for teaching self-control skills to children. Some have been developed specifically for use in a school setting, while others may be used individually or in groups (Kendall & Hollon, 1979).

A specific self-control technique you may want to consider is the Turtle Technique. Originally designed as a self-control method for children experiencing classroom learning problems, the procedures can be applied to a variety of children with many types of concerns. A more extensive presentation of the Turtle Technique is given in Schneider and Robin (1976) and from the *Turtle Manual.*[*]

Basically, Turtle involves teaching children four steps. The first step is learning to respond to the cue "turtle." When you or the parents say the word "turtle" the children are to respond by closing their eyes, pulling their arms close to their bodies, putting their heads down, and curling up like a turtle pulling into its shell. This will need to be practiced until the children can respond quickly to the cue.

The second stage of the Turtle process is learning to relax while pulled into the turtle position. Relaxation training may take several forms. Chapter Six presents relaxation methods for adults that can be adapted to children. Another method is to have the children tense all their muscles while in the turtle position, hold the tension for a few seconds, then relax all their muscles at once. As therapist, you will need to monitor whether the children are, indeed, relaxed. Thus, in the second stage, when children hear the word "turtle," they will first assume the turtle position and then relax as completely as possible.

The third step of the Turtle Technique is to teach children alternative problem-solving strategies. For this, you will need to help them identify problem areas. For each problem area, several alternatives are discussed with the children, and the consequences of each alternative are considered. They are then taught to identify the alternative with the best results. If you are going to ask parents to help you institute the Turtle self-control procedure, you may have to teach the children problem-solving steps similar to those that the parents have learned:

1. What's my goal?

---

[*]Available from the Point of Woods Laboratory School, Department of Psychology, State University of New York, Stony Brook, New York 11794.

2. What am I doing now?

3. Is what I'm doing helping me to achieve my goal?

4. If it isn't, what do I need to do differently? List several choices.

5. Which is the best choice?

At the third stage, children are required to pull into the position, relax, and begin the problem-solving steps.

The fourth step is to incorporate the Turtle process into family practice around the house. Just as children learn to do time-out at a simple hand signal, so they can learn to do the Turtle exercise just from the cue word "turtle." However, to maintain the new behavior, parents will need to praise their children for doing the procedure well.

Most often the Turtle Technique is introduced to children in the form of a story:

TH: So, sometimes mom and dad may tell you to do something, and when you don't do it, they begin to get angry. When this happens, you start to get mad because you think they are picking on you. A good thing to remember at those times is how a turtle handles conflict. Do you know how a turtle behaves when it gets in trouble? It pulls into its shell, doesn't it? Let me tell you about one turtle that used to get in trouble a lot. His name was Timmy, Timmy the Turtle.

Timmy used to do things around the house, and sometimes those things were OK and he and his mom and dad got along just fine. But sometimes Timmy would forget to do the things his parents wanted, and they would get upset with him and start fussing. That would upset Timmy, and he'd get mad and start fussing back, and pretty soon the house would be full of fussing turtles. You can just imagine how noisy that would be!

Well, one day Timmy was told to pick up his toys before he could play outside. Well, Timmy forgot...you know how turtles can forget sometimes. And he started playing with a friend. Then he heard his mom calling him, and he decided he'd run away because he just didn't want to be fussed at again. So he ran away, or at least as fast as turtles can run, which of course isn't very fast.

As he lumbered down the road, he came across Old Mr. Tortoise, the wisest turtle in the area. Mr. Tortoise saw Timmy and asked him why he looked so sad. Timmy told Mr. Tortoise what had happened, and explained that sometimes he would just get so mad that he didn't know what to do. Then Timmy would start yelling at his parents and get in really bad trouble.

Mr. Tortoise smiled and said that he could understand that, because a long time ago, before he became so wise, he also would get upset and angry and just blurt out things that would get him in trouble. Timmy was surprised about this and asked him how he learned not to do that. Mr. Tortoise said, "Well, Timmy, I just learned to use my natural protection...my shell." Mr. Tortoise went on to tell Timmy that the way he handled conflicts was to pull into his shell, breathe deep and relax...calm down a little. Then he would think about the predicament he was in and decide how he could handle it. He would come up with about four or five ideas and then figure out what would happen if he did each one of those things. Finally he would choose the best one for him and act on it. That's how he got to be so wise.

Well, Timmy was really excited about that idea. So he ran, as fast as turtles can run, back home; and when he got there he heard his mom calling out in an angry voice. Timmy went to her and told her he was sorry for running away, but he had talked with Mr. Tortoise and Mr. Tortoise had told him how to handle things better. He said "Watch!" and he pulled into his shell, relaxed, and came out smiling. Then he picked up the toys like he was told to do earlier. Timmy kept practicing pulling into his shell, relaxing, and considering a plan on how to handle things until he got really good at it. Then he and his mom and dad stopped getting so upset. In fact, his mom and dad started practicing doing the same thing when they got upset because they knew that if Mr. Tortoise had told Timmy about it, it must be good. And they all got a lot happier living together.

Well, what do you think...does that sound like something you could use? I have a feeling it is, so what I'd like to do now is have us practice it, practice being like turtles.

Techniques other than Turtle may be used. If you decide to work with the child on classroom disturbances, you will want to look over several of the procedures for classroom teachers reviewed in the Kendall and Hollon (1979) text.

Chapter Fifteen

DIFFICULT CLINICAL POPULATIONS

Child rearing is stressful even for middle-income, two-parent families. Investigations consistently reveal that marital satisfaction declines after the birth of the first child (Bram, 1974; Feldman, 1971; Glenn & Weaver, 1978; Houseknecht, 1979; Renne, 1970; Ryder, 1973) and rebounds after the last child leaves (Burr, 1970; Rollins & Cannon, 1974). For client families, the stress is even greater because of more severe parent-child conflicts. Personal problems, poverty, or being a single parent often serve to compound the situation. As a result, such families not only are more likely to experience problems with their children (Hollingshead & Redlich, 1958) but they traditionally fare poorly in treatment (Hersch, 1968; Overall & Aronson, 1963).

Even within the restricted domain of behavioral or social-learning-oriented parent training programs, there is growing consensus that these clients are harder to work with. In a survey of 16 such parent training programs, it was reported that approximately 40% of the families had serious difficulty in acquiring and maintaining the skills taught (O'Dell, 1982). This fact, which parallels our own experience in working with such families, has motivated us to pay more attention to increasing the therapist's effectiveness with this population. For the remainder of this chapter, we will outline various procedures and tactics we have found helpful. We also have included a brief discussion regarding use of this program when child abuse is one of the presenting problems.

REDUCING PRETREATMENT ATTRITION

The first problem therapists face in working with this population is the large percentage of clients who fail to follow through after the initial request for help. Hunt (1961), for example, found that 24% of the families who applied to a child guidance clinic quit during intake. Of those families who did complete intake and were considered appropriate, 18% refused the treatment offered. It is also true that many of the families who are referred but refuse to participate in treatment are likely to be the least cooperative and most frustrating to the therapist who has to work with them. Bernal & Kreutzer (1976) found that excuses clients make during the intake period can be a significant predictor of later problems in cooperation.

Nonetheless, a large portion of these families will have demonstrated a real need for services. They often have serious problems with their children and lack the resources to resolve these problems on their own. For this reason, pretreatment attrition has been referred to as the "Achilles' heel" of the community mental health movement. Fortunately, there are steps that you can take to reduce pretreatment attrition for families who have demonstrated their need for services. We would like to acknowledge the suggestions of Dr. Steven Szykula and the staff at the Helena Family Teaching Center. In their experience, once these procedures were instituted, pretreatment attrition was cut in half (Szykula, Fleischman, & Shilton, 1982).

While the Helena group made many of the suggestions put forth in this chapter, the one they felt was most important was having the referral agent serve as an extended member of the treatment team. Thus referral agents, whether they were the family's physician, a school teacher or counselor, or a caseworker, were asked not only to make the referral but to introduce the family to the therapist and participate in an initial "get-acquainted" meeting. If family members elected to enter treatment, the referral agent was then kept abreast of their progress. Referral agents were also asked to express an ongoing interest in the family's treatment progress during subsequent contacts. If family members withdrew prematurely, the referral agent was asked to help them reestablish contact with treatment.

DEVELOPING YOUR RELATIONSHIP-BUILDING AND OTHER CLINICAL SKILLS

Clients will not remain in treatment unless they experience a client-therapist relationship in which they feel cared for, understood, and supported. In addition, they must believe you are competent. Low-income and single-parent families are usually particularly skeptical about the worth and skill of therapists. Thus, you will need to spend time carefully building a relationship and becoming sensitive to their needs. You will have to take extra care when explaining what treatment is and what it requires of them. Because they tend to have more problems implementing the program at home, you should focus special attention on preproblem solving. Finally, remember that they will most likely carry out the program if you indicate you expect them to. You can communicate this expectation by the way you present assignments, by the fact that you will be monitoring their performance, and by responding to difficulties with problem solving techniques rather than encouraging excuses.

Some of the most difficult families to work with are those who do not want to be in treatment but have been referred under the order of some third party. This may include families whose children have (a) experienced considerable difficulty in school, (b) had trouble with the law and been ordered by a juvenile court to come for family therapy, or (c) have exhibited signs of abuse and have been referred by a welfare or child protection agency. These families generally approach therapy with a hesitant, defensive, and often angry or even openly hostile attitude.

When beginning with a hostile family referred by an outside agency or under legal sanction to seek treatment, you will need to keep two points in mind. First, family members are probably doing the best they can given the circumstances of their lives. Your job is to help them change the circumstances, to teach them more effective ways to deal with each other. Second, responsibilty for resolving their problems resides with them, not you. Thus, you should not react to their hostility by becoming defensive. Rather, present the program as clearly and supportively as you can, then request their cooperation with the program. If they refuse or respond aggressively, draw them back to their problem. For example:

TH: So that's what the program involves. Again, it will take us about 3 months, and it will require some effort on your part each day to try out the things I'll be teaching you.

FATHER: (In a hostile tone) Yes, I understand all that. But just why the hell should we do all this?

TH: Good question. First, as you said, you've been having difficulty getting your children to mind. I think we can help you with that. Second, the problem seems to be getting worse and it's likely to keep on getting worse unless you do something about it now. Third, Child Protective Services is going to press formal charges if you don't try to make some changes in your family. I can help you make those changes, if you want; or we can decide to do nothing for now and risk having your children removed from your home. I'd like to help prevent that, but only you can decide whether it's worth your time and effort. I guess you have to weigh your options. Which do you think you'd prefer?

USING PARENTING SALARIES AND OTHER TANGIBLE REINFORCERS

For many families, the promise of reaching their desired goals is not a sufficient reinforcer to maintain their initial performance in treatment. For these families, money or other tangible reinforcers can be highly effective in improving their performance. Fleischman (1979) reported on a study that compared the effects of a "parenting salary" on the performance of both middle-income, two-parent families and low-income and/or single-parent families. The parenting salary was $1 per day paid contingently for cooperation. Cooperation was assessed on the basis of whether the parents attempted the various tasks in the treatment. Performances were monitored during daily phone conversations with the parents and during weekly sessions. Assignments varied depending on the particular family and the phase of treatment but typically included such behaviors as observing the child, recording the number of rewards given, time-outs imposed, and the like. Instances of incorrectly performing assignments were not counted against the family but regarded as areas in which clients needed further instruction.

The results demonstrated that the parenting salary had a powerful impact on the performance of low-income and/or single-parent families. Previously, this group had cooperated only about 50% of the time; they now performed the assignments 85% of the time. Middle-income and/or two-parent families appeared to benefit less from the salary, possibly because their performance was already relatively high. Families in this group who received the salary performed at the 94% level versus 90% without it. The impact that salaries had on the attrition rate of the low-income families was particularly noticeable. All of the families who did not receive a salary failed to complete the program, while all of those who did receive a salary completed the program.

To persons who believe that benefits gained from therapy should be reward enough, the use of parenting salaries may seem unconventional. However, in our experience, families rarely, if ever, object to such a system, nor does it take away from their eventual accomplishments. Furthermore, families who drop out of treatment represent a considerable investment of therapist time with minimal benefits to the family. For the families who participated in the aforementioned study, the agency spent an average of $77 per family, the range being from $52 to $191. Taken from a financial perspective, if one includes in the cost of treatment staff salaries, agency overhead, and the social cost of failure, parenting salary monies seem to represent worthwhile expenditures. Another consideration for the use of a parenting salary with low-income parents is that treatment, even if free, usually involves some costs for carfare, baby-sitters, and the like. The ability to earn even a few dollars per week to cover these costs can make a real difference in their ability to attend sessions.

Parenting salaries are not the only form of tangible reinforcers that can be used. Indeed, some other alternatives may be even more effective. For example, a program applying the social learning intervention with groups of low-income parents reported for child abuse in Toronto, Canada, replaced parenting salaries with raffle tickets that were earned for performance of assignments. The tickets were then deposited in a drum and a winner was drawn at the next meeting. Prizes included coupons for two meals in a fast-food restaurant, two movie tickets, and money for baby-sitters. This type of procedure has additional advantages: (a) it is less costly than paying every family a dollar a day; (b) it can encourage certain types of appropriate family activities or give the parents an occasional break from their household and/or child care duties; and (c) it adds an element of fun. Interestingly, the group in Toronto reported that after approximately 3 weeks it was possible to fade the prizes, since the parents had discovered that their progress and the enjoyment of participating in the sessions were reward enough.

An alternative to a parenting salary is a breakage fee or deposit system. Eyberg and Johnson (1974) tested the effects of having parents pay twice the initial treatment fee and then charging instances of nonperformance against the parents' account. This procedure was also found to have an effect on parental performance, although not as marked as in the study by Fleischman (1979). The families in Eyberg and Johnson's study were more middle-class and therefore may have been less responsive to tangible reinforcement. The use of breakage fees, however, creates a problem with families who cannot afford to pay even for the initial treatment, let alone provide a deposit.

INCREASING THE PACE OF TREATMENT

At first glance, it would appear that accelerating the pace of treatment would not be an effective tactic in motivating difficult families. However, keep in mind that a major reinforcer for families is the change they see in their children's behavior. Families whose patience is thin or whose problems are oppressive, will probably drop out unless change is made rapidly. Thus, one way to encourage these families to remain in treatment is to speed up the scheduling of sessions. For example, a group recently conducted by one of the authors was scheduled for three meetings a week for 4 weeks.

There are several other advantages in developing an accelerated schedule. It reduces the need for between-session monitoring by the therapist. Second, particularly during summer when vacations tend to disrupt attendance, condensing treatment avoids the loss of momentum. Third, the rapid pace underscores the urgency of working on the problem and effecting a change.

Moving quickly is also important during intake. Many families seek treatment only when problems reach crisis level; if help is delayed and the problem temporarily subsides, they may lose interest in the treatment program. For this reason, we recommend that intake interviews be conducted as soon after the initial call as possible, and that treatment begin directly.

WORKING WITH SINGLE PARENTS IN GROUPS

As described in Chapter Thirteen, the program can be provided to clients either individually or in groups. Christensen, Johnson, Phillips, and Glasgow (1980) found both formats equally effective in changing child behavior, although treating families individually required approximately twice as much therapist time as the group format. Unfortunately, Christensen et al. (1980) provided no information indicating whether one of these treatment formats may have been more effective with a particular group of clients such as single-parent families or those experiencing greater stress in their daily lives. While we cannot offer any experimental proof in this regard, our experience would support using groups when working with single-parent families, particularly when the parent is socially isolated.

There are several reasons for making this recommendation. Although these points are covered in Chapter Thirteen, we have summarized them here as they apply to single parents. First, seeing some members of the group learn, apply, and succeed with the treatment procedures can serve to encourage the others. Simply being able to share one's successes and even setbacks works to overcome the sense of isolation and defeatism.

Second, a group format can facilitate the movement from therapist-led to client-led treatment. The principal way to foster independence is to have the client take the initiative in developing strategies or programs to address particular child behavior problems. With a group, if the individual cannot come up with any suggestions, you can solicit other members' ideas. Surprisingly, parents who can't seem to generate their own programs often can help others with their problems. Eventually, the parents should be able to function more independently. In the meantime, the presence of the group allows you to take the first step toward making someone else a resource for solutions.

Third, the behavior of parents in a group conforms to the same laws of reinforcement that shape our behavior in other settings. If parents can gain attention and recognition by acting helpless or contrary, those behaviors will increase. On the other hand, if such behaviors are tactfully ignored and participation is supported, parents will perform more effectively. A group setting allows you to shift your attention from parent to parent to maximize appropriate group behavior. The advantage for parents is that in the long run they get more out of treatment.

The fourth advantage of the group format is the social outlet it provides for single parents. Allowing time at the end of each session for socializing, providing coffee and pastry at the first meeting and asking someone else to bake something for the next meeting, sharing phone numbers and use of a phone network, and encouraging parents to form car pools will further develop social interaction. Also, because the treatment calls for only limited personal sharing as opposed to more in-depth self-disclosure, group cohesiveness tends to develop rapidly.

MAKING SPECIAL ARRANGEMENTS

Low-income and single parents have particular burdens that create obstacles to their participation. Their concerns about housing, health care, legal matters, and employment often require therapists to extend their help beyond the target child behavior problems. For example, you may find yourself assuming the role of caseworker *and* therapist and devoting session time or special sessions to providing information on available services.

Another problem faced by low-income families and single parents in particular is the need for child care while the parent or parents attend the program. Some agencies equip a room with suitable toys and games to occupy the children during therapy meetings. A less satisfactory but still workable arrangement is to have toys in your office for young children to play with while you talk to their parents.

The best solution, particularly in working with groups, is to arrange for outside child care. If funds are not available, you might consider having each parent pay a small fee and pooling the money to hire a baby-sitter.

You also need to be flexible regarding the time and place of meetings. Often working parents can meet only in the evenings or on weekends. Families who lack adequate transportation may have difficulty traveling to your office. Holding treatment in a neighborhood church or school will make it easier for parents to attend and give you a greater appreciation of their living conditions. You will also be more visible in the community, a definite asset in building your credibility and making your services known to those who may need them most.

REDUCING STRESS

For overly stressed parents, there are several ways you can reduce the pressures, particularly those arising from child rearing. In Chapter Fourteen, we discussed interventions to help the demanding or attention-seeking child play independently. For overburdened mothers, especially those with young children, knowing there will be times during the day when they will be free of demands can be immensely calming. For working parents, teaching their child to allow them 15 to 30 minutes of peace when they first arrive home can also lower stress and set the stage for a calmer evening.

Much of the work on stress reduction can come under the guise of setting up for success. Chapter Five presents several suggestions in this area such as planning for the parents to have a night out; getting parents to trade off some of the child-management chores; and putting parents in touch with personal growth, educational, or vocational development programs, and various self-help groups. These techniques often mean dealing with parents' emotional reservations ("I wouldn't feel comfortable doing that," "My child needs me") and with practical issues (money, baby-sitting). You can approach money and child care problems by helping to set up a baby-sitting cooperative. In this arrangement, each parent in the group is given 20 coupons. Then, for each half hour of baby-sitting parents provide for others, they are paid one coupon. These coupons can then be exchanged for child care as they need it. The advantage is that the system doesn't cost anything, and it helps keep families in touch with each other.

DESIGNING TASKS AROUND CLIENTS' LIMITATIONS

Especially with difficult families, you need to follow the specific recommendations and cautions listed for each of the procedures described in this book. For example, stressed or anger-prone parents will find it difficult to withhold attention from their children's noxious but harmless behavior. As a result, time-out is a more appropriate technique for them to use. It has the double advantage of being effective and giving parents a chance to regain composure. Second, recognize and respect other demands placed on the clients. Do not make treatment all-consuming. Keep the assignments simple and the number of tasks to be monitored few. If a situation is coming up that may interfere with the parents' performance, adjust the effort required of them accordingly.

APPLYING SELF-CONTROL PROCEDURES

The self-control procedures (relabeling, self-talk, relaxation, stress reduction) are the primary means of preparing the overwrought parent to respond more effectively to the stresses of child rearing. As discussed in Chapter Six, these procedures can be used with parents who are depressed, anxious, stressed, and explosive.

With depressed parents, for instance, you can use self-control procedures to help them recognize their negative thoughts, develop more positive alternatives, and become more self-reinforcing. Keep in mind that when parents are learning to use child-management procedures, they should reinforce themselves simply for carrying out the tasks. As the procedures take effect, parents should be taught the importance of congratulating themselves on the changes they have achieved.

For anxious, stressed, and anger-prone parents, the relaxation exercises are especially beneficial. Parents who are so distressed that they cannot maintain their calm "under fire" can use relaxation exercises twice a day. Even after the parents have mastered the key treatment components and you begin to move towards generalization and termination, do not ignore these procedures. Monitor the use of them throughout and encourage the parents to see the importance of these components in coping with stress in a wide variety of settings.

REINFORCING CLIENT BEHAVIOR

Little needs to be added here about the importance of reinforcement in strengthening behavior. For depressed, anxious, or stressed clients, frequent and enthusiastic reinforcement from you is doubly important. One advantage of the program's structure is that it creates many opportunities to reinforce clients for behaviors such as carrying out assignments, roleplaying during the sessions, and proposing solutions to problems. Frequent between-session phone calls not only allow you to spot client performance problems before they become serious but provide more opportunities to reinforce the family.

Because your attention is often reinforcing in itself, exercise care about how you handle episodes of nonperformance. If the client does not attempt an assignment, or misapplies what you have taught, avoid being merely "supportive" without tactfully confronting the client about this behavior. Otherwise, the client will learn that your concern and support can be gained as readily for talking about problems as it can for performing, making performance even less likely. We find this pattern particularly applies to "agency-wise" parents, that is, parents who go from agency to agency without making any lasting changes. With *all* clients, you should respond to their lack of performance by first making sure they understood the assignment. If they didn't, reexplain and practice. If they understood but for some reason didn't attempt the assignment, probe for the reason. After pinpointing the difficulty, have them problem solve how they could overcome it or how the tasks might be modified to accommodate realistic limitations. Then be generous in reinforcing their efforts at problem solving.

WORKING WITH ABUSIVE FAMILIES

In recent years there has been a shift in thinking concerning the nature and treatment of child abuse. Now less emphasis is placed on psychiatric maladjustment of the parents and more attention is given to what has been termed "the ecology of child maltreatment" (Garbarino & Gilliam, 1980). This new concept is especially compatible with a social learning model, particularly as it relates to family intervention. In this approach, child abuse is viewed as the outgrowth of three factors: certain parental deficiencies, stress, and isolation.

The parental deficiencies include several already described: inadequate skill at managing stress, ignorance of normal child development and the resulting unrealistic expectations placed upon the child, lack of skill in teaching and encouraging appropriate behavior, and lack of effective alternatives to physical punishment to control the child. This last deficiency is especially important because of evidence that abused youngsters are more likely to be "difficult" and out of control (Reid & Taplin, 1977). Indeed, a large percentage of abuse incidents occur in the context of disciplinary episodes.

Stress in abusive families comes from many sources besides parent-child conflicts. Abusive parents frequently suffer from depression, anxiety, and problems controlling their anger. Problems within and outside the family such as marital conflicts, alcohol abuse, and difficulties with relatives, friends, and neighbors are also common. Finally, many abusive families suffer from obvious situational stresses including poverty, poor housing, employment problems, and single parenthood.

Isolation from friends, family, and community resources also plays a significant role in abusive families. Isolated parents have little respite from their children, which not only increases stress but means the child must meet many of the parents' social needs, a task for which the child is unprepared. Isolation also deprives parents of the opportunity to observe more effective parenting or to share information and concerns. Finally, isolation enables a family to hide parenting behavior that otherwise would not be condoned.

The program described in this book provides a sound plan for improving the self-control and child-management skills of these parents. In addition, once parents become more proficient at managing their children appropriately and the level of child-induced stress is reduced, the focus of treatment can be shifted to addressing situational stresses and overcoming isolation. While the specific contents of this latter intervention will depend on the client's particular circumstances, you should adhere to the instructional, problem-solving, and assignment-based format of the earlier phases of treatment.

One particularly important issue in working with abusive families is the relationship between yourself and the protective services worker, if one is involved. Therapists who have used this program within a protective services setting generally recommend that treatment be carried out by someone other than the worker responsible for investigating and monitoring the family. The reasons for this suggestion are twofold. First, the protective services worker is often called away for crisis work and court-related tasks and cannot provide the consistent teaching and supervision necessary to retrain the parents effectively. Second, the protective services worker may not be able to form a trusting relationship with the client because of the potential for legal sanctions inherent in the work. This is not to suggest that you should disregard your legal responsibility to report further abuse or to keep the protective services worker abreast of the clients' progress. Nonetheless, most caseworkers with whom we have worked report they prefer separating the responsibilities of the treatment agent and the protective services worker.

When treatment is provided by an individual or agency outside the protective services system, it is particularly important to keep the protective services worker well informed about the nature of treatment. The worker can then deal with any recurring crises in a way that builds upon what parents have learned rather than feeds their fear that they can't handle things themselves. Also, the worker needs to know which community resources clients have contacted during the latter phase of treatment so that the worker can help clients become more independent of the protective services system.

In conclusion, we suggest that abusive families should not be regarded as different from other families in conflict; it is only that their range of problems is often greater and the consequences more serious. Before applying this program to such families, we would suggest that you use it first with less disrupted families where progress is likely to come sooner and the results of failure are less potentially harmful. Once you are familiar with this program and comfortable administering it, you should find using this model to treat such a difficult population rewarding for both you and your client families.

References

Achenbach, T.M. The child behavior profile: I. Boys aged 6 through 11. *Journal of Consulting and Clinical Psychology*, 1978, *46*, 478–488.

Achenbach, T.M., & Edelbrock, C.S. The classification of child psychopathology: A review and analysis of empirical efforts. *Psychological Bulletin*, 1978, *85*, 1275–1301.

Alexander, J.F., Barton, C., Schiavo, R.S., & Parsons, B.V. Systems-behavioral intervention with families of delinquents: Therapist characteristics, family behavior, and outcome. *Journal of Consulting and Clinical Psychology*, 1976, *44*, 656–664.

Alexander, J.F., & Parsons, B.V. Short-term behavioral intervention with delinquent families: Impact on family process and recidivism. *Journal of Abnormal Psychology*, 1973, *31*, 219–225.

Arnold, J., Levine, A., & Patterson, G.R. Changes in sibling behavior following family intervention. *Journal of Consulting and Clinical Psychology*, 1975, *43*, 683–688.

Bahm, A.K., Chandler, C., & Eisenberg, L. *Diagnostic characteristics related to service on psychiatric clinics for children*. Paper presented at the Thirty-Eighth Annual Convention of Orthopsychiatry, Munich, Germany, 1961.

Bandura, A. *Principles of behavior modification*. New York: Holt, Rinehart & Winston, 1969.

Bandura, A. *Social learning theory*. Englewood Cliffs, N.J.: Prentice-Hall, 1977.

Barton, C., & Alexander, J.F. *Delinquent and normal family interaction in competitive and cooperative conditions*. Paper presented at the Annual Meeting of the American Psychological Association, New York, 1979.

Baumrind, D. Authoritarian versus authoritative parent control. *Adolescence*, 1968, *3*, 255–272.

Beck, A. *Depression: Causes and treatment*. Philadelphia: University of Pennsylvania Press, 1972.

Beck, D.F., & Jones, M.A. *Progress on family problems: A nationwide study of clients' and counselors' views on family agency services*. New York: Family Service Association of America, 1973.

Bernal, M.E., & Kreutzer, S.L. Relationship between excuses and dropout at a mental health center. *Journal of Consulting and Clinical Psychology*, 1976, *44*, 494.

Blechman, E.H. The Family Contract Game: A tool to teach interpersonal problem solving. *Family Coordinator*, 1974, *23*, 269–281.

Blechman, E.H., Olson, D.H., Schornagel, C.Y., Halsdorf, M., & Turner, A.J. The Family Contract Game: Technique and case study. *Journal of Consulting and Clinical Psychology*, 1976, *44*, 449–455.

Bram, S. *To have or have not: A social psychological study of voluntarily childless couples, parents-to-be, and parents.* Unpublished doctoral dissertation, University of Michigan, 1974.

Burr, W. Satisfaction with various aspects of marriage over the life-cycle. *Journal of Marriage and the Family,* 1970, *32,* 29–37.

Christensen, A., Johnson, S.M., Phillips, S., & Glasgow, R.E. Cost effectiveness in behavioral family therapy. *Behavior Therapy,* 1980, *11,* 208–226.

D'Augelli, A.R. Nonverbal behavior of helpers in initial helping interactions. *Journal of Counseling Psychology,* 1974, *21,* 360–363.

Dooley, D. Selecting nonprofessional counselor trainees with the Group Assessment of Interpersonal Traits (GAIT). *American Journal of Community Psychology,* 1975, *3,* 371–383.

D'Zurilla, T.J., & Goldfried, M.R. Problem solving and behavior modification. *Journal of Abnormal Psychology,* 1971, *78,* 107–126.

Ellis, A.A. *Reason and emotion in psychotherapy.* New York: Stuart, 1962.

Ellis, A.A. A cognitive approach to behavior therapy. *Interactional Journal of Psychotherapy,* 1969, *8,* 896–900.

Ellis, A.A., & Abrahms, E. *Brief psychotherapy in medicine and health practice.* New York: Springer, 1978.

Eyberg, S.M., & Johnson, S.M. Multiple assessment of behavior modification with families: Effects of contingency contracting and order of treated problems. *Journal of Consulting and Clinical Psychology,* 1974, *42,* 594–606.

Feldman, H. The effects of children on the family. In A. Michel (Ed.), *Family issues of employed women in Europe and America.* The Netherlands: E. Brill, 1971.

Flanagan, J.C. The critical incident technique. *Psychological Bulletin,* 1954, *51,* 327–358.

Fleischman, M.J. Using parenting salaries to control attrition and cooperation in therapy. *Behavior Therapy,* 1979, *10,* 111–116.

Fleischman, M.J. A replication of Patterson's "Intervention for boys with conduct problems." *Journal of Consulting and Clinical Psychology,* 1981, *49,* 342–351.

Fleischman, M.J. Social learning interventions for aggressive children: From the laboratory to the real world. *The Behavior Therapist,* 1982, *5,* 55–58.

Fleischman, M.J., & Szykula, S.A. A community setting replication of a social learning treatment for aggressive children. *Behavior Therapy,* 1981, *12,* 115–122.

Forehand, R.L., & McMahon, R.J. *Helping the noncompliant child.* New York: Guilford Press, 1981.

Garbarino, J., & Gilliam, G. *Understanding abusive families.* Lexington, Mass.: Lexington Books, 1980.

Glasser, W. *Reality therapy.* New York: Harper & Row, Colophon, 1965, 1975.

Glenn, N., & Weaver, C. A multivariate, multisurvey study of marital happiness. *Journal of Marriage and the Family,* 1978, *40,* 269–282.

Goldstein, A., Sprafkin, R., Gershaw, J., & Klein, P. *Skillstreaming the adolescent.* Champaign, Ill.: Research Press, 1979.

Goodman, G. *Companionship therapy: Studies in structured intimacy.* San Francisco: Jossey-Bass, 1972.

Gottman, J., Notarius, C., Gonso, J., & Markman, H. *A couples' guide to communication.* Champaign, Ill.: Research Press, 1976.

Haase, R.F., & Tepper, D. Nonverbal components of empathic communication. *Journal of Counseling Psychology,* 1972, *19,* 417–424.

Herbert, E.W., Pinkston, E.M., Hayden, M.L., Sajewaj, T.E., Pinkston, S.,

Cordua, G., & Jackson, C. Adverse effects of parental attention. *Journal of Abnormal Psychology*, 1973, *6*, 15–30.

Herman, B., Passmore, J., & Horne, A. *Treating cognitively impulsive children using academic materials and peer models*. Paper presented at the Ninetieth Annual Convention of the American Psychological Association, Washington, D.C., 1982.

Hersch, C. The discontent explosion in mental health. *American Psychologist*, 1968, *23*, 497–506.

Hollingshead, A.B., & Redlich, F.C. *Social class and mental illness: A community study*. New York: John Wiley, 1958.

Hops, H. Social skills training for isolated children. In P. Karoly & J. Steffen (Eds.), *Enhancing children's competencies*. Lexington, Mass.: Lexington Books, 1982.

Hops, H., Fleischman, D.H., Guild, J.J., Paine, S.C., Walker, H.M., & Greenwood, C.R. *PEERS: Procedures for establishing effective relationship skills*. Eugene, Oreg.: CORBEH (University of Oregon), 1978.

Horne, A. Aggressive behavior in normal and deviant members of intact versus mother-only families. *Journal of Abnormal Child Psychology*, 1981, *9*, 283–290.

Horne, A., & Fuelle, J. *Problem-solving interactional patterns of impulsive and reflective children and their mothers*. Paper presented at the Fifteenth Annual Convention of the Association for the Advancement of Behavior Therapy, Toronto, Canada, 1981.

Houseknecht, S. Childlessness and marital adjustment. *Journal of Marriage and the Family*, 1979, *41*, 259–265.

Hunt, R.G. Age, sex, and service in a child guidance clinic. *Journal of Child Psychology and Psychiatry*, 1961, *2*, 185–192.

Jacobson, N., & Margolin, G. *Marital therapy: Strategies based on social learning and behavior exchange principles*. New York: Brunner/ Mazel, 1979.

Kendall, P.C., & Hollon, S.D. *Cognitive-behavioral interventions: Theory, research, and procedures*. New York: Academic Press, 1979.

Kirby, E.A. *Measurement and modification of attention span and self-control among hyperactive children*. Paper presented at the Third Annual Indiana Conference on Child and Adolescent Disorders, Brown County, Indiana, 1981. (Available from Dr. E.A. Kirby, Indiana State University, Terre Haute, IN 47809.)

Kirby, E.A., Glynn, M., & Manos, R. *A comparison of cognitive-behavioral and behavioral strategies for modifying impulsive and inattentive behaviors of hyperactive children*. Unpublished manuscript, Department of School Psychology, Indiana State University, 1980. (Available from Dr. E.A. Kirby, Indiana State University, Terre Haute, IN 47809.)

Kirby, E., & Horne, A. *Cognitive self-control and behavioral strategies for modifying children's behavior*. Paper presented at the Ninetieth Annual Convention of the American Psychological Association, Washington, D.C., 1982.

Lambert, M.J., DeJulio, S.S., & Stein, D.M. Therapist interpersonal skills: Process, outcome, methodological considerations, and recommendations for future research. *Psychological Bulletin*, 1978, *85*, 467–489.

Lavelle, J.J. Comparing the effects of an affective and a behavioral counselor style on client interview behavior. *Journal of Counseling Psychology*, 1977, *24*, 173–177.

Lederer, W., & Jackson, D. *Mirages of marriage*. New York: Norton, 1968.

Levitt, E.E. Research on psychotherapy with children. In A.E. Bergin & S.L.

Garfield (Eds.), *Handbook of psychotherapy and behavior change*. New York: John Wiley, 1971.

Liebert, R., Sprafkin, J., & Davidson, E. *The early window: Effects of television on children and youth* (2nd ed.). Elmsford, N.Y.: Pergamon Press, 1982.

Mahoney, M. *Cognition and behavior modification*. Cambridge, Mass.: Ballinger, 1974.

Mahoney, M.J., & Arnkoff, D. Cognitive and self-control therapies. In S. Garfield & A. Bergin (Eds.), *Handbook of psychotherapy and behavior change*. New York: John Wiley, 1978.

Maultsby, M.C., Jr. *Help yourself to happiness*. New York: Institute for Rational Living, 1975.

McCord, W., & McCord, J. *Origins of crime*. New York: Columbia University Press, 1959.

McCroskey, J.C., Larson, C.E., & Knapp, M.L. *Introduction to interpersonal communication*. Englewood Cliffs, N.J.: Prentice-Hall, 1971.

McMahon, R.J., Forehand, R., & Griest, D.L. Effects of knowledge of social learning principles on enhancing treatment outcome and generalization in a parent training program. *Journal of Consulting and Clinical Psychology*, 1981, *49*, 526-532.

Meichenbaum, D. *Cognitive-behavior modification*. Morristown, N.J.: General Learning Press, 1974.

Meichenbaum, D. *Cognitive-behavior modification*. New York: Plenum Press, 1977.

Meltzoff, J., & Kornreich, M. *Research in psychotherapy*. New York: Atherton Press, 1970.

Morris, H.H., Jr., Escoll, P.J., & Wexler, R. Aggressive behavior disorders of childhood: A follow-up study. *American Journal of Psychiatry*, 1956, *112*, 991-997.

O'Dell, S.L. Enhancing parent involvement training: A discussion. *The Behavior Therapist*, 1982, *5*, 9-13.

Ollendick, T., & Cerny, J. *Clinical behavior therapy with children*. New York: Plenum Press, 1981.

Overall, B., & Aronson, H. Expectations of psychotherapy in patients of lower socio-economic class. *American Journal of Orthopsychiatry*, 1963, *33*, 421-430.

Patterson, G.R. An empirical approach to the classification of disturbed children. *Journal of Clinical Psychology*, 1964, *20*, 326-337.

Patterson, G.R. Interventions for boys with conduct problems: Multiple settings, treatments, and criteria. *Journal of Consulting and Clinical Psychology*, 1974, *42*, 471-481.

Patterson, G.R. *Families: Applications of social learning to family life*. Champaign, Ill.: Research Press, 1975.

Patterson, G.R. The aggressive child: Victim and architect of a coercive system. In L.A. Hamerlynck, L.C. Handy, & E.J. Mash (Eds.), *Behavior modification and families* (Vol. I. Theory and research). New York: Brunner/Mazel, 1976.

Patterson, G.R., & Brodsky, G. A behaviour modification programme for a child with multiple problem behaviours. *Journal of Child Psychology and Psychiatry*, 1966, *7*, 277-295.

Patterson, G.R., & Hops, H. Coercion, A game for two: Intervention techniques for marital conflict. In R. Ulrich & P. Mountjoy (Eds.), *The experimental analysis of social behavior*. New York: Appleton-Century-Crofts, 1972.

Patterson, G.R., Jones, R., Whittier, J., & Wright, M.A. A behavior modification technique for a hyperactive child. *Behaviour Research and Therapy*, 1965, *2*, 217–226.

Patterson, G.R., McNeal, S.A., Hawkins, N., & Phelps, R. Reprogramming the social environment. *Journal of Child Psychology and Psychiatry*, 1967, *8*, 181–195.

Patterson, G.R., Reid, J.B., Jones, R.R., & Conger, R.E. *A social learning approach to family intervention* (Vol. I). Eugene, Oreg.: Castalia, 1975.

Platt, J., Scura, W.C., & Hannon, J.R. Problem-solving thinking of youthful incarcerated heroin addicts. *Journal of Community Psychology*, 1973, *1*, 278–281.

Platt, J., & Spivack, G. Problem-solving thinking of psychiatric patients. *Journal of Consulting and Clinical Psychology*, 1972, *39*, 148–151. (a)

Platt, J., & Spivack, G. Social competence and effective problem-solving thinking in psychiatric patients. *Journal of Clinical Psychology*, 1972, *28*, 3–5. (b)

Platt, J., & Spivack, G. Means of solving real-life problems: Psychiatric patients versus controls, and cross cultural comparisons of normal females. *Journal of Community Psychology*, 1974, *2*, 45–48.

Reid, J.B. *Reciprocity and family interaction*. Unpublished doctoral dissertation, University of Oregon, 1967.

Reid, J.B. *A social learning approach to family intervention* (Vol. II). Eugene, Oreg.: Castalia, 1978.

Reid, J.B., & Taplin, P. *A social interactional approach to the treatment of abusive families*. Unpublished manuscript, Oregon Research Institute, 1977.

Renne, K.S. Correlates of dissatisfaction in marriage. *Journal of Marriage and the Family*, 1970, *32*, 54–66.

Roach, J.L., Gursslin, O., & Hunt, R.G. Some social-psychological characteristics of a child guidance clinic caseload. *Journal of Consulting Psychology*, 1958, *22*, 183–186.

Robins, N.L. *Deviant children grown up: A sociological and psychiatric study of sociopathic personality*. Baltimore: Williams & Wilkins, 1966.

Rogers, C.R. *Counseling and psychotherapy*. Boston: Houghton-Mifflin, 1942.

Rogers, C.R. The necessary and sufficient conditions of therapeutic personality change. *Journal of Consulting Psychology*, 1957, *21*, 95–103.

Rogers, M., Lilienfeld, A.M., & Pasamanick, B. *Prenatal and parental factors in the development of child behavior disorders*. Baltimore: Johns Hopkins University Press, 1954.

Rollins, B., & Cannon, K. Marital satisfaction over the family life cycle: A reevaluation. *Journal of Marriage and the Family*, 1974, *36*, 271–282.

Rutter, M. Protective factors in children's responses to stress and disadvantage. In M. Kent & S. Rolf (Eds.), *Primary prevention of psychopathology* (Vol. III). Hanover, N.H.: University Press of New England, 1979.

Ryder, R. Longitudinal data relating marriage satisfaction and having a child. *Journal of Marriage and the Family*, 1973, *35*, 604–606.

Sawhill, I., Peabody, G., Jones, C., & Caldwell, S. *Income transfer and family structure*. Washington, D.C.: Urban Institute, 1975.

Schneider M., & Robin, A. The turtle technique: A method for the self-control of impulsive behavior. In J. Krumboltz & C. Thoresen (Eds.), *Counseling methods*. New York: Holt, Rinehart & Winston, 1976.

Schorr, A.L., & Moen, P. The single parent and public policy. *Social Policy*, 1979, *9*, 15–21.

Schumaker, L.B., Hovell, M.F., & Sherman, J.A. *Managing behavior, part 9: A home-based school achievement system.* Lawrence, Kans.: H & H Enterprises, 1977.

Shure, M., & Spivack, G. Means-ends thinking, adjustment, and social class among elementary-school-aged children. *Journal of Consulting and Clinical Psychology*, 1972, *38*, 348–353.

Shure, M., Spivack, G., & Jaeger, M. Problem solving thinking and adjustment among disadvantaged pre-school children. *Child Development*, 1971, *42*, 1791–1803.

Siegel, J.M., & Spivack, G. A new therapy program for chronic patients. *Behavior Therapy*, 1976, *7*, 129–130.

Spivack, J., Platt, J.J., & Shure, M. *The problem-solving approach to adjustment.* San Francisco: Jossey-Bass, 1976.

Spivack, J., & Shure, M. *Social adjustment of young children: A cognitive approach to solving real-life problems.* San Francisco: Jossey-Bass, 1974.

Stuart, R.B. *Helping couples change: A social learning approach to marital therapy.* New York: Guilford Press, 1980.

Szykula, S.A., & Fleischman, M.J. *Child abuse treatment: Reducing costly out of home placement through effective intervention.* Unpublished manuscript, 1983. (Available from S.A. Szykula, Primary Children's Medical Center, University of Utah School of Medicine).

Szykula, S.A., Fleischman, M.J., & Shilton, P.E. Implementing a family therapy program in a community: Relevant issues on one promising program for families in conflict. *Behavioral Counseling Quarterly*, 1982, *2*, 67–78.

Teuber, H.L., & Powers, E. Evaluating therapy in a delinquency prevention program. *Journal of Psychiatric Treatment*, 1953, *21*, 138–147.

Thibaut, J., & Kelley, H. *The social psychology of groups.* New York: John Wiley, 1959.

Truax, C.B., & Carkhuff, R.R. *Toward effective counseling and psychotherapy: Training and practice.* Chicago: Aldine, 1967.

Truax, C.B., & Mitchell, K.M. Research on certain therapist interpersonal skills in relation to process and outcome. In A.E. Bergin & S.L. Garfield (Eds.), *Handbook of psychotherapy and behavior change: An empirical evaluation.* New York: John Wiley, 1971.

Wahler, R.G. Oppositional children: A quest for parental reinforcement control. *Journal of Applied Behavior Analysis*, 1969, *2*, 159–170.

Wahler, R.G. The insular mother: Her problems in parent-child treatment. *Journal of Applied Behavior Analysis*, 1980, *13*, 207–219.

Wahler, R.G., & Fox, J.J. Solitary toy play and time out: A family treatment package for children with aggressive and oppositional behavior. *Journal of Applied Behavior Analysis*, 1980, *13*, 23–39.

Wahler, R.G., & Moore, D.R. *School-home behavior change procedures in a "high risk" community.* Paper presented at the meeting of the Association for the Advancement of Behavior Therapy, San Francisco, December 1975.

Walter, H., & Gilmore, S.K. Placebo versus social learning effects of parent training procedures designed to alter the behavior of socially aggressive boys. *Behavior Research and Therapy*, 1973, *4*, 361–377.

White house conference on families: National organizations issues resource book. Washington, D.C.: U.S. Government Printing Office, 1980.

Wiltz, N.A., & Patterson, G.R. An evaluation of parent training procedures to alter inappropriate aggressive behavior of boys. *Behavior Therapy*, 1974, *5*, 215–221.

Woody, R.H. *Behavioral problem children in the schools.* New York: Appleton-Century-Crofts, 1969.

Zax, M., Cowen, E., Rappaport, J., Beach, D., & Laird, J. Follow-up study of children identified early as emotionally disturbed. *Journal of Consulting and Clinical Psychology,* 1968, *32,* 369–374.

Index

About the Authors

MATTHEW J. FLEISCHMAN

Matt has considerable experience as both a researcher and a clinician. He is Staff Psychologist at the Sacred Heart General Hospital Adolescent Care Unit, Eugene, Oregon, and conducts a private practice specializing in the treatment of children, adolescents, and families. Previously he was Project Director at Family Research Associates, where he investigated community applications of behavioral technologies.

Matt is a graduate of Antioch College and received his doctorate from the University of Oregon in 1976. He has worked with incarcerated delinquents and severely emotionally disturbed children, and as a graduate student was a clinical assistant in the Social Learning Project at Oregon Research Institute. After completing his doctorate he was Principal Investigator on the TEACH project, a multi-site implementation and evaluation study of social learning treatment programs. Matt is married and has a son.

ARTHUR M. HORNE

Andy has had a varied background and wide experience working with children and families. After completing a bachelor's degree from the University of Florida, he worked in junior and senior high schools as a teacher and counselor, actively involved in helping children and their families.

Andy completed his doctorate at Southern Illinois University in 1971 and since that time has been at Indiana State University. He has taught in the counseling program, conducted research on counseling children and parents, worked with public and private schools, and provided training, supervision, and therapy in juvenile correctional facilities.

Currently Andy is the Director of Training of Counseling Psychology at Indiana State University, Terre Haute, Indiana. He is the coeditor of *Family Counseling and Therapy*.

JUDY L. ARTHUR

Judy received her undergraduate degree from the Wallace School of Community Service and Public Affairs at the University of Oregon in 1976. She also earned a master's degree in Psychology from the University of Oregon in 1980. Judy has been involved in NIMH-grant-supported research since 1977. The focus of this research has been on conduct disordered children and their families and, more recently, on clinically depressed mothers and their families. In addition to her work as a family therapist and therapist trainer, Judy has gained extensive experience and expertise in the development of direct observation assessment procedures. Currently she is the Project Coordinator for the Family Studies Project at the Oregon Research Institute. She also remains active in development and evaluation of community-based treatment programs through her work as a consultant with Moore/Arthur Associates.